The
Eighteenth
Century
1688–1815

MODERN BRITISH FOREIGN POLICY

General Editor: MALCOLM ROBINSON
Headmaster, Queen's College, Taunton

Tudor Foreign Policy   P. S. CROWSON
Stuart and Cromwellian Foreign Policy   G. M. D. HOWAT
The Eighteenth Century, 1688–1815   PAUL LANGFORD
The Nineteenth Century, 1814–80   PAUL HAYES

In preparation
The Twentieth Century   PAUL HAYES

By the same author
The First Rockingham Administration, 1765–1766   (1973)
The Excise Crisis: Society and Politics in the Age of Walpole   (1975)

MODERN BRITISH FOREIGN POLICY

The Eighteenth Century 1688–1815

Paul Langford

ADAM & CHARLES BLACK
LONDON

941.07

First published 1976
A. & C. Black Ltd
35 Bedford Row, London WC1R 4JH

ISBN 0 7136 1652 0 (cased)
    0 7136 1662 8 (paperback)

Printed in Great Britain by
Billing & Sons Limited
Guildford, London and Worcester

Contents

Preface

No book of this kind can be written without extensive dependence on the scholarship of others. My debts are acknowledged in detail elsewhere but it would be churlish to evade declaring my obligations not merely to the founders of the modern school of diplomatic historians concerned with the eighteenth century, the Lodges, Horns and Thomsons, but also to those, such as Professor Anderson, Professor Hatton, Professor Roberts, Dr Gibbs and Dr Spencer, who have in recent years cleared new paths through the jungle of international relations in the age of the Elightenment. It is one of the primary aims of this book to bring to the general reader the results of such scholarship. It has also been my objective to create something like a unified picture of British foreign policy in the eighteenth century. For the shades and tones of the picture I am entirely responsible, and indeed I have not hesitated to colour it to my taste. However, I have also endeavoured to ensure that the important subjects and themes all appear in their proper relationship. It is something of a paradox that so much attention should have been lavished on eighteenth-century politics in recent years and yet that so little has been done to place foreign policy, to contemporaries a constant and often dominating preoccupation, squarely in the overall domestic context. To provide students with a running commentary which allows them to do this for themselves is the ultimate justification for this book.

Lincoln College   *Paul Langford*
Oxford

PART I

Foreign Policy
and its Setting

1 The Machinery of Foreign Policy

Foreign policy in Britain, like that of almost all European states, was primarily the responsibility of the monarch. Whatever the pretensions of Parliament, English kings had traditionally guarded the prerogative of conducting relations with other governments with extreme jealousy. Charles II was typical in chastising the Commons for 'not only directing him to make alliances, but by pointing out to him what those alliances should be, and with whom they should be made; that the power of makeing peace or warr only belonged to himselfe, and if that was taken from him he should only have the name of a King'.[1] This was not simply a matter of entrenched royal prerogative. On the contrary even the opponents of courts were generally prepared to admit that the secrecy of deliberation and immediacy of action required by the exigencies of relations between the states of Europe required an executive instrument less blunt and cumbersome than that provided by the legislature. As a result the monarchy retained throughout the eighteenth century greater powers in this sphere than in most. Understandably, too, most rulers were concerned not merely to preserve but to exercise this prerogative. William III, George I and George II all had continental commitments which they tended to place above those of their adopted country, Holland in the first case, Hanover in the others. All three spent long periods of their reign away from England, a habit which even drove Parliament to legislate against such absences. Indeed the clause in the Act of Settlement of 1701 which with the conduct of William III in mind, prevented royal travel overseas without parliamentary permission, had to be repealed on the accession of the Hanoverian line out of deference to the wishes of George I.

[1] *Memoirs of Sir John Reresby* ed. A. Browning (Glasgow 1936), p. 123.

All three monarchs were accused of neglecting British interests and even of unconstitutional or at least imprudent reliance on foreign advisers. The influence of Keppel and Bentinck in the 1690s and of Bernstorff and Robethon in the early years of George I's reign was after all a matter of common knowledge and is amply attested by all the evidence. On the whole Englishmen accepted the diplomatic implications ultimately because they had to, unless they were prepared to restore the Stuarts to the throne. Even so Holland and Hanover successively provoked great political debates and even crises. The last years of William III's reign were embittered by a violent attack on the policies of continental involvement which had dominated the previous decade; similarly in the mid-1720s, in the late 1730s, in the mid-1740s, and even in the mid-1750s, the cry of Hanover was exploited to great effect by politicians. Nor was this all mindless xenophobia. There were moments when British interests obviously were sacrificed to purely electoral concerns for example. The convention which provided for Hanoverian neutrality in July 1741 was an obvious infringement of the interests which George II should have protected as King of England in defence of those for which he cared as Elector of Hanover. Similarly great horror had been expressed twenty-five years earlier when George I blatantly used the Royal Navy in the electoral interest. However, though there was talk in George I's reign of separating the British and Hanoverian successions by bestowing the electorate on a junior branch of the royal family, little serious consideration was given to such a solution, and the Hanoverian connection remained a fundamental fact of political life. It was not possible to give the throne to foreigners without taking on some of their foreign responsibilities, a lesson which Englishmen found it difficult but necessary to learn.

Queen Anne and George III did not present quite the same problems as the other monarchs of the period; Queen Anne for the obvious reason that she had no foreign connections, other than her husband's Danish affiliations, George III because he ostentatiously renounced Hanoverian policies in his endeavours to appear a patriotic British monarch. Eventually he learned to regret the postures he took up at the beginning of his reign and particularly in his latter years was by no means uncaring of Hanoverian concerns. Even so the contrast with the reigns of his grandfather and great-grandfather was marked. This is not to claim that either Queen Anne or George III was insignificant in foreign policy. Queen Anne was limited by her sex and her sickness but was not a negligible force in the politics of her reign. George III had very much his own ideas. His attachment to an Austrian rather than Prussian alliance was a matter of consequence in the politics of the 1760s when his opponents differed strongly with him, and in the diplomacy of the War of American Independence he played a crucial part. Nor, for example, was he above going over the heads of his ministers to correspond directly with the British ambassador at the Hague on matters of state policy towards the Dutch Netherlands. Neither George III nor his predecessors had a *secret du roi* in the classic fashion of the French monarchy under Louis XV, but they were not mere ciphers in foreign policy.

If the king was universally recognised as the constitutional authority in the matter of relations with other states, he was also provided with a formal departmental structure to assist him. Immediately responsible for the conduct of the king's business were the two Secretaries of State for North and South, who before 1782 divided foreign policy between them. In 1782 the modern division between a Home and Foreign Secretary, each with unified responsibility, was established. Below these officers who were important ministers with cabinet rank, stretched the bureaucracy, such as it was in a relatively small and economical government machine like Whitehall. In London a handful of under-secretaries and clerks formed the core of the system; overseas a small number of ambassadors in the key posts of Western Europe headed a large body of envoys and lesser officials, between them looking after relations with states as diverse as Turkey and Tuscany, Sweden and Switzerland, Poland and Portugal. It is not easy to judge the quality of this machinery, even compared with the other diplomatic systems of Europe, though the plausible criticisms were many and obvious. How could a consistent and coherent policy be evolved by two Secretaries of State responsible for relations with different parts of Europe; how could the apparent corruption of the patronage system permit the rational staffing of a corps of men whose expertise and technical efficiency were vital to the nation's security; how indeed in an age of amateurism and oligarchy could diplomatic talent emerge at all? On the other hand, answers to such questions were not entirely lacking. For instance the division of duties between the Secretaries was much less damaging than might have been expected. In practice one or other was recognised as the superior, and in any case significant policy decisions had to be thrashed out with the king and with other ministers. The Duke of Newcastle expected his colleague as Secretary of State to be absolutely subordinate, and while he had to resort to repeated dismissals in the late 1740s and early 1750s, Harrington, Chesterfield and Bedford all being sacrificed before the compliant Holderness was found to be satisfactory, he inevitably got his way. Earlier in his career, in the 1720s, Newcastle had had himself to defer to the greater power and prestige of Townshend as Secretary. In consequence the formal creation of a single Foreign Secretaryship in 1782 by no means had a dramatic effect in practice. A far greater problem was the system of appointment which characterised the political world of the eighteenth century. Rank, influence, wealth, parliamentary pull, all seemed to leave ability and merit far behind. There were many grotesque examples at all levels in the diplomatic services. Secretaries of State like Suffolk who knew no French at all, like Wellesley, of whom his brother complained 'I wish that Wellesley was castrated; or that he would like other people attend to his business and perform to';[1] envoys like Aberdeen, sent in 1813 to do diplomatic battle with Metternich and the crowned heads of Europe, without the aid of either the French language or diplomatic experience; ambassadors like Bute at Madrid whose secretary considered him 'as fit to be ambassador as I am to be Pope of Rome';[2] ministers like Sir Horace Mann, who spent nearly fifty years at Florence hosting travellers on the Grand Tour, or like Sir Charles Hanbury Williams whose bright ideas and appalling prejudices bedevilled British policy in Germany in the 1750s. 'Most of our ministers abroad', wrote Chesterfield, 'have taken up that department occasionally, without having ever thought of foreign affairs before; many of them without

[1] *Spencer Perceval: The Evangelical Prime Minister, 1762–1812* by D. Gray (Manchester 1963), p. 275.
[2] *Ambassadors and Secret Agents* by A. Cobban (London 1954), p. 14.

speaking any one foreign language; and all of them without manners which are absolutely necessary towards being well received, and making a figure at foreign courts. They do the business accordingly —that is, very ill'.[1] At home ministers often totally unversed in the arts of diplomacy and officials capable of losing treaties and omitting to correspond with envoys; abroad a bizarre blend of great aristocrats and insignificant adventurers intent only on their own profit— this was a less than impressive picture. On the other hand it was no worse than that presented by most diplomatic services. With the exception of France which had a vast and universally admired diplomatic bureaucracy, and Russia, which greatly improved its organisation in the course of the eighteenth century, it may be doubted whether other European monarchies had a notably more effective machine than did the British. Moreover there was, towards the end of the eighteenth century, a distinct improvement, a growing professionalism which was reflected in the remarkable activities of men like Eden, Harris and Ewart in the courts of Europe. The career diplomat had arrived if not triumphed by 1800, and indeed the new spirit of the diplomatic service provoked extreme criticism among many. Burke claimed that 'those in power here, instead of governing their Ministers at foreign Courts are entirely swayed by them', a charge which Sir James Harris, who claimed to have 'never yet received an instruction that was worth reading', would have been proud to sustain.[2] In fact such allegations were exaggerated; the like of the Younger Pitt were not easily dominated by their diplomatic agents. None the less, the charge was a tribute to the growing skill and specialisation of the service by the end of the eighteenth century.

In any event contemporary Europe was not inclined to blame Britain's diplomats for the weaknesses and failures, such as they were, of its foreign policy. Rather the cause was seen in the extraordinary powers which Parliament claimed, though technically of course the legislature had little or no standing in foreign policy. Negotiations

[1] *The British Diplomatic Service, 1689–1789* by D. B. Horn (Oxford 1961), pp. 93–94.
[2] *The Correspondence of Edmund Burke* ed. T. W. Copeland (Cambridge 1958), vi, p. 357; *The British Diplomatic Service, 1689–1789* by D. B. Horn (Oxford 1961), p. 3.

were conducted, treaties made, war declared by the monarch as head
of state, and in international law peoples were committed by their
sovereigns without being recognised as actual parties to the decisions
made by them. However in practice the House of Commons, in
particular, had long sought to influence and even override the
foreign policy of the executive. Financial exigencies had compelled
monarchs such as James I and Charles II to make at least some
concessions to parliamentary feeling. Moreover the Revolution of
1688, which simultaneously strengthened the position of Parliament,
and enthroned a king whose priority was to obtain English consent
to a vigorous continental foreign policy, was bound to increase this
tendency. Parliamentary pressure was constant in the 1690s and
came to a head at the end of the decade when it was revealed that
the king and his ministers had been negotiating the Spanish Partition
Treaties with Louis XIV without consulting the legislature. The
result, quite apart from creating a major political crisis, was to
establish a significant statutory restriction of the royal prerogative.
The Act of Settlement of 1701, which was to take effect on the
accession of the House of Hanover, required the crown to make war
in defence of its foreign dominions only with Parliamentary consent.
The further stipulation of parliamentary approval to permit the
monarch to visit his electoral dominions was too insulting and offensive to be retained when the Elector of Hanover actually succeeded
in 1714. None the less, in a small but significant way, the Act of
Settlement clearly marked the advance of the legislature into an area
which had traditionally been regarded as inviolably the crown's.
It was not surprising then that throughout the eighteenth century
the executive normally made a practice of presenting treaties to
Parliament for formal approval; certainly nothing quite comparable
to William III's action in unilaterally committing his British subjects
to sweeping guarantees of continental arrangements was ever
attempted again.

   More important still than the fact that treaties were formally laid
before Parliament was the extensive preliminary consultation which
soon became inseparable from the making of foreign policy. After
the establishment of the civil list in 1697 it was out of the question to
expect the crown itself to contribute significantly to the waging of

war or the prosecution of an ambitious military or foreign policy. Every parliamentary session in the eighteenth century witnessed a major debate on foreign policy, either when the crown requested supplies for the armed forces, or for other specific purposes, or at the beginning of each session when the formal King's Speech to Parliament was expected to animadvert on the international situation. And a vote against ministerial policy was a matter of the utmost seriousness. No government could afford to provoke parliamentary displeasure at its foreign policy, when its credibility abroad rested on its ability to procure financial assistance at home. Understandably the executive did not find this parliamentary dependence, almost unique among European states, to its liking. British diplomats like William Eden complained that while the parliamentary session was in progress it was futile to expect directions from ministers preoccupied with defending their record in the House of Commons. The ministers themselves found it irksome to have to explain the most elementary principles of continental politics to country gentlemen, who as Eldon once remarked, 'are always thinking for themselves and yet never know their own minds'.[1] More seriously, parliamentary discussion of confidential negotiations was profoundly embarrassing. Walpole complained bitterly of investigations which 'might have very bad influence on our affairs abroad',[2] while Castlereagh similarly pointed out the restricting effects of parliamentary sovereignty on diplomatic activity. 'It is almost impossible to make foreigners understand the delicacies and difficulties of our Parliamentary system. . . . In our system concealment is not practicable for any length of time, and when the stipulations are canvassed they are impeached upon every extreme case that ingenuity can suggest as falling within their possible operation'.[3] It was indeed a common complaint among continental sovereigns, many of whom were limited only by their own caprice or whim, that perfidious

[1] *Spencer Perceval: The Evangelical Prime Minister, 1762–1812* by D. Gray (Manchester 1963), p. 260.

[2] *The Parliamentary Diary of Sir Edward Knatchbull, 1722–1730* ed. A. N. Newman (Camden 3rd Ser., xciv), p. 57.

[3] *The Foreign Policy of Castlereagh, 1812–1815* by C. K. Webster (London 1931), p. 101.

Albion could not be depended upon for constancy when her Parliament was so powerful. In fact this charge was often greatly exaggerated, notably by Frederick II in the 1760s. But it was useful ammunition in propaganda warfare and was not always entirely without a vestige of plausibility.

Still more embarrassing was the growing power and influence of the parliamentary opposition in Britain. In almost every continental state there was a battle between factions at court, which provided foreign diplomats with openings for mischief-making, and in certain cases, notably Poland and Sweden, the result was almost anarchy. But Britain was the only major power in which a formal opposition was capable of seriously damaging the objectives of government abroad. Few foreign ambassadors could resist the temptation to dabble in opposition politics, and even the Tsar Alexander I, on an official visit to London in 1814, infuriated his royal host by making up to the Whigs. Occasionally such activities rebounded on their authors as in 1727 when the Austrian ambassador, Count Palm, attempted to meddle in parliamentary politics and burnt his fingers badly in doing so. But there can be no denying that the privileged position of opponents of government in a country which prided itself on its libertarianism, was potentially damaging to the international credibility of the crown and its policies. The most extreme case is perhaps that presented by the activities of Robert Adair, an agent of the Foxite Whigs, who visited Russia at the time of the Ochakov crisis almost as shadow official representative to the court of Catherine the Great. Indeed Foxite cooperation with Russia was something of a scandal; Burke declaimed against 'setting on foot communications with foreign powers, leading to concert and cooperation with them in measures hostile to the King's Government', and the administration were not without justification in considering 'the idea of Ministers from Opposition to the different Courts of Europe a new one in this country' which 'would go very near to an impeachable misdemeanour'.[1] A recognised and constitutional opposition was not an unalloyed blessing, at least in the view of those charged with making foreign policy.

[1] *The British Diplomatic Service, 1689–1789* by D. B. Horn (Oxford 1961), p. 41; Historical Manuscripts Commission, *Fortescue MSS*, ii, p. 144.

The position of Parliament both reflected and reinforced a still more fundamental fact of political life in Britain—the power of public opinion. Nothing is more difficult to define as a precise concept or to delineate as a practical force, yet no element in politics was ultimately more important. The public interest could be expressed in a number of ways. One of the most striking characteristics of British politics for example, was the very great influence of the press. 'Scarce anything is ever debated in Parliament that is not first canvassed without doors', it was noted in the early eighteenth century, at a time when the metropolitan and provincial press was growing rapidly.[1] After the effective abolition of formal state censorship with the lapsing of the Licensing Act in 1695 the way was open for the emergence of a vigorous and outspoken newspaper and pamphlet press. By the end of the eighteenth century indeed, many even in England felt that the freedom of the press represented a significant threat to the conduct of foreign policy. Napoleon was driven formally to complain of the incessant abuse directed at him by the London newspapers after the Peace of Amiens, and more seriously there was considerable concern at home when *The Times* printed reports of the naval manoeuvres of the French and Spanish fleets before Trafalgar and so informed their commander that his movements were known to the Royal Navy. Nor was it merely that the press was free enough to embarrass government in its dealings; by contrast with many of its continental rivals it was so widely read, and taken as so representative of public opinion, that it was ignored at peril. Wellington's remark, at the height of the war with Napoleon, that the newspapers had come 'to rule everything in this country' was only a slight exaggeration.[2] The nineteenth century was to add still further to this influence, but it was the eighteenth that witnessed its firm establishment.

The public itself had other ways of expressing its concern with foreign policy. Particularly in the early eighteenth century, for example, parliamentary elections provided ample opportunity for a clear statement on international affairs. To a great extent the over-

[1] Quoted by G. C. Gibbs, 'The Revolution in Foreign Policy' in *Britain after the Glorious Revolution, 1689–1714* ed. G. Holmes (London 1970), p. 41.
[2] *Spencer Perceval: The Evangelical Prime Minister, 1762–1812* by D. Gray, p. 131.

whelming Tory victory at the polls in 1710 derived from general and acute concern at developments in the War of Spanish Succession, and it is not too much to say that the Oxford Ministry was borne faster to the making of peace in the Treaty of Utrecht than it wished to proceed. One of the strongest arguments employed in 1716 on behalf of the Septennial Act, which required elections to Parliament at seven-year instead of three-year intervals, was the need to reduce the electorate's influence on foreign policy. Men like Stanhope and Carteret, who had elaborate and carefully thought out plans in foreign policy, were incensed by the instability of policy dictated by triennial elections and insisted that 'no foreign power would enter into alliance with us lest the next Parliament should annul what this had done'.[1] Nor were electors restricted to voting at the polls. Addresses and petitions to Parliament and the Crown were recognised means of bringing popular pressure to bear on the making of policy. Particular petitions came near to causing national crises, for example the Kentish Petition of 1701 which fiercely castigated Parliament for insufficient support of the continental schemes of William III; but still more important were the great campaigns which collected support from all over the country. The addresses in favour of peace in 1710, the instructions in support of war against Spain in 1739, the addresses on the loss of Minorca in 1756, the petitions for an inquiry into the failure of the Walcheren expedition in 1809, expressed the deep concern of propertied opinion at large and vitally affected the conduct of national policy.

In the last analysis however the importance of the public's view was something which came across not in specific newspapers, elections, or petitions; rather it was reflected at every level and in every facet of political life. The constant anxiety of politicians to safeguard themselves against popular anger—men like Newcastle and Henry Fox, expert in the intrigues of court and arts of government, were obsessed with this preoccupation, and the obvious authority of those who could claim fairly or otherwise to represent popular wishes (Pitt the Elder was the outstanding example)—amply testify to the importance of the public. In the eighteenth century foreign policy was almost always the most important matter before

[1] *Stanhope* by B. Williams (Oxford 1932), p. 197.

the political nation. Apart from the duty to maintain law and order, one which government normally fulfilled with little difficulty, the conduct of relations with foreign states was overwhelmingly the most important responsibility of the executive. The key functions of modern government, in terms of social welfare and economic regulations, were scarcely a significant element in the everyday business of administration, even if Parliament discussed them. Thus the pride of place given to foreign affairs in the press was an authentic tribute to the interest attached by the public to them. News from abroad was usually the most important category of information purveyed and clearly took precedence over all but the more sensational news at home. No doubt this was true in most countries, but what was striking in Britain was the degree of importance attached to popular interest in these matters. Foreign envoys, apart from being shocked by the limitations thus placed upon the freedom of action of the crown, its ministers and even Parliament, quickly learned to recognise their significance. The French observer who remarked that Carteret had not the popular qualities necessary in what he described as *un état républicain* could hardly have made such a comment elsewhere in a major European state.[1]

If the public at large played a real, though undefined, part in the making of foreign policy, particular sections of the public also had their role. However, in a country where power was as diffused among king, ministers, bureaucrats and parliamentarians as in England, the function of pressure groups was bound to vary. Naturally the consistently strongest lobbies were drawn from businessmen who had a powerful vested interest in influencing the foreign policy of the state. Monopoly companies like the Levant and East India Companies, formal committees like those of the West India and North American merchants, loose interest groups like the merchants trading to Spain, all had strong views on particular aspects of relations with foreign states and expected them to carry weight either in the councils of state or in the legislature. This was not necessarily for the general good since it was possible for particular interests to obtain an undue share of influence either through in-

---

[1] *Recueil des Instructions données aux Ambassadeurs et Ministres de France*, xxv—2, ed. P. Vaucher (Paris 1965), p. 350.

tensive political activity or through the aid of powerful political connections with an axe to grind. The parliamentary opposition was always ready to remind government of its responsibilities towards the business community. As Carteret once remarked, 'Royal navies are kept by merchants, and must protect the merchants'.[1] A classic case of ministerial impotence in the face of the concerted activities of economic pressure groups occurred in the 1730s. The outbreak of war with Spain over the depredations in American waters, owed much more to the power of organised lobbying than to sensible argument or informed deliberation. The South Sea Company made life for Britain's negotiators intolerable with its refusal to accept the most reasonable concessions which could be extracted from the Spanish authorities. Similarly the great outburst of anger which forced Walpole into war owed much to the propaganda and pressure deployed by the great merchants of London in alliance with a vociferous parliamentary opposition. As it happened there was a strong case for arguing that the war which resulted (the War of Jenkins' Ear) did far more damage to traditional trade with Spanish America through Old Spain than could possibly be compensated by aggressive action in the Caribbean. But unfortunately for them the merchants who organised the Iberian trade were unable to compare with their West Indian colleagues in terms of political influence. 'This branch of trade by Old Spain to America', one contemporary commented, 'has ever been neglected by our ministers and ever will, as it lies among a set of people who can't be clamorous, vizt. Roman Catholics and Jews'.[2]

No less important than the mercantile bodies were the financial interests of the City, on which government depended for the raising of money, and the manufacturing interest, which with the growth of industrialisation in the second half of the eighteenth century was to outstrip all other pressure groups. The influence of the Great (later General) Chamber of Manufacturers under Garbett and Wedgwood in the 1780s was particularly marked. Faced with its attack on aspects of the Eden Treaty with France, the Younger Pitt himself was driven to denounce 'a few manufacturers collected in a certain Chamber of

[1] *War and Trade in the West Indies* by R. Pares (Oxford 1936), p. 48.
[2] ibid., p. 61.

Commerce' who would 'save Parliament the trouble of legislation'.[1] This was very much a foretaste of things to come; the implications for governments of the growth of manufacturing industry were made clear when the British were faced with Napoleon's economic blockade embodied in the Continental System. In 1812 for example, when Perceval's ministry repealed Orders-in-Council which had been deemed an essential part of economic warfare against Napoleon, but which brought down on the heads of ministers the fury of business men faced with ruin, Castlereagh confessed that he did 'not like to own that we are forced to give way to our manufacturers'.[2] No doubt British ministers rarely enjoyed having to take note of the desires of others; but it was one of the distinguishing features of British foreign policy in the period that neither the crown nor its servants nor Parliament could make even relatively small decisions without taking into account the wishes of those they ruled. In the age of enlightened despotism this situation both baffled and impressed continental statesmen. Whether it weakened or strengthened the processes of foreign policy, whatever the prejudices of those who little liked the limitations upon their freedom of action, is another matter.

---

[1] J. M. Norris, 'Samuel Garbett and the Early Development of Industrial Lobbying in Great Britain' in *Ec. Hist. Rev.*, 2nd Ser., x (1957–58), p. 460.

[2] *Castlereagh* by C. J. Bartlett (London 1966), p. 111.

2 The Objectives of Foreign Policy

In a structure of diplomatic decision-making as complex as that which existed in Britain, it was not to be expected that aims and objects would be simple and clear-cut. In fact a whole range of objectives was pursued at various points. Early in the period, the highest priority accorded internal security was one which made foreign policy peculiarly important and also peculiarly hazardous. It is obvious enough that the defence of the Bill of Rights which bestowed the throne on Mary Stuart and her husband, and of the Act of Settlement which provided for the Hanoverian Succession, involved a dramatic and extensive revolution in foreign policy. But the temptation presented to foreign states by the existence of a continuous Jacobite threat to the British succession in the first half of the eighteenth century was not a passing one. Every ministry between 1689 and 1750 had to treat the Jacobites and their potential foreign connections as a serious matter, bearing heavily on the conduct of foreign policy, and some were obsessed with the dangers involved. One of the most striking changes in British foreign policy, that represented in the Anglo–French alliance of 1716 and thereafter, derived its *raison d'être* from the succession problem on each side of the English Channel and ran directly counter to many other interests which would naturally have dictated Anglo-French animosity. Every state of any consequence, notably Spain, France, Austria, Sweden, Prussia and Russia, meddled at one time or another in Jacobite intrigues, with important results for Whitehall. The Jacobite threat is frequently treated in terms of a handful of ludicrously ineffectual intriguers and two serious but short-lived rebellions. For those charged with conducting relations with other countries, it was a great deal more.

The problem of a contested succession imposed strains on strategy as well as on diplomacy, and so paved the way for one of the eighteenth century's major contributions to the development of maritime power. Invasion was, of course, an ancient and to some degree perpetual menace so far as Englishmen were concerned. However, a combination of incessant Jacobite intrigues, growing Anglo-French tension and ever increasing commercial dependence on overseas trade, made the war at sea of central significance to British governments. As a result this period produced key concepts which were to characterise British strategic thinking well into the twentieth century. The very term a 'fleet in being' was first employed by Torrington in the 1690s,[1] and thereafter quickly became an established feature of strategic planning. Moreover, it was in the course of the eighteenth century that the idea of the two-power naval standard, a maritime force capable of dealing with the fleets of France and Spain simultaneously, gained currency, and that recognition of the central importance of blockade as a weapon for use against the continental powers developed. In practice, of course, there were naturally many problems. Neither Chancellors of the Exchequer nor country gentlemen in Parliament were always ready to finance the naval expenditure desired by the strategists, nor were the seamen themselves always able to overcome the technical problems involved—witness the failure of the Royal Navy successfully to master the art of bottling up the main French fleet in Brest, until the War of the Austrian Succession.

If British strategic planning was concerned first and foremost with the navy it does not follow that there were no other strategic objectives to be borne in mind by the diplomats. However, broadly speaking, it is true that statesmen, concerned though they might be with the preservation of the continental balance of power, did not have to consider at all seriously the possibility of making territorial gains in Europe. After the sale of Dunkirk in 1662 there was no significant attempt to take over a channel port for example, despite the obvious advantages to be derived from such a foothold on the Continent; in this area the principal aim was rather to restrict

[1] *England in the Reigns of James II and William III* by D. Ogg (Oxford 1955), p. 357.

French construction of naval facilities and fortifications. The harbours at Dunkirk and Mardyke featured in virtually every set of diplomatic negotiations between the two countries, and while the attempt to prevent the French maintaining a naval capability in the Channel was largely impracticable, it was none the less a permanent bone of contention between Paris and London. Moreover Britain was bound to be concerned with the lands lying along the North Sea and Channel coast. The preservation of Belgium in neutral or friendly hands was central to allied war aims in the War of the Spanish Succession, played a vital part in the War of the Austrian Succession, and was an important issue in the Revolutionary and Napoleonic Wars. Indeed, though the old Spanish Netherlands were technically in Austrian ownership after 1713, British statesmen like the Duke of Newcastle were not above describing them as a 'kind of common country in which we, the Dutch, and the Empress-Queen are all interested'.[1] Similarly Holland itself, a declining force in the eighteenth century, was strategically important; in 1787 the Younger Pitt risked war to prevent it becoming a French satellite and in 1793 he actually went to war for the same reason. No minister in London could afford to stand by while a potentially hostile power ensconced itself in the Low Countries.

Further north lay a commitment which was less welcome but equally pressing. From 1714 the electorate of Hanover was the personal property of the kings of England; though it had been a preoccupation of politicians in the early eighteenth century to ensure that this state of affairs would not involve British subservience to Hanoverian interests, in practice the electorate had a large measure of influence on policy. Throughout the reigns of George I and George II Hanover was inevitably a central element in the calculations of British ministers, and the subject of constant controversy. Moreover the electoral connection seemed to bring in its train extensive involvement in continental intrigue and warfare, with heavy expenditure in terms of blood and treasure, and the consequent diversion of resources vitally needed in the Americas, in Africa, in India and on the high seas. Yet in retrospect there is a strong case to

[1] *Sir Charles Hanbury Williams and European Diplomacy* by D. B. Horn (London 1930), p. 149.

be made on behalf of the Hanoverian connection. For Hanover presented to the French an alluring bait which she might have done well to leave alone; though the electorate was of little consequence in its own right, as a possession of the King of England it had enormous potential value as a bargaining counter. Like Flanders, Hanover could be a trump card when played at peace negotiations to recover vulnerable colonial territories overseas. Moreover the British could scarcely avoid being distracted from other commitments by the need to keep a close watch on northern Germany. French intervention in German affairs was in any case traditional and it was all too easy to substitute a casual march to the Weser and Elbe for a more hazardous assault on Britain's coasts or colonies. Indeed in the wars of the mid-century the French staked their future as an imperial power on success in the German theatre. They did not do so merely because the King of England was also Elector of Hanover, but none the less the vulnerability of Hanover played a significant part in their calculations. Yet the result was paradoxical. In the event it was the British who succeeded in limiting their involvement on their continent, the British who witnessed France squander her resources in central Europe, the British who, in Pitt's phrase, conquered America in Germany. With the possible exception of brief periods under Carteret and Newcastle, the underlying priority accorded the colonial and maritime war was rarely threatened, despite the allegations to the contrary which poured from 'patriotic' presses. There were of course many factors at work in the fortunes of the Seven Years' War, the attitudes of the eastern European powers, the basic superiority of the Royal Navy, and so on. But in the last analysis the Hanoverian connection probably worked to the advantage rather than the disadvantage of the British. Nor was it entirely coincidence that in the War of American Independence when Hanover was left peacefully to its own devices, and when the Bourbons committed their resources to overseas instead of continental warfare, Britain was decisively, indeed almost catastrophically, defeated as an imperial power. The despicable electorate was not necessarily a millstone around English necks.

Outside the northwestern corner of Europe the main strategic interest was located in the Mediterranean where, by the late eighteenth century, it was possible for a British official to declare, 'the presence of a British squadron in the Mediterranean is a condition upon which the fate of Europe may almost be said to depend'.[1] In this area it was the legacy of William III and Marlborough which proved crucial. The possibility created by French designs on the Spanish Succession, that the Mediterranean might become a Bourbon lake, precipitated in Whitehall a concern with Mediterranean strategy which was to remain an enduring feature of British policy. Initially it seemed that Lisbon's port facilities might be vital and great weight was placed on the achievement of the Methuens in securing Portugal's accession to the Grand Alliance. Indeed, many European statesmen came to regard eighteenth-century Portugal as, in Choiseul's words, 'an English colony'.[2] However, with the capture of Gibraltar in 1704 and of Minorca in 1708 the emphasis switched naturally to the Mediterranean proper. Gibraltar remained British, despite serious consideration of returning it, by Stanhope in 1718, Sunderland in 1721, Newcastle in 1747, Pitt in 1757 and Shelburne in 1782, and despite determined enemy attack, notably in the War of American Independence. Though public opinion was wedded to the retention of Gibraltar, the case for keeping or abandoning it was delicately balanced; Stanhope was not alone in believing that its naval value was insignificant and its diplomatic disadvantages in terms of Anglo-Spanish friction severe. On the other hand, much depends on an assessment of the trading advantages obtained with a secure post at the meeting point of Europe and North Africa, and much too on a judgement of the extent to which the interests of a rising imperial power like Britain, and those of a decaying imperial power like Spain, were in any case bound to clash in the eighteenth century. Less the subject of controversy, but more difficult to retain, was the island of Minorca. The naval advantages of a fine base from which both to watch the French Mediterranean fleet at Toulon and to protect British trade to the Levant were obvious. However, it proved unexpectedly awkward

[1] *The War of the Second Coalition, 1798–1801* by A. B. Rodger (Oxford 1964), p. 30.
[2] A. Christelow, 'Economic Background of the Anglo-Spanish War of 1762' in *Jnl. Mod. Hist.*, xviii (1946), p. 27.

to defend this valuable acquisition. Minorca was lost temporarily in 1756, and for good in 1781. But a power with growing Mediterranean and even Middle Eastern interests needed something more than Gibraltar. The Revolutionary and Napoleonic Wars amply demonstrated the value of a temporary naval base like Sicily, and more importantly of a permanent one like Malta. British statesmen were slow to grasp the full significance of Malta and acquired an interest in it largely in response to French intervention in the island. But by 1815 it had come to be seen as a vital element in Mediterranean strategy.

In retrospect the most striking feature of Britain's diplomatic and strategic policy is not its interest in European objectives but rather its concentration on new worlds overseas. To a great extent this was part and parcel of the basic rejection of purely territorial gain as an overriding aim of British statesmen. In an age of mercantilism there was nothing extraordinary about concern with economic profit; however, the priority accorded commercial objectives in British policy was almost unique in Europe, and reflected not merely the interested designs of particular mercantile pressure groups but rather the general drift of public, parliamentary and ministerial opinion. Particularly during the reign of Queen Anne the intense hostility of the country gentlemen towards the growing commercial and financial interests of the City tended to reinforce their traditional antipathy towards trade. However, as the eighteenth century wore on this antipathy steadily evaporated, until the landed classes subscribed as much as any to the notion that the wealth of the country ultimately depended on its commerce and industry. Trade, as Walpole was never tired of repeating, actually relieved rather than increased the burden of taxation upon the land; moreover it provided for the gainful and tranquil employment of the poor, those legions of potential troublemakers with whom the propertied classes were so constantly preoccupied. In practice of course, the activities of businessmen were enormously diverse and even conflicting. However, certain points stand out. First and foremost Englishmen were seduced by the glitter of the Indies. Time and again in the eighteenth century government and indeed society at large proved extraordinarily rash in support of schemes intended to strengthen

Britain's share in colonial and overseas trade. The result was to bedevil foreign relations with complications which would certainly not have arisen but for commercial ambitions. No doubt it was true that enmity towards Spain, which was so characteristic a feature of British attitudes in the eighteenth century, was to some extent a result of a Bourbon presence at Madrid. However, it was also the product of commercial competition; if the war of 1718 stemmed from a preoccupation with the Spanish threat to the balance of power, the war of 1739 was the most direct result of bitter conflict in the South American trade. No less significant was rivalry with the French in which commercial differences, though almost inextricably entangled with considerations of power politics, were crucial, particularly in the great colonial and maritime confrontation which finally exploded in the Seven Years' War. In India and Africa, in the West Indies and Canada, on the Mississippi and in the fisheries, it was trade rather than dominion that was at stake. The tea and spices of the East, the gum and slaves of West Africa, the fur and fish of Canada, the sugar and coffee of the Caribbean, all were at issue in the mounting hostility between the courts of George II and Louis XV. Such examples could be multiplied. In an age which valued commerce as the ultimate source of power, and which had as yet little interest in novel doctrines of free trade, this naked economic competition was central to diplomatic and military conflict. Relations with Russia were for long dominated and always influenced by the need to protect a trade which provided valuable raw materials for British industry and the Royal Navy—witness the treaties of 1734 and 1766. Particularly in the early eighteenth century relations with the Austrians were severely affected, and often adversely, by the need to protect the position of the East India Company as well as of British trade with Belgium, and with the hereditary Habsburg lands. Especially at lower levels commerce could completely outrank other considerations. In many German and Italian posts the British envoy was first and foremost a business agent. The office of Ambassador to the Porte at Istanbul was exceptional in being actually financed by the Levant Company, but it was also symptomatic of the importance which was attached both by merchants and ministers to the advancement of commercial interests abroad.

With the advantage of hindsight, it would be easy to mock the reliance which government placed on the eldorados they were apt to see on every hand. Traditional as well as more novel avenues to prosperity were often overrated. Typical were the Newfoundland fisheries which contributed substantially to the bitterness of Anglo-French and to some extent of Anglo-Spanish relations in the eighteenth century. The belief at Versailles that the loss of the French share in the fisheries would beggar three provinces was matched in England by the stern conviction of generations of politicians that the benefits of the fishery, both in terms of direct commercial profit and in terms of national defence and naval recruitment, were incalculably great. In the Seven Years' War Choiseul would concede almost anything rather than the fisheries, while on the other side of the English Channel, Pitt regarded their exclusive possession as an absolute priority. 'England's gold and silver', he called them.[1] Yet there is little by way of conclusive evidence that the contribution of the fisheries, particularly in an age of industrial expansion, deserved the overall economic significance attributed to them. Equally dubious was the value attached to the opening of the Pacific trade in the 1780s and 1790s. Englishmen were led to risk war over Nootka Sound in 1790, for a trade in fur and fish which was trivial at the time and which even in the long run was unlikely to be very great. On a larger scale similar doubts may be expressed as to the entire economic orientation of government strategy in this period. If any age was an age of war, it was the eighteenth century, and it is reasonable to ask whether repeated bouts of severe and often trade-based warfare could benefit the economy. At least in the case of Britain, however, it can be argued that war, though frequently damaging to particular sections of commerce and industry, was generally stimulating in its effect. The impetus given to the development of technology, particularly by government expenditure on the metallurgical industries, was striking; no less important was the fact that Britain's relative success in the wars of the eighteenth century markedly increased her share of world trade. In any event, the critical

[1] J. O. McLachlan, 'The Uneasy Neutrality: A Study of Anglo-Spanish Disputes over Spanish Ships Prized, 1756–1759' in *Cambridge Hist. Jnl.*, vi (1938–40), p. 70.

fact is that it is impossible to discuss foreign policy in the period without giving weight to the role of economic forces. The remarks of one Secretary of State, Lord Holderness, may stand for all. 'I am convinced you will agree with me in one principle, that we must be merchants while we are soldiers, that our trade depends upon a proper exertion of our maritime strength; that trade and maritime force depend upon each other, and that the riches which are the true resources of this country depend upon its commerce'.[1]

Internal and external security, strategic and economic advancements, these were the normal and natural preoccupations of statesmen and those to whom they were responsible in the eighteenth century. Only slightly less important however were the sometimes less rational considerations which operated at one level or another in the making of foreign policy. In a state like Britain, where neither the desires of the monarch nor the projects of the minister were necessarily sufficient to override the wishes of politicians on the one hand, or the propertied classes and even the public at large on the other, the role of prejudice was indeed extensive. Understandably in the light of earlier history, strong predispositions and presumptions were entertained. Dislike of the French was axiomatic despite the fact that Cromwell and his immediate successors in power had frequently supported the French alliance: 'We do naturally love the Spaniard and hate the French', Pepys had remarked.[2] Certainly national loathing for everything French was a consistent feature of public opinion in the period. Admittedly it did not prevent the Anglo-French *entente* which was the policy of Stanhope and Walpole; on the other hand it did much to defeat the progressive scheme of Bolingbroke who sought to create a commercial partnership with France, and played a critical part in preventing that realignment of the Western powers which seemed distantly possible in the 1770s, and which would unquestionably have been in Britain's long-term interest. The long Revolutionary and Napoleonic Wars greatly exacerbated national animosity towards the French but they

[1] A. H. John, 'War and the English Economy, 1700–1763' in *Ec. Hist. Rev.*, 2nd Ser., vii (1954–55), p. 339.

[2] Sir R. Lodge, 'English Neutrality in the War of the Polish Succession' in *Trans. Roy. Hist. Soc.*, 4th Ser., xlv (1931), p. 142.

did not by any means create it. As the diplomat James Harris remarked, it was 'a truth inculcated into John Bull with his mother's milk, viz. that France is our natural enemy'.[1]

Other antipathies were scarcely less influential. Despite the long period of relatively harmonious relations with Madrid in the late seventeenth century, constant disputes over colonial trade in the eighteenth century brought out intense anti-Spanish feeling, repeatedly and amply attested by the public uproar associated, for example, with the Spanish depredations of the 1730s, the Falkland Islands crisis of 1770, and the Nootka Sound affair in 1790. A prejudice which receded as the rivalries underpinning it vanished was that against the Dutch. Hostility towards the aggressive businessmen of Holland had a long pedigree, and even in the War of the Spanish Succession when the Dutch were allies in the cause of the Grand Alliance, the Tory party nourished a bitter hatred of them. Indeed in the years after the accession of William of Orange, domestic and foreign politics were heavily entangled and the feelings which were later to centre in distaste for Hanover were then expressed against the Netherlands. 'If you would discover a concealed Tory', it was expressed in 1706, 'speak but of the Dutch and you will find him out by his passionate railing'.[2] Anti-Dutch feeling reached its zenith in the furore over the Barrier Treaty in 1710; thereafter it was overtaken by the continuing menace of the Bourbons and by Holland's decline as a world power. Indeed, the connection between the incidence of national interests and the sway of these national prejudices may appear to suggest that the latter were little more than symptoms of the former. To a great extent this was doubtless the case. What matters however is that there was in the English a deep fund of xenophobia on which interested parties could draw almost at will. This does not make it less important than more specific and consistent attitudes of mind. On the contrary, the mindless patriotism of the community at large was a devastatingly potent force which on occasion could sweep away even those who sought to ride it. The power of public opinion is not easily analysed in any period,

[1] *Ambassadors and Secret Agents* by A. Cobban (London 1954), p. 89.
[2] A. D. McLachlan, 'The Road to Peace, 1710–13' in *Britain after the Glorious Revolution, 1689–1714* ed. G. Holmes (London 1970), p. 199.

let alone in the eighteenth century, but that it existed can scarcely be doubted. The antics of politicians when the gale of public opinion blew strongly on issues of foreign policy, as in 1739, in 1756, and in 1790, were ample evidence of that. No doubt in other countries too this often irrational and damaging force was present. But in Britain political and constitutional conditions gave it a much more effective role than was the case in most European states.

Nor indeed were statesmen themselves devoid of prejudice and predisposition in their conduct of foreign policy. The Younger Pitt was unusual, for instance, in claiming that there were no eternal animosities or friendships. 'To suppose', he remarked in Parliament in 1787, 'that any nation could be unalterably the enemy of another, was weak and childish. It had neither its foundation in the experience of nations nor in the history of man'.[1] Yet in practice most ministers believed in such enmities and amities. It is difficult, for example, to account for the recurrent anxiety of British statesmen to pursue an alliance with Austria when it had ceased to be an obviously valuable commodity except in these terms. The 'old system' of William III, with its reliance on the Habsburg alliance, and described as the 'evil genius of Britain' by Bolingbroke,[2] was ever an object of many politicians, even in the late eighteenth century. Other elements in the Whig creed, the Revolutionary 'contract' of 1688–89, the Protestant succession and toleration, liberty and property, were banal and generally unobjectionable. But the 'old system' was a more serious matter, since it bore on constant realities of politics where there was a grave and authentic choice. Time and time again in the mid-eighteenth century politicians like Pelham and Newcastle, and indeed like George III (hated by so many Whigs yet fundamentally so intensely Whiggish in his political convictions), hankered for an Austrian alliance long after Habsburg policy had clearly removed it from the realm of either possible or desirable objectives. And in the 1790s when a German alliance against France once again became plausible, the natural advantages of a Viennese policy were inevitably cited. 'My own manner of thinking,' Carmarthen, as the Younger Pitt's Foreign Secretary declared, 'with respect to Austria and

[1] *The Younger Pitt: The Years of Acclaim* by J. H. Ehrman (London 1969), p. 493.
[2] *The British Diplomatic Service, 1689–1789* by D. B. Horn (Oxford 1961), p. 23.

Prussia remains, and probably ever will remain, unshaken: the first ought to be the *perpetual*, as it is the *natural* ally of England, the second one can, I apprehend, be but an *occasional* one'.[1]

The one prejudice which can rarely be detected in the minds of those in power is in some ways the most interesting one, and yet at the same time the most difficult to pin down. Religion, a key factor in the international disputes of the seventeenth century is generally, and with considerable justice, treated as something of an irrelevance in the stately but none the less naked realpolitik of the eighteenth. Yet religion was not something that could be ignored in a society where popular opinion could carry the influence it did in Britain. As in domestic politics the mob itself had a way of fiercely defending the Church of England against nonconformists, Methodists and papists, so in international affairs it had an instinctive liking for Protestant crusades long after European statesmen had ceased to regard religion as a serious issue. Heavily intermixed with the popular antipathy to the Bourbon powers in terms either of power politics or pure xenophobia was a significant portion of religious bigotry. Ministerial interest in such questions was largely limited to the concern of early eighteenth-century administrations with the Papacy's involvement in Jacobite intrigues, and with such purely coincidental manoeuvres as the bullying of the Vatican to procure the release from a papal prison of Lord Peterborough, whose eccentric activities on the Continent led him into trouble in 1717. But it was not possible to ignore the concern of the press and the public with religious affairs. The prosecution of Protestants in the Empire and in Poland, and above all the massacre at Thorn in 1724, was, for example, a contributory factor in the feeling in England which permitted Townshend to adopt an aggressive stance towards Austria in the mid-1720s, and which even provoked talk of a war 'in defence of Luther'.[2] Similarly the alliance of Prussia, which Newcastle and Pitt developed simply for reasons of national security, struck a remarkable chord of religious emotion during the Seven

[1] *Great Britain and Prussia in the Eighteenth Century* by Sir R. Lodge (Oxford 1923), pp. 163–64.
[2] G. C. Gibbs, 'Britain and the Alliance of Hanover, April 1725–February 1726' in *Eng. Hist. Rev.*, lxxiii (1958), p. 423.

Years' War. Unlikely figure though he was, Frederick II was to Englishmen the Protestant hero.

Though religious feeling gradually lost ground, it was to some extent replaced in the late eighteenth century by a more specific and in some ways more effective moral force. The rapid growth of the crusade against slavery as an international institution was bound to have an effect on British foreign policy. Particularly in the last years of the Napoleonic Wars when Castlereagh was laying the basis for a peace settlement, the moral fervour of the middle classes, translated into specific pressure on the question of the slave trade, could not be neglected. Thus Wellington remarked on the 'degree of frenzy existing here about the Slave Trade. People in general appear to think it would suit the policy of the nation to go to war and put an end to that *abominable* traffic, and many wish we should take the field on this new crusade'.[1] The inclusion of the eventual abolition of the commerce in slaves among the peace terms agreed at Vienna was entirely a result of this pressure. Nothing could be more powerful testimony to the extent to which British statesmen, in great measure by contrast with their continental colleagues, were compelled to listen to the voice of those they served, and to adopt aims and objectives which lay outside the customary preoccupations of European courts.

[1] *The Foreign Policy of Castlereagh, 1812–1815* by C. K. Webster (London 1931), p. 413.

3 The Pattern of Foreign Policy

Whatever the pressures on those responsible for the direction of foreign policy, whatever the aims they and their associates set themselves, to a great extent foreign policy was bound to be shaped by circumstances beyond British control. The shifting pattern of international relations in Europe interacted with domestic forces to produce a complex pattern in which it is not always easy to discern clear or consistent lines. None the less it is possible to outline some of the central themes in the development of British foreign policy, and some of the significant changes affecting the diplomatic context in which it operated. The period began with a dramatic recasting of the traditional framework of policy not merely in England but in Western Europe generally. In England the Revolution of 1688, by enthroning William of Orange, reversed thirty years or more of largely pro-French policy in favour of an aggressively anti-French one. In European terms the change of sovereign in England strengthened the will and capability of Louis XIV's enemies and opened a generation of bitter and costly warfare on an unprecedented scale. In twenty years of hostilities between 1689 and 1714, interrupted only by the brief interlude which followed the Peace of Ryswick in 1697, Britain's primary interest concerned the need to protect her Protestant succession. There were other themes too, notably the preservation of the European balance of power in the face of Louis XIV's designs first on the Netherlands and Germany and subsequently on the Spanish empire generally. But fundamentally what was at issue for Englishmen was the security of their succession, first embodied in the rule of William of Orange and his wife Mary, subsequently in that of Mary's sister, Queen Anne, and finally in default of Protestant heirs of the Stuarts, in the settlement of the English and Scottish thrones on the Hanoverian dynasty. It is no exaggeration to claim that the defence of the Bill of Rights and the Act of Settlement was the central aim of foreign policy until 1720 and an essential part of it until the 1750s. Yet in the process of this defence, Britain's status in Europe changed astonishingly. Admittedly the Nine Years' War was a desperate affair in which little was gained but much saved. A serious threat of invasion, a massive onslaught on trade, both were defeated as much perhaps by luck as judgement. By contrast the War of the Spanish Succession, no less defensive in concept, transformed Britain into a power of the first rank, capable of determining the fate of Europe. Marlborough's victories, which humbled the mighty power of the Sun King, prevented Italy and the Netherlands from falling into French hands, while the capture of Gibraltar and Minorca helped to preserve the Mediterranean balance of power. However, the financial and economic strains of such a war were colossal and when even Marlborough finally began to falter in Flanders, it was not to be expected that the propertied classes would continue to support so devastating a burden. The Treaty of Utrecht, willed by the nation and negotiated by Harley and St John, was the subject of bitter denunciation by Whigs at the time and thereafter entered the Whig mythology of Tory atrocities. Yet it was a sensible and necessary peace, as well as one which registered a new peak in Britain's international standing. French historians have perhaps exaggerated in seeing the Peace of Utrecht as creating an era of British hegemony,[1] but it undoubtedly reflected a major change in the balance of power between the states on either side of the English Channel and indeed in Western Europe generally. The age of French dominance was drawing to a close, albeit without the spectacular débâcle in Paris and Madrid for which Marlborough had worked, and new powers, Britain, and even Prussia and Russia, were moving towards the centre of the stage.

The reign of George I, which began almost as soon as the Peace of Utrecht had been ratified, was dominated by two themes, one traditional, one novel. To a great extent the foreign policy of Stanhope and even subsequently of Townshend and Walpole was

[1] See, for example, *La Prépondérance Anglaise* (*1715–1763*) by P. Muret (Paris 1942).

determined by the threat to the succession. Between 1714 and 1720 a series of dynastic crises was surmounted; the 'fifteen' was defeated and Spanish and Swedish support for Jacobites neutralised. More startling was the diplomatic revolution brought about by the Anglo-French alliance of 1716, an alliance negotiated by a French court concerned with the plight of the Regent and the doubtful prospects of a young and ailing French king in Louis XV, and a British court equally nervous as to its own permanence and stability. This novel alignment was employed to great effect in the Mediterranean, where the courts of Vienna and Madrid still refused to accept the partition of the Spanish empire agreed at Utrecht as definitive. Spain, which seemed the more reckless of the two discontented parties was firmly disciplined by the diplomacy of Stanhope and Dubois which brought Austria, though not the United Provinces, into a system of collective security, the so-called Quadruple Alliance of 1718, and by the armed force of the Royal Navy which shattered the Spanish fleet at Cape Passaro and compelled the Spaniards to bring their grievances to an international congress at Cambrai. In the north, peace was only partially the aim of the ministers of George I. The interests of Hanover were uppermost in the mind of the new king and—a sinister foretaste of things to come, so it was thought—the British navy was used in the Baltic in support of electoral interests, first to force the Swedes to disgorge Bremen and Verden, the petty acquisitions for which the Hanoverians lusted, and then to prevent the Russians, under the impressive leadership of Peter I, from filling the now obvious power vacuum in the Baltic. At home the strains of this northern policy temporarily split the Whig party and initiated that most characteristic of Georgian preoccupations with the allegedly malign influence of the Hanoverian connection.

The 'age of Hanover' in British foreign policy was to last for some thirty years. However, though all policy making was bound to be in some measure affected by the influence of Hanover, a variety of approaches were adopted to the basic problems of Britain's role in Europe. Under Townshend in the 1720s, the emphasis was in many ways reminiscent of Stanhope. The French alliance remained the centre-plank of London's strategy, and again the primary problem concerned the enmities of Austria and Spain, particularly their rivalry in Italy. Townshend however, was confronted with an entirely novel twist to this situation. So disillusioned were both Madrid and Vienna at the extent of Anglo-French cooperation that in desperation they were driven into each other's arms. The resulting Alliance of Vienna in 1725 overturned the system inaugurated by the Quadruple Alliance of 1718 and set Europe by its ears. Whether Townshend's policy, which consisted of instant response and confrontation, signalised in a great opposing Alliance of Hanover, was prudent, is matter for debate. In any event, between 1726 and 1729 the armies and navies of Europe were on a war footing and in the case of Britain and Spain there was open conflict on the high seas. In the end Spain and Austria were brought to climb down but not before the Continent had once again faced the prospect of all-out war and not before Sir Robert Walpole, Townshend's brother-in-law and ally, had grasped the dangers implicit in Townshend's positive but adventurous policy in defence of the balance of power and Anglo-French hegemony. In 1730, with Townshend at the apparent height of his prestige and power, Walpole struck. Henceforward he was not only First Lord of the Treasury and 'Prime Minister' as he had been since 1721, but effectively Foreign Minister as well.

Walpole's foreign policy is easier to characterise than that of almost any other eighteenth-century minister. In a word it was peace. Above everything Walpole wanted peace, peace to maintain the political and financial security with low taxation and domestic tranquillity which were his own peculiar contributions to the constitutional stability of the day, peace to permit the consolidation of the Hanoverian succession and the neutralisation of the Jacobite threat, peace to keep himself in power at court and in the Commons. In some respects the results were dazzlingly successful. It was, for instance, Walpole who solved the Austro-Spanish disputes at least for the present. British offices were used to mollify both powers, to arrange a compromise in Italy which allowed the Spaniards in part to get their way there and the Emperor to obtain guarantees for the peaceful accession of his daughter to the Habsburg throne. And when the ancient rivalry of Habsburg and Bourbon did finally burst forth in the inaptly named War of the Polish Succession in 1733, it was Walpole who managed to keep Britain out of the

European conflagration despite the pressure brought to bear by the king and queen at home and by the Austrians abroad. These years of peace during times of significant international tension were arguably disasterous for the cause of the Pretender. Not until Walpole's fall were the Jacobites given an opportunity for invasion and rebellion and it is possible that the enterprise which by 1745 stood little chance of success might in 1735 have worn a quite different aspect. On the other hand there were undoubted disadvantages to Walpole's policy. For one thing the effective cost of peace at any price was the loss of the French alliance. Under Fleury France remained ostensibly friendly, but in practice she moved steadily out of the British orbit, first under the impact of Walpole's double dealing to settle Austro-Spanish differences in 1731, and subsequently in an anxiety to join Spain in a new raid for Austrian booty. The First Family Compact of the Bourbons in 1733 was precisely the spectre which had haunted Whigs since the failure of the Grand Alliance to prevent Philip V's accession to the Spanish throne early in the century. Perhaps in the long run it was inevitable; but in the short run it was to a marked extent Walpole's responsibility. Nor was isolation the only penalty which followed from Walpole's policy. By the late 1730s powerful interests at home were incensed by alleged Spanish depredations against legal and illegal British trade with the Spanish Indies. Though Walpole strove all he could to arrest the slide to war, and nearly succeeded with the Convention of the Pardo in 1739, he was finally overwhelmed by the combined force of political opponents in alliance with vested commercial interests and a responsive public opinion. Walpole was not made to manage war, and by 1742 repeated failure in the West Indies campaigns and elsewhere had cut away his support in administration. However, when it came his fall was merely part of a complex pattern of political developments throughout Europe.

Thanks to the death of the Emperor Charles VI in 1740 and the massive Bourbon and Hohenzollern onslaught on the inheritance of his daughter Maria Theresa, the War of Jenkins' Ear quickly became absorbed in that of the Austrian Succession, one of the most confusing periods of diplomacy and warfare even in the eighteenth century. In appearance it was also one of the least conclusive. The

Treaty of Aix-la-Chapelle in 1748 effectively returned Britain to her pre-war position *vis à vis* both France and Spain, despite nearly a decade of warfare on a truly worldwide scale for the first time. Yet it also registered two changes which were to be of the utmost importance for the future. For one thing the war discredited a 'Hanoverian' or 'continental' foreign policy and prepared the way for the grand strategy of the mid-century. Between 1742 and 1744 Carteret conducted British foreign policy with an exclusively European orientation and threw his own remarkable talents as well as his country's resources into remodelling the balance of power on the Continent. By 1744 it was clear that he had lost credibility abroad and power at home. Though Newcastle and for that matter Pitt were subsequently to be much concerned with the need for allies in Europe, Carteret's failure spelt the demise in Britain of an authentically continental policy of the kind which France herself operated. Significantly, 1744 saw the capture of Louisburg in Canada and 1746 the loss of Madras in India; though these conquests were restored at the Peace they strengthened the new and growing concern of statesmen on both sides of the Channel with overseas interests.

Indeed for Englishmen the age of empire had begun, an age in which maritime and colonial strategy, so ardently advocated by Tories at the beginning of the century and for long apparently neglected, were to move to the centre of the stage. In the short run this era was to be marked by the staggering successes of the Seven Years' War under the elder Pitt; in the longer term it was to be soured by the isolation of the 1760s and the imperial humiliation which stopped only just short of catastrophe in the War of American Independence. At the time it was easy to attribute the success to the elder Pitt, and the failure to Lord North. In retrospect it is possible to give more weight to the shifting patterns of continental power politics. The most striking developments of the mid-century were the rise of Russia, which in successive wars asserted its claim to rank with Austria and with France, and of Prussia, which despite the colossal strains imposed by the adventures of Frederick II, decisively completed its transition from German to European power status. So far as Britain, with its eyes increasingly on North America, was concerned, the crucial question turned on the attitude of France towards the tremendous conflict building up in central Europe. Already in 1740 the French had prepared to intervene in the Anglo-Spanish confrontation taking place in the West Indies, only to be distracted by the deceptive prospect of a share in the partition of the Habsburg Empire. In the 1750s their dilemma was equally if not more marked since the basic conflict between French and British colonists in North America, in the Neutral Islands of the West Indies, and via the monopoly East India Companies, in India, was fast reaching the point of explosion. In this situation it was the French who made the decisive blunder and became inextricably involved in German politics once again, pledging themselves to support Vienna's attempt to regain Silesia from Frederick II, and devoting resources to the European theatre which could have not merely saved but extended their empire around the world. Britain, as it happened, played a crucial role in the alliances which registered this orientation of French policy; indeed it was Newcastle who by insuring Hanover's security with both Prussian and Russian subsidy treaties, pushed France and Austria together, and so precipitated the Diplomatic Revolution of 1756–57. But for Britain, these alliances were of secondary rather than primary concern. They were indeed a vital part of world strategy, as Pitt's ready adoption of Newcastle's policy in its broad outlines signified, but they were not the material part. Plassey, Louisburg, Goree, Guadaloupe, Quebec, Martinique, and with Spain once more in the ring, Havana and Manila, these were the fruits of a slightly modified but none the less authentic 'blue-water policy'. The peace made by the young George III soon after his accession was bitterly attacked by the politicians who had wanted an all-out war policy, and who considered its many gains inadequate. But it was without doubt an extraordinarily striking achievement for a Britain which only three-quarters of a century before had been seen by most Europeans as little more than a client state of France. Marlborough's victories and Pitt's triumphs, which had together brought about this transformation, had their origins in different strategies; Marlborough's was primarily continental, Pitt's primarily maritime. But in each case it was the change of emphasis in a context of French inflexibility which proved decisive.

1763 was a turning-point in British foreign policy and in the pattern of European diplomacy generally, but it was one whose full significance British statesmen were slow to grasp. Two central facts should have been clear to them, firstly that French and Spanish humiliation in the Seven Years' War was almost bound to lead to a war of revenge at a later stage, and secondly that the prospects of obtaining reinsurance alliances of the kind negotiated in the first half of the eighteenth century were dim. Russia and Prussia had little interest in sustaining an overweening British supremacy against the Bourbons, at any rate without firm promises of compensating support on the Continent, and Austria was firmly attached to her new alliance with France. A rapprochement between the courts of Louis XV and George III was the only obvious way of breaking out of this diplomatic circle, and was indeed seriously considered at a number of points. But French statesmen were not anxious to give up their plans of revenge, nor would British public opinion have readily accepted an alliance with the Bourbon powers. The only option left, that of massive naval armament, with a permanent maritime superiority over all-comers was ruled out by the need for economy after years of costly warfare.

Successive ministries, of every political complexion, sought a way out of this dilemma in the 1760s. It was ironic that after the final collapse of Jacobitism it should be more difficult to find allies than it had been while the succession itself was in such danger. Yet little could be done in the existing pattern of international relations, and though the foreign policy of the 1760s was neither consistent nor particularly competent, it is difficult even in retrospect to see how it could have been improved. Unfortunately what the post-war governments did succeed in doing was to pick a quarrel with their own increasingly self-confident American colonists in the worst possible circumstances for Britain and the best for her enemies. The dangers inherent in isolation after the Seven Years' War were made explicit in the War of American Independence, and it was scarcely surprising that ultimately the British proved incapable of overcoming their own rebellious colonies, in league with the united force of France and Spain, and without the assistance of a European diversion or continental allies. In particular the central fallacy of 'patriot' politicians, that European alliances merely weakened domestic interests, was amply exposed to view. What is remarkable is not that in this emergency Britain partially succumbed and in so doing lost a vast empire in America, but rather that so much was saved from the wreck at the peace treaty of Versailles in 1783.

Disaster brought about that rethinking of foreign policy which success had signally failed to achieve, and in 1783 statesmen proved more ready to review the position than they had been in 1763. Many of the ideas touted not merely by the pundits but by politicians like Shelburne and Pitt, were less than sensible, and Shelburne's vision of an international peace based on extensive economic cooperation with America and Western Europe inevitably foundered on the rocks of tradition and prejudice. None the less, there gradually emerged in the 1780s a new assessment of Britain's international position. Under the Younger Pitt there was much that was either ill-considered, like his attitude in the Ochakov crisis, or traditional, like his policy in the Nootka Sound affair. But there was also much that was new, like the Eden Treaty with France in 1786, and the gradual reform of imperial institutions. Above all the Dutch crisis of 1787 led the court of George III out of isolation into a powerful alliance with Prussia, and re-established it as a major force in European politics. French decline after the triumphs of the American War was deceptive, and ultimately to be reversed by the Revolution, but if anything was clear by 1790 it was that Britain was far from being the shattered power pictured by many contemporaries in the light of the disasters of the American War.

The reconstruction of the 1780s was crucial, as it turned out, not merely because it restored Britain as a great power, but also because it prepared her to play a part in defending the European order against the threat represented by an age of revolution and an era of French aggrandisement. It was not of course inevitable that Britain would take up arms against the French Revolution. On the contrary, the Younger Pitt and most of his colleagues were clear that the Revolution must be opposed not for its assault on the *ancien régime* but only if it attempted to interfere with the settled state system on the Continent. In fact long after Prussia and Austria had resorted to violence the British government was attempting to maintain its neutrality. In the end it was the obvious threat represented by the

French Republic to the independence not merely of Belgium, already conquered, but even of Holland, which proved decisive. Moreover, though George III's ministers thereafter dabbled in royalist intrigues and conspiracies, they were insistent that they were fighting not to reverse the changes carried out in France between 1789 and 1793 but merely to protect British continental and colonial interests and to safeguard the balance of power in Europe. However, this turned out to be a difficult task. Not until 1802 in the Peace of Amiens did it prove possible to reach even a temporary compromise with the French. In the intervening period there were two great European coalitions, both subsidised by London, and both ultimately shattered by the force of French arms, a depressing series of military failures both in western Europe and in the West Indies, and perhaps the most punishing war in British history to date.

It says much for British stamina that when the Napoleonic Empire turned out to be as dangerous a menace to the liberties of Europe as its republican predecessor, there was no hesitation about returning to the fray. If anything the war was more depressing than before. Apart from the control of the high seas which the victories of Nelson secured, there was little from which to draw comfort. To the disunity of successive and costly coalitions, and the military ineffectiveness of the British war effort, were also added new and alarming developments, notably the naked economic warfare embodied in the Continental System, and the inexorable advance of hostilities with the United States. The strains of war in a country already in the throes of her first industrial crisis were colossal. Yet they were overcome. Technically, Britain's contribution to the destruction of Napoleon was limited essentially to the Peninsular War and the financing of the Fourth Coalition. But it was also sustained by a record of twenty years, grim and undefeated resistance to the power unleashed by the French Revolution, and directed against the traditional structure of Europe.

It was fitting that Britain's role in the peace settlement of 1815 should reflect her now undoubted hegemony on and beyond the high seas and her recognition in Europe as a power second to none. The measures for the containment of France, the arrangements for collective security enshrined in the Congress system, the re-creation of a modified *ancien régime* in the territorial remodelling on the Continent, all owed much to British diplomatic efforts. But above all, 1815 and the years immediately after were to reveal the essential nature of Britain's conception of her own role in the world. The British remained in Europe and yet they were not of it; where Metternich and Alexander I talked casually of intervention to put down every petty rebellion against their system of organised reaction, British statesmen would only intervene if the balance of power or their own overseas interests, particularly in the east, were likely to be affected. Ever since 1689 the British had accepted their association with Europe; but in 1815, as for most of the preceding century and a quarter, they conceived that association as a strictly limited liability.

PART 2

The Defence
of the Succession
1688–1721

4 The Price of Revolution, 1688—1702

If the Glorious Revolution of 1688 was a revolution in anything (and recent historians have tended to stress its more conservative aspects and underlying continuity), it was in foreign policy. This was not because those who instigated the appearance of William of Orange in England and those who acquiesced in James II's effective dethronement, were particularly concerned with the affairs of Europe at the time. Rather it was because accepting William of Orange meant accepting a great deal else. William was nothing if not a continental statesman; his overriding concern was the protection not merely of the Dutch Netherlands, but of the liberties of Europe in general against the growing power and interference of Louis XIV's France. Moreover the French king, whatever his differences with his English cousins in the past, had no intention of standing idly by while the House of Orange unseated that of Stuart. Together these two forces, the continental concerns of the new king and the interest of France in the English succession, forced Englishmen into a major change of attitude towards the continent. Cromwell and Charles II had actually aided and abetted the rise of French power, and even the somewhat equivocal James had shown little interest in directly opposing it. Moreover three wars had been fought against the Dutch between 1652 and 1674. If, in the face of Louis XIV's mounting campaign to extend French influence in Germany and the Low Countries, any policy seemed to follow logically from the legacy of these years, it was one of neutrality if not actual junction with the French. Yet at one stroke the affairs of 1688 changed all that. Almost overnight Englishmen found themselves committed to alliance with Holland, to cooperation with the great league of powers marshalled by William to resist French dominance (the so-called League of Augsburg) and to a full-scale war against France. This is not to claim that the war was not to the advantage of England at the time, or that William of Orange's new subjects were sacrificed on the altar of Dutch interest. On the contrary, the treaties which were negotiated between London and the Hague in 1689 and which provided the detailed arrangements for English participation with the League of Augsburg against Louis XIV were in no sense a surrender to Dutch objectives. The United Provinces were after all totally committed to war, and were in no position to drive a hard bargain in terms of the means by which the war at sea and on land was to be waged and in terms of the allies' respective contributions to the war effort. Moreover the war, variously known as the Nine Years' War, King William's War and the War of the League of Augsburg, could as easily have been described as the War of the English Succession. It was not possible to unseat James II without protecting his successor, and there can be little question that in 1689 the political nation accepted the regrettable necessity of a major continental war for the first time since Elizabeth's Spanish war in order to safeguard the succession.

As a strategic exercise the Nine Years' War was frustrating but ultimately successful. In all the crucial theatres of war the French offensive was halted, if not decisively. By 1690 the Jacobites had been largely brought to heel in Scotland, while in the same year the Battle of the Boyne signalised the securing of William's succession in Ireland. At sea, national humiliation in the battle of Beachy Head in the summer of 1689 was salved by a crushing victory in 1692 at La Hogue. In the Netherlands a depressing series of French advances, Mons in 1691, Namur and Steenkirk in 1692, and Neerwinden in 1693, was finally blunted by one of William III's rare personal victories with the recovery of Namur in 1694. This was not a very distinguished or dazzling record, and indeed the victor of the Boyne and Namur was not by any standards a great general; yet his achievement was sufficient to bring Louis XIV, if not without reluctance and not without extended negotiations, to the concessions which were essential if even a fragile peace were to be made. The treaties made at Ryswick in September 1697 between England, France, Spain and the United Provinces, effectively ended the war, though it remained for a disgruntled Emperor to come in at the end of October. To appease his continental opponents, Louis XIV was compelled to make territorial concessions; to buy off the English he had to concede the most crucial point of all, recognition of the Revolution of 1688. The recognition was inevitably grudging and qualified. William had demanded, and with greater victories would have obtained, complete acceptance of his own legitimate right to the throne of England and Scotland, a promise from the French king to disown James II and Mary of Modena, and even the expulsion from French territory of the royal family and all those associated with it. But given the limited nature of the military advantage gained by the allies and given the impossibility of humiliating Louis XIV to the point of utter indignity, the compromise achieved was worth having. William himself was recognised formally as king; but despite assurances allegedly given in the preliminary negotiations there was no actual repudiation, let alone expulsion, of James II. The latter had not helped his own cause by flatly rejecting a variety of compromises considered on both sides of the English Channel, ranging from his own acceptance of the Polish Crown as compensation for the loss of the English, to the succession of his son, after an appropriate Protestant education, to the English throne. Even so Louis XIV declined to betray the man he regarded as king by divine right of England.

The Peace of Ryswick, inaptly named since only the formal completion of the treaties took place at the congress summoned to Ryswick, brought to a moderately satisfactory end an uninspiring war, at any rate from the Englishman's point of view. Yet in retrospect the Nine Years' War can be seen as one of significance far beyond its purely military or diplomatic impact. As has been seen, by its very origin it involved a major revolution in British foreign policy and a degree of commitment to continental warfare which had not been paralleled since the reign of Elizabeth I. Not surprisingly then, it displayed a number of novel features of the utmost importance. Even to contemporaries it was obvious, for example, that the scale and cost of this war were quite unprecedented. On average the Nine Years' War involved the British taxpayer in liability for a sum of something like £5 million per annum. The means by which this sum was found is more a part of financial than diplomatic history; yet it was also more important to diplomatic history than any amount of actual diplomacy. The establishment of the Bank of England, the creation of the National Debt, these were symptoms, though hardly likely to be recognised as such at the time, of a new and as it turned out critical approach to the whole problem of financing heavy national expenditure. A system which permitted the raising of vast sums of money at short notice and without impugning the credit or stability of the state, was almost beyond the dreams of European statesmen. Yet in England in the years after the Revolution, the foundations were laid for precisely such a system and one which was to grow and endure in the following decades and centuries. William of Orange himself saw clearly the significance of this admirably acceptable way of finding resources to fight a colossally expensive war, by borrowing based on parliamentary guarantee, and not merely on royal authority. 'Take care', he told Parliament, 'of the public credit, which cannot be preserved but by keeping sacred that maxim, that they shall never be losers who trust to a parliamentary security'.[1]

If the financial consequences of the Nine Years' War were heavy with implications for the future, so were its strategic lessons. The fundamental fact about the Nine Years' War was that it was a continental war of a kind long unwaged by Englishmen. In the short run it was obvious enough that William of Orange's drive against the French offensive in the Low Countries would have to be supported and subsidised. But it did not take many years of expensive and depressingly futile campaigning before there emerged a school of opinion which recognised the inevitability of continued involvement in the war but which also offered an alternative strategy. The crucial stage in the process perhaps occurred with the bloody defeat at Steenkirk in 1692, when to many it seemed that unfeeling Dutch generals had sacrificed great quantities of English blood in a hopeless cause. This view was not entirely accurate but neither was it without some colour of plausibility, and it was not to be expected that there would be unthinking acquiescence in England. In fact there was a

[1] *England in the Reigns of James II and William III* by D. Ogg (Oxford 1955), p. 413.

storm of protest. As Nottingham, one of the more amenable Tories remarked, 'it was not likely the Parliament would be of opinion that so great a share of the expense should be or could be spent in Flanders'.[1] In the event, at any rate during the Nine Years' War, Parliament accepted the necessity for the campaign in Belgium. But there was none the less a growing belief that there must be other and equally effective, while less wasteful, means of curbing French power. It was on the high seas, in onslaught on French trade and the French navy, and in the colonies, at the sources of French colonial and maritime power, that the main concentration of the English war effort should take place, so the argument ran. In particular the navy must be utilised as an offensive weapon. Thus Admiral Rooke insisted that 'blocking up the enemy fleet in their principal port, insulting their coast, and burning their towns at the same time, must, in all humble opinion, expose them to the world, make them very uneasy at home, and give a reputation to his Majesty's arms'.[2] Early attempts in this direction, with combined operations against the French coast and in the West Indies, were not encouraging. However, this 'blue-water strategy' was to be revived repeatedly in the following century and indeed at times became something of an orthodoxy. Its political attractiveness, both in terms of possible financial economies, and in terms of the support to be gained by a policy which eschewed direct involvement on the continent of Europe, was never negligible, and indeed at times overwhelming. Later on, 'patriotic' Englishmen liked to see it as England's traditional policy and were wont to link it in particular with the much approved practices of Elizabeth I. But it would be more realistic to see its emergence together with the consequent inauguration of the great debate between the merits of continental and maritime policies, as one of the important legacies of the Nine Years' War, and less directly of the Revolution of 1688.

Even at the time peculiar importance was attached to elements in the blue-water strategy which all saw as essential, whatever the underlying pattern of war. For example, contemporaries were well

[1] *William III* by S. B. Baxter (London 1966), p. 305.
[2] *William III and Louis XIV. Essays 1680–1720 by and for Mark S. Thomson* ed. R. Hatton and J. S. Bromley (Liverpool 1968), p. 66.

aware that the navy was acquiring a more and more important role. Admittedly, the accent in retrospect must again be on the implications rather than the immediate effects of change. Neither the battle of Beachy Head nor that of La Hogue bestowed great credit on their victors, and neither was properly exploited. But more telling was the growing and indeed quite novel importance attached, for example, to the maintenance of a fleet in the approaches to Brest, ready to blockade the enemy before it could emerge either to spearhead an invasion of the British Isles or an onslaught on the colonies. Comparable was the despatch of a fleet to the Mediterranean, a theatre far, at least in theory, from traditional British interests, to counter the French naval presence in the south. In neither case were the immediate results entirely satisfactory. At no point in the Nine Years' War did the Royal Navy master the difficult art of permanently blockading the French Atlantic fleet, and naval operations in the Mediterranean were maintained for only two years. But in the long run both strategies were to pay handsome rewards.

More important than these dawning symptoms of a new era in British foreign and strategic policy was one simple and overriding fact. Above all else the Nine Years' War was one which operated on a new and alarming level. Total war is a term reserved for the era of the French Revolution or even later; yet war in the 1690s, at least in so far as it involved Britain, made devastating and essentially novel demands. Politically, for example, the war unleashed an exceedingly dangerous crisis. For the first time in a century the threat of invasion was a real one. In 1689 and 1690, with Scotland and Ireland apparently aflame with rebellion, the menace posed by French invasion plans was intensely disturbing. Only the crass mismanagement of the French navy after the great victory of Beachy Head prevented England's enemies from launching a lethal assault on its shores. Again in 1696 there was an invasion scare as well as a conspiracy at home, culminating in the Fenwick plot and several months of extreme political tension. In terms of the economy the extraordinary dimensions of the crisis of the 1690s were also obvious. The war against trade was a vital element in the strategy of both sides, and especially in that of the French. Vauban's belief that ultimately the maritime powers would be reduced more by a war on their commerce than on their navies or armies, was by no means without support. This was after all the great age of French privateering, the age of Jean Bart, and the most spectacular blow of all— the French interception of the great Smyrna Convoy in June 1693— was merely the most striking, and one which provoked a considerable political crisis in London. Like the invasion plans, like the desperate financial crisis, this war on business merely reflected a basic fact: that Englishmen, as a result of the revolution they had engineered in 1688, now found themselves in a new and sinister era of instability.

In view of the many pressures which a great European war brought to bear on all aspects of English political and economic life, it was not surprising that its so-called author came in for considerable criticism. William III was not in any case the most attractive of figures, but what made him peculiarly liable to objection was undoubtedly his allegedly Dutch bias. It was repeatedly charged against him, not altogether without reason, that English generals and statesmen were consistently discriminated against in favour of Dutch; his frequent absences abroad, amounting to sixty-two months in a short reign, not merely during the war but thereafter, laid him open to the charge that he was unduly negligent of domestic interests; above all his blatant use of English patronage and Irish lands to feed the demands of Dutch favourites, together with his refusal after the Peace of Ryswick entirely to disband his armies, raised a storm of protest, which played into the hands of the new and powerful country party led by Robert Harley. The result was repeated refusals by Parliament to pass the usual Mutiny Acts between 1698 and 1701, a bitter attack on William's Whig ministers, including even an attempt to impeach them, and that frontal attack on the royal prerogative, the Act of Settlement. The Act of Settlement, though notionally concerned with providing for the peaceful accession of the House of Hanover on the death of William and subsequently of Princess Anne, was also intended to reduce the powers to which the new rulers would succeed. For the moment, the stipulations in the Act, that no war should be fought for the defence of interests not exclusively British without parliamentary consent, and that the king should not be permitted to leave British shores without the agreement of Parliament, were suspended until the accession of the Hanoverians. But nothing could more clearly have indicated the depth of feeling and indeed indignation which was William of Orange's reward for rescuing Englishmen from the dilemma imposed upon them by the policies of James II. Nor is it surprising that William himself was driven to talk of returning to Holland for good during the last years of his reign.

There was admittedly much about William III's character, abilities and record, to justify criticism. Yet it is difficult in retrospect to endorse the charges levelled by his opponents. At bottom William was a responsible and intelligent statesman profoundly concerned with the need to create a stable and lasting peace, as well as to defend his own beloved country. This emerges clearly from his activities in the last years of his reign, between the making of the Peace of Ryswick and the beginning of the War of the Spanish Succession. Though those activities, and in particular his negotiations with Louis XIV, were deeply distrusted by many Englishmen and did much to aggravate his unpopularity, they were neither ill-intentioned nor within the limitations imposed by the circumstances, ill-considered. For once the difficult circumstances arose not from the disputes left by the previous war, though these existed and undoubtedly helped to exacerbate international tensions. Rather they concerned the fate of the Spanish succession on the imminent death of the childless and decrepit Charles II, a fate which long had been a subject for speculation in the courts of Europe. The glittering lure of an empire which comprehended much of the New World, and valuable lands in Italy and the Low Countries as well as Spain itself, was such as to excite the greed of more than one monarch. Moreover, as with most succession disputes, the legal position was impossibly complex. The Bourbons of France, the Habsburgs of the Empire, the ruling house of Bavaria, all had excellent claims to the throne of Spain, though to all there were objections of one kind or another. However, in the long run it was obvious that whatever the arguments, a considerable portion of the empire would have to be divided between Vienna and Paris, the two parties capable of enforcing their own desires and guaranteeing a settlement. So far as William III was concerned, and indeed so far as British as well as

Dutch interests were concerned, the clear priority was to settle these competing claims without resorting to open war, and also to ensure that neither was so favoured as to endanger the balance of power in Europe or in the New World. This fundamental aim, surely a sensible one, was central to the highly secret but critically important negotiations which William and Louis XIV conducted in 1698 and 1699. In the First Partition Treaty of 1698 it was agreed that the electoral prince of Bavaria should inherit the great bulk of the Spanish empire. France was to be compensated by the bestowal of Naples and Sicily on the Dauphin, and Austria by the succession of the Emperor's younger son, the Archduke Charles, to the duchy of Milan. The treaty was neither acceptable to the Spanish court itself which plumped for preserving the integrity of the empire in the hands of the electoral prince, nor to the Austrians, who saw it as giving France a decisive advantage in the Mediterranean. From the British viewpoint too, this seemed a telling criticism; yet it is difficult not to sympathise with William, who saw that France would insist on having mainland Spain if it did not receive substantial concessions in Italy, and who was well aware that a settlement which did not give Louis at least some of his strategic objectives would have to be enforced by a long and costly war. As it turned out however, these arguments were academic; early in 1699 the electoral prince of Bavaria died and by so doing reopened the whole question of the Spanish succession.

The Second Partition Treaty of 1700, negotiated with a haste which adequately indicated the concern of statesmen involved, was an attempt to apply the principle of its predecessor to the new situation. This time the Archduke Charles was to receive Spain, the Indies, and the Netherlands, while the Dauphin would acquire all Spain's Italian possessions, with additional provision for eventual French acquisition of the border province of Lorraine. As before, there were snags. Madrid would never willingly consent to the division of the Spanish patrimony, Vienna considered that it had a clear right to the entire empire after the death of the Bavarian claimant, and neither of the Maritime Powers themselves could be entirely happy at the effective control of the central Mediterranean now vouchsafed to France. In England indeed, the Second Partition

Treaty unleashed a new phase of the domestic political crisis, more, it must be admitted, because of William's alleged temerity in carrying on vital negotiations with little reference to the advice of his English councillors, than because the opposition in Parliament had a clear alternative diplomatic strategy in mind. In any event sensational news from the Continent quickly made the second treaty as irrelevant as the first and faced politicians and public with an extraordinary dilemma. On 1 November Charles II of Spain at last expired, and his own will, made only a month before, became public knowledge. The Spanish empire was to go in its entirety to the French Duke of Anjou, younger son of the heir to the French throne. Still more sensational was the reaction of Louis XIV who at once repudiated the treaty which he had signed less than a year before and announced his acceptance of the will. The possibility which William had dreaded, that Bourbon power would over-night be buttressed by the potentially overwhelming political and economic strength of the Spanish empire, had become fact. For William himself there was only one sensible course; he had struggled, by diplomacy, to avoid violent measures, but when circumstances threatened to bring about a disaster still bigger than the war he had fought to avert, there was little alternative but once again to build an armed alliance to defy the power of Louis XIV.

Unfortunately for William, his subjects in the British Isles were not disposed once again to launch themselves into a massive continental war, which was likely to involve still greater strains than the last. Soon after the death of the Bavarian electoral prince, the king's ministers had warned him of the lack of readiness for renewed war in England. 'There is a deadness and want of spirit in the nation universally, so as not at all to be disposed to the thought of entering into a new war, and that they seem to be tired out with taxes to a degree beyond what was discussed till it appeared upon the occasion of the late elections'.[1] In the fiercely hostile atmosphere prevailing in Parliament it was not surprising that this mood of pacifism endured and indeed strengthened. Harley's country party, which by the last year of William's reign was effectively in complete control

---

[1] *England in the Reigns of James II and William III* by D. Ogg (Oxford 1955), p. 449.

of the House of Commons, did not see why English blood and English resources should be thrown away, as they saw it, in maintaining the trade and independence of the Dutch Netherlands on the one hand, and the antiquated claims of the Holy Roman Emperor on the other. The men who were intent on impeaching the junto, stripping William of his patronage, and severely circumscribing the powers of the future Hanoverian royal family, were hardly likely to be convinced by the arguments of William himself. Yet their attitude was of crucial importance. As the King's Speech informed Parliament at the opening of the session in 1701, 'The eyes of all Europe are upon this parliament; all matters are at a stand till your resolutions are known'.[1] This was no exaggeration. If the enemies of Louis XIV were to forestall this new and most sinister of all threats offered by the power of France, it was essential to obtain the cooperation of the English.

In the end, though only just before his death, William got the war he had reluctantly felt compelled to advise, and so bequeathed to his successor another monumental international struggle which was to shape Britain's role abroad for decades. That he did so was a triumph for his own policies, but it also owed much to accident and good fortune. No one could have predicted for example that Louis XIV would so conveniently have turned out to be his own worst enemy. It was not in the interests of France to bring about a great continental conflagration, and had the French king been skilled and cautious enough to make some parade of protecting British and Dutch interests, war need not have ensued, especially given the strength of the pacifist party in both London and the Hague. And yet Louis acted in a way which was bound to provoke even those least inclined to war in those capitals. For example, almost as soon as he had declared his adherence to the will of Charles II, he also issued letters patent declaring that Philip of Anjou, the successful claimant to the Spanish throne, was not by the mere fact of his succession excluded from inheriting the French throne in default of more direct heirs. Though this proclamation allowed for the succession of another French prince of the blood royal to the Spanish throne in the event of Philip's accession to the French, such a move

[1] *England in the Reigns of James II and William III* by D. Ogg (Oxford 1955), p. 483.

was not calculated to reassure those whose greatest fear was the effective amalgamation of the French and Spanish royal houses. Equally provocative was the assiduity with which Louis set about maximising the potential provided by Charles II's will. Spanish and French nobles were given equivalent status and privileges at each country's court, joint plans for defence were openly discussed, and perhaps most dangerous of all, a combined campaign against the trading power of Britain and the United Provinces was launched. If anything was needed to remind merchants in those two countries that the union of France and Spain in one family would involve a French monopoly of the enormous commercial markets of the Spanish empire, it was this. As Aglionby, the envoy to Spain, pointed out, England would soon 'have no place to send a ship to but the East Indies and their own American colonies'.[1] Yet this was not the limit of French folly. The Dutch garrisons in the Spanish Netherlands were quickly surrounded by French troops, and it was treated as something of a concession when their Dutch contingents were permitted to retire to their own borders. Again in the inevitable negotiations opened at the Hague in 1701, the French took a blatantly unconciliatory line, declining even to reassure those on the other side who were anxious to portray Louis XIV's designs as fundamentally pacific; when the talks broke down in July Louis XIV at once withdrew his ambassador from the Hague and issued an edict putting a complete stop to Anglo-French trade. Yet the crowning folly was still to come. In September 1701 James II died; within days his heir, the Old Pretender, was recognised in France as the legitimate ruler of England, and full support for the Jacobite cause promised. Finally, French troops were sent to the moral support of the Elector of Cologne, effectively a puppet prince, and the neutrality of Germany incidentally violated.

Quite why Louis XIV wilfully provoked a war in the course of 1701 remains something of a mystery. Perhaps he mistakenly regarded war as ultimately unavoidable and sought to push matters to an advantageous and immediate conclusion. Alternatively, and more plausibly, he may simply have made a series of grave mis-

[1] *Trade and Peace with Old Spain, 1667–1750* by J. O. McLachlan (Cambridge 1940), p. 42.

judgements. But whatever the reason he played into the hands of the war party in England. Parliament, at any rate before the general election of 1701, was far from well disposed towards the court of William III. Yet it could hardly be blind to the gravity of events on the Continent. Out of doors a massive propaganda campaign was launched to persuade the representatives of the political nation that interest as well as loyalty to the crown dictated a firm attitude towards France. The celebrated Kentish Petition, one of the most remarkable attempts by electors to influence the deliberations of the legislature in matters of foreign policy, warned M.P.s against flying in the face of a public opinion allegedly deeply impressed with the extent of the danger. Similarly Defoe's *Legion's Petition* accused Westminster of neglecting the clear trading and strategic interests of the country. Against this background Parliament moved slowly but inevitably towards endorsement of the king's policy. After the death of James II and the clearly announced French intention to support his heir, there was little that the pacifist party could do to avert action. As one country gentleman remarked, it was 'absolutely necessary to put a stop to the imposing genius of France',[1] an argument which, with the added stimulus of a general election, at last began to commend itself to the legislature. An Act of Attainder to condemn James III, new oaths clearly renouncing the Jacobite allegiance, and above all resolutions supporting a war against France were rapidly conceded. On 21 February William III fell from his horse, and suffered injuries which with complications were to prove fatal; his death took place a fortnight later. By that time Parliament had sanctioned his arrangements for a Grand Alliance against Louis XIV and Philip V of Spain, and ensured Britain's participation in a war still greater than that which had been initiated by the Revolution of 1688.

---

[1] *England in the Reigns of James II and William III* by D. Ogg (Oxford 1955), p. 477.

5 Emergence as a Great Power, 1702–14

The War of the Spanish Succession in many respects resembled its predecessor. Like the Nine Years' War it was the result, at least as far as British participation was concerned, principally of the need to protect the Protestant Succession in England, and partly of the need to safeguard strategic and commercial interests against the ever present threat of French hegemony. Like the Nine Years' War it involved a frightening commitment on the part of society at large, and a considerable strain on traditional assumptions and procedures. At the height of the war, in 1708–09, no less than 70,000 troops of British origin were maintained as part of the war effort, a remarkable novelty given the relative indifference of Englishmen to continental warfare in the previous century. King William's war had required government borrowing of some £14½ million and Queen Anne's war added another £21½ million. Apart from this a similar sum was raised by actual taxation, and both the interest on the National Debt and the taxation laid a heavy burden on the propertied classes. Nor did the merchants escape. The privateering war which had added a new and alarming dimension to the activities of businessmen, was actually intensified between 1702 and 1714, and the resulting depredations were spectacular. Any notion that the War of the Spanish Succession would prove a more limited affair than its predecessor proved sadly mistaken in the event.

In other respects moreover there were a number of new and disquieting features revealed in the conflict which was William III's final legacy to his subjects. In many ways it created far more tensions and divisions, and had much more serious political consequences than the Nine Years' War. This was even true, for example, at international level. Like any coalition the League of Augsburg had by no means been without its stresses and strains. But the Grand Alliance arranged in 1701 was peculiarly subject to disputes and dissensions. Quite apart from the jealousies to which the lesser allies were subject, there was only a limited degree of cooperation among the 'big three'. Between the British and the Dutch there were incessant bickerings; over the war at sea, where the Dutch demanded a strategy which would permit their trade with neutrals and enemies to continue unhindered, and where their ally favoured a brutally restrictive strategy, and on land, where the States General were only with the greatest difficulty persuaded to allow their troops to stray from Dutch frontiers. Still more irksome was the attitude of the Austrians, whose war aims, military strategy and basic distrust of the Maritime Powers were constant problems. Godolphin's remark that 'Vienna has not one thought that is not directly opposite to the interest of the allies',[1] may have been as much a comment on British intolerance as Austrian perversity, but it testifies none the less to the utter lack of fellow feeling between the statesmen who determined relations between the two states.

However, the differences which impeded the effectiveness of the Grand Alliance were far less serious than the bitterness and divisiveness of politics in England itself during the War of the Spanish Succession. Party conflict was at no point in the remainder of the eighteenth century as intense as under Queen Anne. Particularly on the land, deep economic distress, aggravated by the burden of war taxation, fuelled the rage which was spent on the great issues of the post-Revolution period, the question of religious toleration, the problem of the succession, and above all, the matter of the war itself. Even the Tory country gentlemen, with the help of a vociferous public opinion, had recognised the need to fight the French, albeit reluctantly, but they were never entirely happy about the war. Though they could scarcely argue openly for peace in the early years of the new century, they lost no opportunity of urging alternatives to the war aims and strategy of the Whigs, who were either influential or dominant in government from 1702 to 1710. It was argued for example, in a further development of that debate which had begun to emerge during the previous war, that a blue-water rather than

---

[1] *England under Queen Anne* by G. M. Trevelyan (London 1965 edn.), ii, p. 307.

continental strategy was required. The early, if limited, success of
the navy under Admiral Rooke, at Vigo Bay in 1702, together with
the spectacular intervention of the Spanish Porto Bello treasure fleet
in 1708 did much to reinforce such arguments. Equally compelling
were the combined operations of the war, leading to the capture of
Gibraltar in 1704 and its subsequent retention, together with the
taking of Minorca in 1708. Yet the blue-water school was never a
really serious contender. For one thing really ambitious schemes
overseas went badly adrift in practice. The campaigns in the West
Indies succeeded only in securing St Kitts while the Tory ministry's
great Quebec exhibition of 1711 foundered on inadequate leadership.
Moreover, cold logic suggested the fatuity of combating the vast
power of Louis XIV in the colonies. No doubt significant French
reverses in the West Indies or in North America would have been
valuable at any peace negotiations; but if British refusal to engage in
the continental conflict resulted in the overrunning of the Spanish
and Dutch Netherlands by French armies and the total alienation
of the Spanish mainland and empire into French hands, they would
not weigh greatly in the diplomatic scales. The unceasing argument
of the Whigs, that continental ambitions could only be defeated on
the Continent, was in the last analysis an unanswerable one.

An alternative tack however was the Tory demand, which emerged
early in the war, to devote allied resources to the Iberian peninsula
rather than to the Low Countries, Italy or Germany. The notion
that if the war were principally about the Spanish Succession, it
might best be fought in Spain, was superficially an attractive one,
and certainly accorded ill with the Whigs' insistence on the need to
campaign for the most part in the obvious theatres of central and
north-western Europe. Moreover peninsular successes like those of
Peterborough in 1705–06 and the welcome accorded Archduke
Charles of Austria in Catalonia together with his coronation as
Charles III of Spain, provided the advocates of a truly Spanish war
with valuable ammunition. Even here though there were difficulties.
Britain's allies, for example, were less than fully convinced of the
wisdom of concentrating their main efforts in Spain. The Emperor
Leopold, whose younger son was intended to succeed to the Spanish
throne, had been himself much more concerned about the Italian

dominions ruled from Madrid than about the Spanish homeland, and the same attitude was taken by his successor, Joseph. Similarly the Dutch had not the least enthusiasm for adventures over a thousand miles from their own borders, and more importantly from their beloved barrier in the Spanish Netherlands. Moreover the Spanish people, not for the last time, declined meekly to conform to the desires of continental statesmen. Apart from the basically separatist aspirations of the Catalans, there was little real or sustained opposition to Philip V in Spain; any hopes entertained in England that it would be none the less possible to make Charles III the effective ruler of Spain were defeated at Almanza in 1707 and Brihuega in 1710.

More important than the practical difficulties in the way of the blue-water and peninsular strategies, however, was one central fact of crucial significance; in John Churchill, Duke of Marlborough, the British had finally produced a general and statesman who was not merely fitted to assume the mantle, but far better fitted to carry out the ambitions of William of Orange. In the divisive politics at home, Marlborough passed at one time for a Tory, at another for a Whig; in fact he was first and foremost a soldier and indeed a statesman of truly European stature. 'I will endeavour', he once remarked, 'to leave a good name behind me in countries that have hardly any blessing but that of not knowing the detested names of Whig and Tory'.[1] Marlborough had the clearest possible conception of the war, one which indeed exceeded that of William III himself. On land his initial object was to crush Louis XIV's attempt to combine with his German allies against not merely the Italian and Belgian provinces of Spain but the heartland of the Habsburgs themselves. Ultimately the great land war on which Louis XIV had launched his troops so confidently must be turned into a direct assault on the frontiers of France, and he who had so long assumed that the Low Countries were the Bourbon corridor to Germany, must be shown that they were also the allied avenue to Paris. In other theatres a holding operation, though often an aggressive one, was envisaged. In Spain, everything possible, short of diminishing the allied effort elsewhere, could be done to obstruct and divert Philip V and his French supporters; Italy must be kept out of Franco-Spanish hands, and the

[1] *England under Queen Anne* by G. M. Trevelyan (London 1965 edn.), i, p. 437.

Mediterranean, where Marlborough took up William III's far-seeing strategy to provide a continuing British presence, was to be firmly prevented from becoming a French lake. More important than the strategy however, so far as politics at home were concerned, was the fact that it was carried out, at least for the first four years, with devastating success. Blenheim and Ramillies, the great victories which destroyed the French threat in Germany and the Habsburg lands and wrested control of Belgium from the hands of the Bourbons, were triumphs of a kind not merely novel to European eyes, but peculiarly astonishing when laid to the credit of an Englishman by other Englishmen. Even the isolationist country gentlemen found it difficult to object to a war policy which yielded the spectacular victories achieved in these years. As one contemporary observed, Blenheim was 'a pleasing spectacle to the generality, being more for their four shillings in the pound, than they ever saw'.[1] Further Steenkirks in this period would have done much to destroy the British will to fight; instead Blenheim, Gibraltar and Ramillies carried all before Marlborough and the Whig strategy not merely on the Continent but in the no less important political arena of Westminster.

Even so the political effectiveness of Marlborough's victories was necessarily limited. It only required a degree of military failure or stalemate for a measure of hostility to the conduct of the war to develop. That stalemate began in 1707, with the complete failure of an attempt on Brittany, the breakdown of an allied assault on Toulon, the critical defeat at Almanza in Spain, and the growing impasse in Flanders. Thereafter, though there was no catastrophic reverse, allied progress in the war gradually ground to a halt. Marlborough was never defeated in the Low Countries, but his further victories of Oudenarde and Malplaquet were not such as to inspire continued faith in his genius; as one of his commanders remarked of Malplaquet, 'I hope in God it may be the last battle I may ever see. A very few of such would make both parties end the war very soon'.[2] As it happened the Whigs stuck to their strategic guns with grim deter-

---

[1] A. D. McLachlan, 'The Road to Peace, 1710-13' in *Britain after the Glorious Revolution, 1689-1714* ed. G. Holmes (London 1970), p. 201.

[2] *England under Queen Anne* by G. M. Trevelyan (London 1965 edn.), iii, p. 42.

mination, but by 1709 the writing on the wall was clear for all, particularly the Tories, to see.

It was not military setbacks alone which made many in England seriously begin to doubt the wisdom of continuing the war. Rather the strategic deadlock merely brought to a head the underlying diplomatic problems created partly by the war itself as conducted by the Whigs, and partly by the very success which Marlborough had early achieved. At bottom the difficulty which emerged was one of defining British war aims. In the first instance the war had been entered upon with clearly limited objectives. Technically the Grand Alliance had provided for the establishment of the Habsburgs in the Italian provinces of Spain, together with the erection of a defensive barrier for the Dutch in the formerly Spanish Netherlands which were otherwise to pass to the sovereignty of the Austrians. The British for their part were to receive satisfaction for Louis XIV's impudent backing of the Pretender, and guarantees for the Protestant Succession. The irony was that even these terms, which had been seen as dangerously extensive, and to many represented an excessive commitment on the part of Englishmen, had within four years of the beginning of the war been largely achieved. Between them the armies of the allies cleared all of Italy apart from Sicily, as well as Belgium; Louis XIV who in one way or another was making peace overtures almost throughout the war from 1705, could hardly claim the sovereignty of these territories, nor when it came to the point would he have declined to give some form of acceptable recognition to the Protestant Succession in Britain.

Unfortunately by the time the original war aims of the Grand Alliance had come clearly within its grasp, new and much more embarrassing objectives had been added, and the cry of 'No peace without Spain' had been heard. Originally Englishmen had been less concerned by the prospect as such of a Bourbon upon the throne of Spain, than by the possibility of a joint Franco–Spanish alliance which that prospect created. When eventually they went to war it was not least because Louis XIV seemed intent on demonstrating quite gratuitously that he was determined on the effective union of the two kingdoms. However, with the war under way the arguments for insisting not merely that Philip V of Spain should never accede to the throne of France, but that he should be replaced on the Spanish throne itself by the Habsburg Archduke Charles, were strengthened. The skill of the Methuens in negotiating the accession of the Portuguese to the Grand Alliance and so providing the British with useful naval facilities, not to say a launching platform for the campaign against Spain, has long been recognised. But not the least result of their activities was to place on record the allies' readiness to hold out for the expulsion of the French royal family from Madrid. Pedro II of Portugal, who had actually concluded an alliance with France and was in no hurry to change sides, could not be expected to do so without such a specific guarantee of the elimination of Bourbon influence in the peninsula. That guarantee, not without objections from the Dutch and even the Austrians themselves, was given in the Triple and Quadruple Alliances signed in Lisbon in 1703, and so added a new war aim to the list drawn up in the original Grand Alliance. Thereafter the prosecution of the war in Spain became a consistent if secondary theme in the war, ironically not least because Tory opponents of Marlborough saw in it a useful weapon with which to attack the continental strategy of the Whigs. In 1707 the House of Commons firmly resolved for example, 'that no peace can be honourable or safe for her majesty and her allies if Spain and the Spanish West Indies be suffered to continue in the power of the House of Bourbon'.[1] Still more important, the Whig Ministry which in 1708 finally consolidated its hold on ministerial power, was so carried away in its enthusiasm for the Spanish war, both on strategic and on commercial grounds, that it launched a major diplomatic initiative which had the most significant consequences. In order to secure the complete support of the increasingly war-weary Dutch, not only for the guaranteed accession of the Hanoverian line, in the now relatively near event of Queen Anne's death, but also for the establishment of Charles III in Spain, a new treaty of alliance was negotiated, the celebrated Barrier Treaty of 1709, which gave to the Dutch a promise of almost everything they desired in relation to the post-war creation of garrisoned fortresses in the Spanish Netherlands. To place an Austrian rather than a French prince in Madrid, so it seemed, England was prepared to make almost any sacrifice of

[1] *England under Queen Anne* by G. M. Trevelyan (London 1965 edn.) ii, p. 345.

blood and treasure, and even to devote herself to the establishment of the Dutch in Belgium.

By the time the Barrier Treaty was made a number of forces were combining to explode the assumptions on which it rested. For one thing the evident absurdity of insisting on the expulsion of Philip V from Spain was clearly revealed in the peace talks which took place with Louis XIV's negotiators in 1708, 1709, and 1710. The disasters which beset France in these years, both in terms of the desperate military situation and the still more serious famine and economic hardships at home, were quite sufficient to bring the French king to reasonable terms on the substantive points at issue in the war. On Belgium, on Italy and on the English Succession he was brought to agree to concessions as great as could be expected from a monarch who had not actually surrendered his own capital. The one sacrifice he would not make was to force his grandson to abandon the Spanish throne. Thus in the 1709 negotiations, he broke off discussion of the peace preliminaries, after the allies issued an ultimatum requiring the expulsion of Philip from Spain, and similarly in 1710, though he was apparently ready to offer subsidies to those charged with removing the Spanish king, he would not give any absolute guarantees of Philip's departure. To all but the most partisan of Whigs there seemed something ludicrous about pressing the French king to expel from Spain a French Prince of the Blood, whom the Grand Alliance itself was quite incapable of removing. 'If I were in the place of the King of France,' Marlborough wrote to his Dutch colleague Heinsius, 'I should venture the loss of my country much sooner than be obliged to join my troops for the forcing of my grandson'.[1] On the other hand, it was asserted by the Whigs that Louis XIV was acting a double part and could not be trusted in his promise that he would do his best to influence Philip in favour of renunciation. For this view there was probably some justification. Though Philip of Anjou was not the most disciplined of princes, and though the Spanish court itself was plainly intent on repulsing the Archduke Charles, it is difficult to believe that some effective French leverage could not have been applied. It was commonly believed that the principal advisers of Philip were either Frenchmen or

[1] *England under Queen Anne* by G. M. Trevelyan (London 1965 edn.), ii, p. 425.

French sympathisers, and in particular the king's mistress, Madame des Ursins, was regarded as a powerful agent of Versailles. Yet when all is said and done it was surely asking too much to force the French to declare war on the Spain of Philip V, especially in the context of growing strategic deadlock in 1709–10. A really effective drive through Flanders towards Paris, or a major advance in the peninsula itself would of course have dramatically altered the position. But apart from a brief success in Spain, quickly extinguished by the defeat of Brihuega in 1711, there was little to suggest that the military issue could be clinched.

The apparent fatuity of the peace negotiations was not the only cause for concern in the public mind in England. By 1709 the tide of war-weariness was growing to dangerous proportions from the point of view of the Whig ministry. However, the latter chose a mode of combating it which proved entirely counter-productive. The trial of Dr Sacheverell for preaching doctrines of non-resistance in 1710 did not directly concern the war at all. But it was mounted by the Whigs as a propaganda exercise to discredit the Tory opposition and brand it as ideologically unsound. Few political stratagems can have misfired more spectacularly. Far from quelling public opposition, the Sacheverell trial raised tumults of a kind and degree unseen since the Exclusion Crisis. It also gave the uneasy coalition that was the Tory party an opportunity to unite in a climate which encouraged emotional union, and the queen, now increasingly hostile to her long-standing servants, Marlborough and Godolphin, a chance to change the administration. It only required a general election, held in 1710 in the heated atmosphere created by the Sacheverell affair, to complete the triumph of a new and powerful Tory ministry under the leadership of Robert Harley.

The new ministers did not enter office specifically to carry through a new policy in foreign affairs. But it could hardly be expected that matters would be allowed to remain the same. The countrywide agitation over Sacheverell, far from evaporating, was quickly turning into a general campaign for peace, not least no doubt because the Tory country gentry of the counties, triumphantly returned to power, were determined to strike while the iron was hot. Moreover the arguments did not grow less compelling abroad. By

1710 the sheer extremity of the crisis in France had created a mood of national stubbornness of a kind which Englishmen were traditionally accustomed to congratulate themselves on possessing. Any hope that the allied armies would achieve a decisive breakthrough in the Flemish sector seemed increasingly remote. Above all, the death of the Emperor Joseph I in 1711 and the succession of his brother, the Archduke Charles, made the Whig cry of 'no peace without Spain' more extraordinary than ever. Successful imposition of Charles on the Spaniards would now recreate the great empire of Charles V, an outcome which even the Austrians had previously denied any desire to bring about. Those who wondered why it was wrong to permit the union of two great empires in the House of Bourbon but not in the House of Habsburg, were not easily answered.

Argument and emotion now clearly pointed to peace and it was fortunate for the Tories that at this moment a combination of party passion and personal interest brought from Jonathan Swift one of the great classics of British polemical literature. The *Conduct of the Allies*, published at the critical moment in November 1711, provided precisely the intellectual stuffing which the peace movement needed. The Barrier Treaty, the insistence on Austrian occupation of the Spanish throne, even the personal integrity of Marlborough, all were ruthlessly and indeed almost unanswerably raked to show how the British had become 'the Dupes and Bubbles of Europe'.[1] If those who had long resented the war and now felt its oppressiveness needed reasoning to reinforce their feelings, Swift's pamphlet more than adequately provided it. In fact, arguments were scarcely necessary. One of the main problems confronting Harley's administration was that opinion in the House of Commons and indeed in the country at large was in such a hurry for peace that diplomatic negotiations were difficult to carry through in a controlled and restrained manner.

The peace which was eventually made, sketched out in its earliest form as soon as 1711 and then translated into a major European peace treaty at Utrecht in 1713, was one of the most contentious in the history of British foreign policy. Whigs like Pitt the Elder, who called it 'that indelible reproach of the last generation',[2] were brought

[1] *The Pen and the Sword* by M. Foot (London 1958), p. 300.
[2] *War and Trade in the West Indies* by R. Pares (Oxford 1936), p. 562.

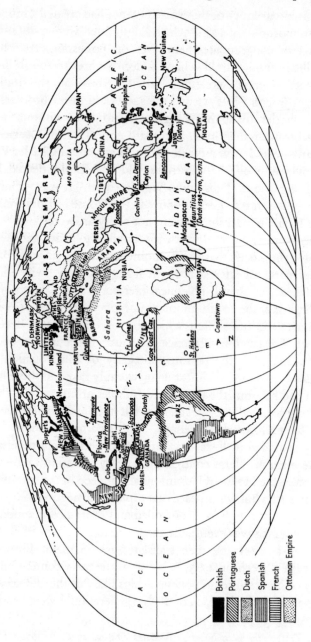

Map 1. The World at the Peace of Utrecht, 1713-15

up to believe that Utrecht was a classic piece of Tory, indeed Jacobite, double dealing, not merely devious but actually treacherous in its betrayal of the soldiers in Flanders and in its desertion of Britain's loyal allies. The villain of this piece was Henry St John, shortly to be Viscount Bolingbroke, who as a confessed Jacobite in 1715 was a more convincing scoundrel than his colleague Harley. In fact all the evidence is that Harley (also elevated to the peerage as Earl of Oxford), was more important in the peace negotiations than St John, and also considerably more devious than his junior. St John was admittedly a thoroughgoing peace maker, but his very commitment in this direction dictated a more direct, less equivocal approach than Harley, who sought to balance the desirability of peace with the need to carry with him the allies. None the less the Whig case had some strong points. The notorious restraining orders sent to Ormonde, Marlborough's Tory successor in the field, which required him to avoid offensive action against the French, and the still more appalling communication of these orders to the French general Villars, in order to hold the war at a standstill while the diplomats worked out a peace formula, was difficult to defend. Nor was the obvious intention of forcing the Catalans, the Dutch and the Austrians to accept terms which conflicted with the agreed objectives of the alliance, easy to justify. In the end the allies had little option but to come in; at least the Dutch signed the Peace of Utrecht in good time, leaving the Austrians to bring up the rear, and then without signing a peace with Spain at all. However, if this aspect of the peace making was distasteful, the difficulty lies in envisaging alternatives. In a country where party had become an overwhelmingly important fact of political life, and at a time when the monarch no longer provided firm leadership let alone a clear and consistent policy, it was inevitable that policies would change and in the process involve the breaking of moral and even legal obligations to allies. There was no means by which the Tories could have avoided making peace after the ferments of 1710. That there was an element of deviousness in the manner that peace was made was no doubt regrettable, but in eighteenth-century politics it was an impeccable statesman who could afford to point the finger of moral obliquity at his colleagues. The Whig attack on the peace of Utrecht would have been more plausible if it had not chimed so conveniently with the political objectives of the Whig party and if Whigs had not proved equally disingenuous in their day.

Viewed purely in terms of national interest, the case in defence of Utrecht is still more compelling. It was by any standards but the inflated ones applied by a generation of Whigs, a valuable peace. French historians have indeed seen in it the establishment of something approaching British hegemony in Western Europe, and St John himself assured his queen that the peace preliminaries contained 'more advantages for your Majesty's Kingdom than were ever, perhaps, stipulated for any nation at one time'.[1] First and foremost the Hanoverian Succession was finally recognised by Louis XIV, for what that recognition was worth, and the Old Pretender repudiated. The latter had had more than one chance of success, notably in 1708 when there had briefly appeared the possibility of a really effective rising in the highlands of Scotland, though misfortune had dogged the resulting rebellion; he was also to have further opportunities, but for the moment he could hardly expect the French king to withhold formal recognition of the Protestant Succession in England. Of scarcely less significance dynastically was the formal separation of the French and Spanish successions with specific promises from all concerned that the two crowns would never be allowed to unite. So far as territory was concerned, the two conquests made in the Mediterranean were retained by Britain at the peace. In one of them the British had a useful base from which to protect their trade. The value of the Rock was to be a constant subject of dispute in the following century and more than one statesman was to feel that its retention damaged Anglo-Spanish relations without commensurate economic or strategic benefits. British public opinion was, on the other hand, to have its own very clear estimate of the utility of Gibraltar. The other conquest, Minorca, was still more valuable. Stanhope was doubtless biased as the commander who had taken Port Mahon in 1708 but few would have disagreed with his assertion that 'England ought never to part with this island, which will give the law to the Mediterranean both in time of war and peace'.[2] The

[1] *England under Queen Anne* by G. M. Trevelyan (London 1965 edn.), iii, p. 206.
[2] *England under George I: The Quadruple Alliance* by W. Michael (London 1939), p. 137.

French navy at Toulon had ample cause to rue the advantage which possession of Minorca was to give the British for much of the eighteenth century.

There were also other consolations. In Canada the French formally ceded Nova Scotia; though that province was to provide something of a headache for British imperial administrators, its cession represented a significant reverse for French designs on British North America. Dunkirk was to be eliminated as a base for French privateering and naval forces, though here too the difficulties of enforcing such good intentions were to prove considerable in practice. So far as allied gains were concerned, British interests were also protected. The Dutch got their barrier in the Netherlands, but without the exclusion of Queen Anne's subjects from their lucrative trade in Belgium. The Austrians were given the greater part of Spain's Belgian and Italian empire, above all the Milanese and Naples, the territories which Vienna had been most anxious to obtain. This was by no means the end of the story in Italy, where the ambitions of Savoy and Spain were to hold up an effective and final settlement for another forty years; on the other hand Harley could fairly claim that Austria had achieved its basic war aims, and also that British interests in the Mediterranean were now served better than they would have been either by the partition treaties or by Bourbon victory in the war.

In some ways the most controversial aspects of the peace treaty revolved about trade. Much though the Tories disliked those who profited by capitalism and commerce, and much though they had objected to the waging of war merely to line the pockets of City merchants, they took care in the peace negotiations to obtain concessions for businessmen which it would be embarrassing for the Whigs to oppose. The real value of the famous commercial agreements with the Spanish court, providing for British participation in the slave trade with the Spanish colonies, and for the annual despatch of a merchantman to Spanish America, is arguable. Those who felt that the ancient trade to mainland Spain which had for so long flourished during the reign of Charles II, and those who similarly valued the entirely illegal but extremely remunerative trade between the British West Indies and Latin America, were probably right to doubt the utility of the new treaties; in practice the South Sea Company, set up to handle the new concessions, was something less than brilliantly successful. None the less, the Tory ministry could reasonably argue that one of the primary aims of the government in 1701, the securing of a major share in the trade of the Spanish empire, to the relative disadvantage of Dutch and French rivals, had been achieved as effectively as was possible by treaty. More contentious still however, was the draft trade treaty with the French, a treaty which to some extent anticipated the Eden Treaty of 1786 and which would have substantially liberalised trade across the English Channel. The agreement was St John's handiwork and foundered on a combination of Tory xenophobia and Whig preference for the Portuguese trade. Great and arguably excessive emphasis was placed on the Methuens' commercial treaty of 1703, and under the pressure of political obstruction and mercantile hostility, particularly in the woollen trade, the trade clauses were predictably lost in the House of Commons. Where Harley was normally dragged along in the wake of the party which he ineptly and rather reluctantly led, St John had a way of being just a little too far ahead of it. In any event whatever the popularity of the peace treaty made by the Tories in 1713, the last laugh was to go elsewhere. Shortly the problem of the succession was once again to play strange tricks both with the fate of politicians and the direction of foreign policy.

6 The Impact of Hanover, 1714–21

Like William III's advent at the Revolution, the death of Anne and accession of George I, Elector of Hanover, in 1714 were events of the most profound significance in the history of British foreign policy. The fact that George I's succession was disputed and indeed contested by arms was indeed important in European rather than purely insular terms. As it happened the hopes of the Pretender and his friends were dashed for a variety of reasons. Strictly speaking the fate of James III was probably settled by his determined refusal, finally and decisively indicated to the Tory ministers in March 1714, just four months before Queen Anne's death, to abandon his religion for the sake of all those in England who would gladly have restored the Stuarts if only they would once again embrace the Anglican Church. Even so the military threat was a serious one. In Scotland and in the northwest the rebellion was quelled not without difficulty, and in the west a much more sinister rising was averted only by the vigorous action of the new king's ministers and by the misfortunes of James III's commander, the Duke of Ormonde. But the crucial factor was the attitude of France, the one power which had the capacity to turn the Jacobite dream into an English nightmare; at the crucial point, in September 1715 Louis XIV died, and was succeeded by his great-grandson Louis XV, with his nephew the Duke of Orleans as Regent. Orleans himself was not without designs on the French throne in the by no means unlikely event of the sickly young king's death. But his position was far too weak at home, where he faced a powerful party of aristocratic opponents, and abroad, where his brother Philip V of Spain was far from neglectful of his own interests at Versailles, to risk bold steps in foreign policy. Initially the Regent was anything but an enthusiast for the Elector of Hanover's cause, and he declined in the event to stop the Pretender making a belated and ultimately useless journey from France to Scotland. None the less effective paralysis of the once strong and centralised will of France made the 'fifteen' an entirely different affair from what it might have been. This is not to underrate the long term threat posed by Stuart claimants to the throne. For virtually forty years the Jacobite menace was to remain a real one, and indeed took shape as something truly dangerous on a number of occasions, for example in 1719, in 1722 and in 1745. And for the statesmen whose concern was to protect the succession during the reigns of George I and George II this threat was never negligible, though their fears were ironically based to a great extent on domestic circumstances. An army of standard size, comparable to those maintained by continental monarchs, would effectively have ruled out the possibility of a Stuart restoration, even with the backing of a major power. But no English prejudice was stronger than that against militarism in general and a large standing army in particular. 'It is a ridiculous thing', remarked Stair, who was both soldier and diplomat, 'for us always to be in such a precarious situation as to be at the mercy of any prince that will send 4 or 5000 men into England'.[1] Absurd it may have been but it was a fact of diplomatic life with which British statesmen had long to contend, and frequently a most important one.

The constant danger of foreign invasion and civil war was not the ·only price which Englishmen paid for having a Protestant Succession unsupported by a large permanent army. It was not to be expected that the Elector of Hanover could be transformed overnight into a conventional patriotic Englishman. As it happened, and for understandable reasons, George I had no great respect for either England or Englishmen. As a tireless supporter of the Empire and the wars against the power of France, British treachery at Utrecht had even made him doubt the wisdom of accepting his new responsibilities. That he did in the end undertake them was perhaps inevitable, but his peculiar concern with European and especially German politics, and above all his personal interest in Hanover, were bound to create

[1] *England under George I: The Quadruple Alliance* by W. Michael (London 1939), p. 193.

problems for his new subjects. With the best will in the world, he was unlikely to see his new kingdom as other than a means of exerting additional influence in continental politics. Thus another parvenu monarch, Philip V of Spain, protested at 'the pride of that King, who acted as if he were the arbiter of Europe, taking away and dividing monarchies as he fancied and raising himself above the sovereigns of Germany, not excepting the Emperor, by means of the power Great Britain gave him'.[1] It was only natural that George I should exploit his position in this manner; even so, as in the case of William of Orange, another Protestant prince who had an axe to grind, the results were to create and perpetuate great difficulties in the conduct of foreign policy.

The Act of Settlement of 1701 had to some extent looked forward to these problems. Designed by an angry country party, which was intent on ensuring that the house of Hanover should not be permitted to follow the house of Orange in using British power for continental purposes, the act had clearly defined likely areas of conflict between domestic and electoral interests. It had stipulated, for example, that only royal orders signed by English privy councillors were valid, with the obvious implication that Dutch and Hanoverian adventurers were not to be formally recognised in the constitution. Technically George I obeyed this injunction, but the spirit of it was repeatedly broken. For one thing, at least until 1720, he relied more upon Hanoverian advisers than upon English. Bernstorff, the Hanoverian minister, together with Robethon, the king's private secretary, exercised a continuing and powerful influence on policy which in the last analysis involved far more than purely Hanoverian commitments. The notion of a double cabinet, applied so mistakenly in the reign of George III, probably had more validity under his great-grandfather, when there were indeed two distinct sets of ministers, Hanoverian on the one hand, British on the other. In the royal closet the advice of Bernstorff certainly counted for more than that of Townshend or Stanhope, at any rate in the early years, and it would have been an imprudent Secretary of State who declined to carry out orders issued by the king, whatever their origin. Moreover it was difficult to keep such orders firmly on the lines clearly laid down by

[1] *Stanhope* by B. Williams (Oxford 1932), p. 330.

English law and convention. Admiral Norris, whose responsibility it was to patrol the Baltic theoretically in order to protect English trade from the ravages of those engaged in the Great Northern War, experienced considerable difficulty in distinguishing between Hanoverian and British orders. Letters from Robethon concerning the directions to be given to naval forces had no legal standing but it was not easy for a servant of the king of Great Britain to ignore the instructions of the Elector of Hanover. George I himself was well aware of the nice points involved, observing to the King of Prussia, who had requested naval cooperation from Norris, that 'we could not give a written engagement, since the providing of the squadron pertains to us as King, and if We gave a written engagement We could not use our German Ministers, but We should have to give it by the hands of English ministers'.[1] However, this explanation, designed for Prussian consumption, was misleading. In practice George I found little difficulty in imposing electoral priorities on his British subjects. Had public opinion in England been fully apprised of the extent to which he did so, the cry against Hanoverianism would have been still stronger than it was.

George I's dual responsibilities and powers might have been less worrying had he been gifted with a broader concept of continental politics, and a less provincial concern with the interests of his electorate. William of Orange had scarcely accepted the throne of England out of a desire to advance the interests of Englishmen as such, but he had unquestionably been a statesman of stature, capable of forming European concepts and strategies which were eminently defensible even in English terms. But George I was narrowly German, if not narrowly Hanoverian. It was inevitable that he would choose to spend much of his time in Hanover rather than in London, and the clause in the Act of Settlement which explicitly forbade the absence of the king from England without parliamentary permission had to be hurriedly repealed by the Whig ministers in the first session of the new reign. A more serious matter was the requirement of the act that no war should be waged for objects other than those specifically British without the sanction of Parliament.

[1] *George I, the Baltic and the Whig Split of 1717* by J. J. Murray (London 1969) p. 178.

George I's principal aims in the years immediately after his accession were quite incompatible with any serious interpretation of this clause. First and foremost he sought to deprive the failing strength of Sweden under Charles XII of the petty territories of Bremen and Verden, an object which like all German or Baltic politics during these years involved extraordinarily complex calculations. Bremen was actually in Danish hands and could only be obtained from Denmark in return for assistance in pillaging Swedish Pomerania. Prussia and Russia also had extensive interests at stake, and in the case of Peter the Great especially these were likely to conflict with those of a Hanover by no means anxious to replace Swedish hegemony in the Baltic with Muscovite. In any event the essential fact was that these calculations could scarcely concern the British. For them the priority in these years was to ensure the maintenance of peace in southern Europe and its achievement in the north. Peace would give merchants the chance to operate under stable conditions once again, and also minimise the risks of Jacobite intrigues among foreign enemies. Here was a potentially severe clash of interests between the king and his new subjects.

In retrospect it is remarkable that these differing objects were reconciled so successfully in the early years of George I's reign, without either totally disillusioning the elector or severely disrupting British politics. No doubt there were many reasons. The 'fifteen' and its attendant crisis bred a reaction in favour of the new dynasty which helped to obscure other problems. The complete discredit and demoralisation of the Tory party, with Ormonde and Bolingbroke tainted in exile, and Oxford and his colleagues proscribed, made the development of a systematic challenge to the policies of the new reign difficult. Moreover for the moment at least the Whigs were united; a ministry headed by a junto of Townshend, Walpole, Stanhope and Sunderland cooperated long enough to drive all but a few Tories systematically from office, to carry through a Septennial Act which by postponing parliamentary elections, kept in being a manageable House of Commons, and generally to establish a strong and united Whiggism in power. The foreign policy of Townshend and Stanhope as Secretaries of State was a sensible compromise, driving through a basically Whig policy, while propitiating the

Hanoverian inclinations of their master, and even stealing some
Tory policies where useful. The aggressive posture towards Sweden
desired by George I, was of course adopted despite Britain's traditional policy of friendship since 1700 towards Stockholm. The price
was a high one, since Charles XII did not hesitate to dabble in
Jacobite intrigues, precisely the kind of polarisation which British
statesmen were anxious to avert. Moreover no one could pretend
that the Act of Settlement was inviolate. In 1715 for example, it was a
naval squadron under Captain Hopson which materially assisted
the Danish conquest of Rügen and so impelled the Danes to pass on
Bremen to the Elector of Hanover. Yet it would be a mistake to
make too much of this affair. George I had his value to his new
subjects and was entitled to expect something in return. Moreover
it was arguable that British economic interests could gain as well as
lose by an anti-Swedish policy. The depredations of Charles XII's
privateers and the aggressive mercantilism of Stockholm had
seriously damaged Baltic trade, which especially in terms of the
provision of naval stores was absolutely vital to Britain. It was not
by any means a fiction that the Royal Navy patrolled the Baltic in the
interest of British merchants. Moreover some caution was exercised
in employing naval units in the cause of Hanover. The full scale
deployment of British forces against the Swedish mainland which
George I's northern allies demanded never in fact took place, and
English ministers were careful to observe the proprieties.

These ministers also had an eye on the continental position
generally. So far as the evident need to end British isolation was
concerned their views scarcely differed from those of George I. It is
possible that the revival in the spring of 1716 of the 'old system' by
alliance with Austria in the Treaty of Westminster, was unduly
influenced by George I's personal predilection for the emperor, as
well as by his anxiety for imperial support against Charles XII.
Moreover the treaty unquestionably involved a dangerous commitment to Viennese ambitions in the Mediterranean. Yet it was a
defensible policy to rebuild a system of alliances which would once
again protect the Protestant Succession, though even here there were
admittedly snags. While the Dutch in the course of the winter of
1715–16 signed a Barrier Treaty which laid the basis for a final

settlement in the Austrian Netherlands, and simultaneously renewed their alliance with Britain, they were entering that period of lethargy which was entirely understandable in the light of Dutch financial exhaustion and economic strain, but which was so to irritate their allies. At the Hague the age of adventures was over. Though Dutch troops were sent to aid in the repression of the 'fifteen' in accordance with treaty obligations, naval activity in the Baltic and diplomatic initiatives in southern Europe were less to the taste of the States General. Yet despite the gradual cooling of Anglo-Dutch relations the revival of the 'old system' seemed to its authors something of a triumph. 'Tis not many months since we had scarce an ally abroad and a dangerous Rebellion at home,' Stanhope remarked in 1716,[1] and the ministers' boast that they had steered Britain through a critical crisis at home and abroad was not devoid of foundation.

In any case, once securely in the saddle the Whigs did not prove narrowly traditional in their concept of foreign policy. With the hated Utrecht settlement an established and largely irreversible fact, they were not unready in practice to let amity succeed aggression in trading relations with the Spaniards. Thanks to the Spanish court's desire at this time to woo the Maritime Powers with a view to obtaining their complaisance in the matter of Madrid's Italian ambitions, the Spaniards proved surprisingly and uncharacteristically pliant in negotiating new commercial agreements. Bubb's treaties of 1715–16, which placed British trade to Old Spain on the highly favourable footing enjoyed in the late seventeenth century, and regulated the new asiento trade with the Spanish empire, were an unexpected bonus for the ministers of George I. In practice there were snags, as in Spanish affairs there always were, but in retrospect it is possible to see the concessions made by the court of Philip V to the merchants of England as something of a high point in the history of Anglo-Spanish trade. Still more sensational was the diplomatic revolution (it could scarcely be called less) which brought France and Britain into alliance in 1716. Admittedly the dual alliance owed more to French policy than British. Stanhope was not originally impressed by the prospect, and it was Dubois, the regent's minister, who,

[1] *England under George I: The Beginning of the Hanoverian Dynasty* by W. Michael (London 1936), p. 28.

reduced to clandestine missions to the Hague and Hanover to waylay Stanhope, initiated the policy in the teeth of opposition at home and abroad. Moreover circumstance largely dictated the coming together of two powers whose basic interests were scarcely compatible. As so often in the eighteenth century the chance fate of ruling houses imposed a bizarre pattern on the diplomatic fortunes of peoples. On the one hand George I desired to keep France out of Jacobite intrigues in the south and Baltic adventures in the north; on the other the regent sought support and reassurance in his rivalry with Philip V of Spain. In each case the uncertainties of the succession were crucial. There was, of course, some diplomatic wrangling, over the fortifications at Dunkirk and Mardyke, over guarantees of the Utrecht settlement, particularly in relation to Austro-Spanish disputes and Dutch interests in Belgium, over differences in the Baltic, where France was loath to employ her traditional influence with Russia, Prussia and Sweden to aggrandise the Elector of Hanover. None the less the negotiations eventually succeeded. The signing of the Anglo-French alliance in November 1716 and of a Triple Alliance to include the Dutch soon after, inaugurated a system which was not technically to be abrogated until 1744 and which indeed did more to establish the Hanoverian succession in Britain than any other single factor. Whether France, as opposed to her ruler, gained by it is another matter; but for Britain, friendship with the one power which probably had the capacity to plunge Englishmen into the civil chaos of the seventeenth century, and at a time when the Jacobite cause was still strong enough to exert real influence among them, was to prove invaluable.

If the Whig ministers of the early years of George I had much on which to congratualate themselves, it was not to be for long. By 1717 the cabinet was deeply divided to the point of disintegration. For this there were many reasons. The harmony which had prevailed at the beginning of the reign quickly gave way to personal conflict between Townshend and Walpole on the one hand, and Sunderland and Stanhope on the other. It was not to be expected that a quadrumvirate of diverse but well-matched talents would share power indefinitely without resorting to a struggle for supremacy. This is not to say that no principles were involved. On the contrary.

Townshend and Walpole were unseated for their opposition to the policies which came to them from Hanover, where George I held court attended by Stanhope. The French alliance was negotiated entirely abroad and left the ministers at home in considerable perturbation. Though they did not oppose the alliance openly, their obvious readiness to protract its completion and their solicitude for Dutch objections to it, endeared them neither to Stanhope nor George I. More important still were the adventures into which the king's Hanoverian connections threatened to lead his servants. By 1717 George I had effectively achieved his basic war aims against Sweden, and was becoming increasingly nervous about his former ally Peter the Great. Russia stood to gain prodigiously by Sweden's collapse as a great power, and more sinister still, seemed to be taking a mounting interest in German affairs. Frederick William of Prussia had already concluded an alliance with the Russians in 1716 and Peter himself was now interfering in the affairs of the duchy of Mecklenburg, bordering on Hanover itself. The prospect of Russian troops permanently in Mecklenburg was infinitely alarming to the elector and negotiations concerning the fate of the duchy seemed to overshadow far weightier topics. An aggravating circumstance was the fact that Bernstorff, the hated Hanoverian minister, had a personal interest in certain Mecklenburg estates which greatly complicated relations between George I and his neighbours. This was too much for Townshend and Walpole, who were driven into the position of successive generations of English politicians, insisting that British policy must not be subordinated to the petty concerns of grasping Hanoverians. 'I can't for my life see', complained Horace Walpole from the Hague, 'why the whole system of affairs in Europe, especially in relation to the interest of England, must be entirely subverted on account of Mecklenbourg'.[1] On the other side Sunderland characterised the protests of his rivals as 'the old Tory notion that England can subsist by itself whatever becomes of the rest of Europe, which has been so justly exploded ever since the revolution'.[2] Whatever the arguments, power rested with the king at Hanover. Moreover, events in the shape of a sensational Swedish

[1] *Stanhope* by B. Williams (Oxford 1932), p. 236.
[2] ibid., p. 243.

Jacobite plot which greatly heightened political tension and increased the pressures on those who maintained that there was no need for drastic measures abroad, did not assist the Townshend clan. By the spring of 1717 Townshend and Walpole were in opposition, the Whig party hopelessly split, and the supremacy of Sunderland, and more particularly Stanhope, assured.

Stanhope's pre-eminence was not altogether novel or complete. He had of course been one of the most celebrated generals of the previous war and since the accession of George I one and perhaps the more influential of the Secretaries of State. Though he became the leading light in the ministry after the Whig split, he held the First Lordship of the Treasury for little more than a year before returning to the Secretaryship and conceding to his ally Sunderland a substantial share of power. Nor did he quite figure in Parliament as Walpole and Pitt were to later. Though he made up to some extent in vehemence and choler what he lacked in rhetoric, he was scarcely the most effective of orators either in the Commons or, from March 1718, in the Lords. None the less, his complete security in the closet and his control of foreign policy at a time when affairs overseas were particularly important, gave him a position which probably placed him before the insinuating Sunderland. In any event he was to dominate foreign policy in these formative years before the establishment of the Walpole regime. This was entirely to his own liking. As Horace Walpole observed, Stanhope's great talent was his 'fruitfull and luxuriant genius in foreign affairs',[1] and few eighteenth-century ministers enjoyed their conduct more than Stanhope. Indeed he set a record in personal diplomacy, which earned him Robert Walpole's scornful description of 'the knight errant of English diplomacy',[2] and which outdid even the later exploits of Carteret and Castlereagh.

Stanhope had won his supremacy by loyalty to the Elector of Hanover rather than the King of Great Britain. Yet he was far from being a mere sycophant. On the contrary he utilised his dominant position in the royal confidence to strengthen the standing of his country abroad and his party at home. Abroad there were two

---

[1] *Stanhope* by B. Williams (Oxford 1932), p. 154.
[2] ibid., p. 322.

obvious priorities. Subject to the interests of Hanover, which by this time were largely secured, it was a matter of the utmost importance to plug the gaps in the Treaty of Utrecht and so establish a lasting peace in southern Europe and at the same time to bring an end to the Great Northern War which threatened to continue interminably. In the south Stanhope's problems were considerable. For one thing Charles VI and Philip V had apparently not yet finished fighting the War of the Spanish Succession. The former resented a peace settlement which had left him with Naples but not with Sicily, while the latter was not reconciled to the alienation of Spain's Italian possessions at Utrecht. There was a somewhat farcical aspect to these disputes with both monarchs claiming the right to appoint Spanish grandees, to control the Order of the Golden Fleece, and generally to assert their claims to ancient imperial prerogatives. None the less, the conflict was a serious one and indeed threatened to engulf the whole of southern Europe in a new counterpart to the northern war. This was made all the more likely by Philip V's choice of a second wife. The extraordinary Elizabeth Farnese enormously strengthened the obsession with Italy which already characterised the Spanish establishment. Her own purely dynastic aspirations were extensive, founded as they were on a desire to find her sons lands in Italy which would compensate them for their lack of expectations in Spain, where Philip's son by his first wife would succeed. Circumstances aided the Farnese ambition in the duchies of Parma, Piacenza and Tuscany, where Elizabeth's family could make plausible claims. Added to this was the considerable ingenuity and energy of Cardinal Alberoni, another Italian import, as the first minister in Spain during these years; all in all the possibility that Spain would plunge the Continent into a new and for Britain alarming war naturally seemed strong.

Stanhope saw the solution as stemming logically from the resurrection of the 'old system' and the creation of the Anglo-French alliance. Together the powers involved must unite to give the law to a Spain bent on putting back the clock in Italy. The result was the Quadruple Alliance of August 1718, a remarkable collective security arrangement which challenges comparison with the congress system of the early nineteenth century. Strictly speaking the alliance was a triple one since the Dutch characteristically failed to accede in the event; none the less it was strong enough, and Stanhope's resolution firm enough, to bring Spain to heel. Despite a lightning journey to Spain to mediate a peaceful settlement, Stanhope showed no reluctance to go to war. In the Mediterranean Alberoni's seizure of Sicily from the Duke of Savoy was countered by the Royal Navy's destruction of the Spanish fleet at Cape Passaro. Moreover a Spanish attempt to launch a Jacobite invasion of England was shattered by the elements at sea, while in Scotland the Pretender's followers were defeated in the skirmish at Glenshiel. Simultaneously a French invasion threatened to wrench the Basque provinces from the grasp of Philip V. Against this devastating campaign there was little to be done. Alberoni was dismissed and Spain formally joined the Quadruple Alliance, agreeing that Sicily should be handed over to Charles VI with compensation for Savoy in Sardinia, and that the Farnese family should be established in northern Italy only under the suzerainty of the emperor. A congress was summoned to Cambrai to settle the details and finally bring to a close the disputes which had arisen from the Peace of Utrecht. For Britain, the war waged briefly in 1718 and 1719, seemed an unqualified success.

Elsewhere too Stanhope's policy was bold yet practical. In the north his task was facilitated by the death of Charles XII, which made peace virtually inevitable. Swedish exhaustion was abetted by the ingenuity of Stanhope's young protegé at Stockholm, Lord Carteret. Thanks partly to his skill, but more to the potential assistance of the Royal Navy in fending off the armies of Muscovy, the Swedes were brought to terms. Denmark and Prussia were bought off, as was Hanover, which duly received Bremen and Verden. A series of treaties in 1719 and 1720 formally closed hostilities between Sweden and all her enemies but Russia. Nor was this the limit of Stanhope's triumph. At home he completed his *tour de force* by simultaneously dishing the Hanoverian ministers and reuniting the royal family and the Whig party. Though Townshend and Walpole had gone into opposition in 1717 in protest at the activities of George I's Hanoverians, it was Stanhope who, by capturing the entire confidence of the king, destroyed their political power in England. The occasion, and it was only the occasion, was the rapprochement with Prussia which was part of the manoeuvring under-taken in the final stages of the northern war as the emphasis changed from hostility towards Sweden to defence of Sweden against Russia. 'At last', Stanhope declared in July 1720, we have 'got a complete victory over the old man [Bernstorff]. The King has twice, in council, before all his German Ministers, overruled him with an air of authority in relation to our negotiation with Prussia'.[1] Though the shadow of Hanover was not to shift from British foreign policy for a long time, the direct influence of Hanoverian ministers in British affairs was at an end. Accompanied as this was by a recon-ciliation with the opposition Whigs, by which Townshend and Walpole recognised the predominance of Stanhope and Sunderland, while their ally the Prince of Wales submitted to the authority of his father, it was a remarkable personal as well as political triumph for Stanhope. It was all the more ironic then that the South Sea Bubble was shortly to shatter the equanimity of the regime, while Stanhope and Sunderland were to die in successive years.

Impressive though his record was, it is not impossible to criticise the policies of Stanhope. One obvious objection was that he had leaned much too far towards Hanover in preserving his power base at court. Hanover had dictated support for the Empire against Spain, hostility towards Sweden and subsequently Russia, an unnatural alliance with the traditional enemy France, and bad relations with Holland. All this had allegedly been necessary to secure to the Elector of Hanover two insignificant duchies in northern Germany. Yet this was not an unanswerable argument. All Stanhope's measures were defensible in terms of British interests, notably the security of the Protestant succession and the preservation of peace and the balance of power on the Continent. Exclusively Hanoverian concerns had not seriously distorted Stanhope's policy, and indeed the predictions of his opponents, who foresaw first major clashes between Britain and Sweden and later naval hostilities between Russia and Great Britain, never in fact materialised. Above all it had been Stanhope who had crushed the influence of George I's Hano-verian servants. If this constituted unnatural slavery to the electorate and its interest, there was much to be said for such slavery.

[1] *Stanhope* by B. Williams (Oxford 1932), p. 371.

A connected charge is that Stanhope was much too quick to take an anti-Spanish line in dealing with the problems of southern Europe. A more favourable attitude towards the ambitions of Madrid might have better preserved the continental balance of power and established British merchants in control of the Spanish American economy. The price was alleged to be a small one—cooperation with Spain's designs in Italy. Thus Bubb, who negotiated the trade treaties of 1715–16, themselves tokens of Spanish readiness to move closer to the court of George I, had stressed that 'The absolute controul over Spain will belong to the highest bidder for the Queen's son'.[1] Yet Stanhope was not particularly anti-Spanish. He had personally travelled to Madrid to negotiate immediately before the war of 1718, subsequently incurring much undeserved criticism for a journey which appeared hypocritical in the light of Cape Passaro. He was also one of those who believed that the return of Gibraltar to Spain was both necessary and wise; indeed he initiated the policy which eventually produced George I's admittedly qualified promise to restore Gibraltar in 1721. Consequently his refusal to countenance Spanish designs on Italy was not the result of mere prejudice or even of Hanover's need to conciliate the Empire. There were excellent grounds for arguing that the re-admission of Spain to southern Italy would open a veritable Pandora's box in international relations and make the reinforcement of the Utrecht settlement impossible. That most Englishmen in a position to judge, agreed with Stanhope's determination to force Spain to abandon her aggressive adventures, was indicated by the extraordinary ease with which Parliament was brought to agree to war in 1718. Those who portrayed Spain as a menace to European peace were readily believed, as was Stanhope's insistence on the need to quell this threat if only to defeat the intrigues of the Pretender. As he declared in the Commons, 'though we might by mean, pitiful methods avoid a war for a few months, sooner or later we must have our share in it, and then the succession to the Crown of Britain might come to be disputed as well as that of Spain'.[2] There was also the matter of trade. Savoy and Austria were both powers which could be tolerated in sensitive Mediterranean areas.

[1] *Stanhope* by B. Williams (Oxford 1932), p. 277.
[2] ibid., p. 291.

But the prospect of a Spanish presence in Sicily was something of a nightmare. Daniel Defoe, for example, argued that 'Great Britain cannot acquiesce in letting Spain possess Sicily, without giving up her trade to Turkey and to the Gulph of Venice . . . her trade to Zant for currants, to Gallipoli for oyl, to Messina and Naples for silk, and in a word, her whole commerce of the Mediterranean. . . . How long [would we] be able to . . . carry on our navigation and commerce with our own people at Jamaica, Barbados, etc., if the naval strength of Spain be suffer'd to grow to such an immoderate and monstrous pitch'.[1] In retrospect these fears may appear exaggerated, but at the time they seemed tolerably well founded. The Tory William Shippen was unhesitatingly sent to the Tower for his insinuations in Parliament about Hanoverian influence in Anglo-Spanish relations; moreover, though the Walpole Whigs launched a massive attack on Stanhope's policy the House of Commons agreed by a great majority to support war 'to check the growth of that naval power, which must otherwise prove dangerous to the trade of three Kingdoms, and to the repose of Europe'.[2]

Ultimately the most compelling case against Stanhope is not that levelled by contemporaries, but that which is vouchsafed by hindsight, the fundamental fact that in one sense his policies failed. For example, the war of 1718 proved to be by no means the end of Spain's mischief-making. The congress of Cambrai, in theory meant to dot the i's and cross the t's of the Quadruple Alliance's settlement of Italy, in fact proved something of a farce; Spain's Italian ambitions were to provoke more than one international crisis in succeeding years and indeed were not finally adjusted until 1748. Similarly, though peace in the north was eventually achieved at Nystadt in 1721, it was not entirely on the lines laid down by Stanhope. Peter the Great was not intimidated by the might of the Royal Navy, Sweden did not regain her losses in the eastern Baltic, and the advance of Muscovy was by no means arrested. Yet it would be harsh to condemn Stanhope on these lines. For one thing he died before these matters were settled; in particular if he had been present,

[1] *England under George I: The Quadruple Alliance* by W. Michael (London 1939), pp. 73–74.
[2] ibid., p. 77.

as he intended, at the congress of Cambrai, it is conceivable that he could have brought his own schemes to a more successful conclusion. Again no statesman could comprehensively settle all the problems left by the Treaty of Utrecht and the twenty years of war preceding it. Stanhope had done much to safeguard the Protestant succession in Britain and deprive the Pretender of a real opportunity to upset it; he had propitiated the northern ambitions of the new monarch without disastrously sacrificing the interests of his country; he had left history with one of the most remarkable examples of pre-emptive war, and in so doing had gone far to induce an uncharacteristic fit of realism on the part of the Spanish court; he had also provided the framework of the peace settlements which were needed to quieten the Baltic after twenty years of conflict. Few British statesmen were to die with such a record of success.

PART 3

The Influence
of Hanover, 1721–54

7 European Entanglements, 1721–31

About the aims and merits of the new men who were to rule foreign policy after the death of Stanhope in 1721 and Sunderland in 1722, contemporaries were initially uncertain. Sir Robert Walpole, the new First Lord of the Treasury, who was to carve out for himself a position of power and prestige quite unlike that achieved by earlier ministers, was at any rate during the early years of his tenure, neither expert nor interested in foreign affairs. Even in Parliament, his element, he found the subject an uncongenial one. 'You know,' he once told his brother, 'I do not love to give long opinions nor reasonings upon foreign politicks'.[1] Though he was later to learn the political necessity of understanding such matters, he never acquired either the basic linguistic skills or the wide knowledge of international affairs which were essential to make him master of them. Admittedly his brother, Horace Walpole, supplied some of his deficiencies. Described with Lord Hervey's customary pithiness as the prime minister's treaty dictionary,[2] Horace at least was a qualified diplomat. Years of experience in two of the major capitals of Europe, Paris and the Hague, a remarkable grip on the minutiae of European affairs, and considerable skill as a negotiator made Horace a vital aide to his brother both in private and in Parliament. However, in 1721 it was Walpole's brother-in-law, Lord Townshend, who as Secretary of State for the North was primarily responsible for diplomatic affairs. Townshend was still at least as important in the Walpole–Townshend establishment as his brother-in-law and still possessed his full confidence. His knowledge of foreign affairs was

[1] *Some Materials towards Memoirs of the Reign of King George II by John, Lord Hervey* ed. R. Sedgwick (London 1931), 3 vols., p. 285.
[2] ibid.

89

considerable, his experience and skill no less so. Moreover his personal relationship with George I and the king's most influential mistress, the Duchess of Kendal, made him a formidable figure in court politics. This was to be demonstrated in his successful ousting of the principal rival to the Walpoles and their allies.

The rival was Lord Carteret, a brilliant young man who seemed well fitted to assume the mantle of his mentors, Stanhope and Sunderland. After a distinguished spell as British representative at Stockholm, Carteret had been given the seals of the Southern Department when a combination of the South Sea Bubble and smallpox had carried off the tainted James Craggs. His knowledge of languages, his lightly-carried learning, his mastery of continental affairs, made him a potentially outstanding director of foreign policy, while his standing with the king suggested a strong political base. Yet Carteret lost much by the death of his protector Sunderland, and had not the ruthlessness or determination which were needed to combat the enmity of the new ministers. His destruction was engineered by a means entirely characteristic of the age. At a time when the will of kings was the principal force in international relations, unfettered either by great ideological principles, or for the most part by popular prejudices, it was entirely appropriate that the destiny of ministers should be decided by court intrigues. The remnants of the Sunderland team, Carteret with George I in Hanover and Sir Luke Schaub at the embassy in Paris, became fatally involved in an elaborate scheme to curry favour with one of George I's mistresses, Countess von Platen. In the view of both, a distinguished marriage between the Countess's daughter and the French family of Vrillière would prove a political asset. But it would be still more telling if a French dukedom were to accompany the bridegroom, and both Carteret and Schaub encouraged the notion that this was a practicable possibility. Unfortunately the Regent of France, though anxious to please his ally, did not regard it as a light matter, particularly in view of his own political vulnerability, and the powerful vested interests of those who cared little for parvenu ducal creations.

Moreover a number of factors were at work against Carteret. Though Schaub endeavoured to assure the French that 'Lord Carteret is the minister of confidence and has the sole conduct of foreign affairs',[1] they were not entirely convinced nor even well disposed. Dubois was inclined to regard Carteret as an uninhibited champion of the Habsburgs and the Walpole group as worthy successors to Stanhope. Already in April 1722 he had greatly assisted the political fortunes of Walpole and his friends by passing the initial information which led to the revelation of the Atterbury plot. A gratuitous betrayal of the Pretender in this manner did much to consolidate the connection between Dubois and the new ministers in England. The latter showed their anxiety to strengthen this connection by sending Horace Walpole to Paris in a deliberate attempt to cut out the official ambassador, Schaub, and kill his influence with the Regent. Though a nominal diplomatic posting was arranged to explain Horace Walpole's activities, the spectacle of two competing accredited ministers at the court of France was a bizarre if, for Townshend and Walpole, useful one. Nor did Carteret's cause prosper elsewhere. At Hanover in 1723 both Townshend and Carteret attended the king, matching stratagem for stratagem. On this occasion the victor was Townshend. His rival had played on George I's fears of Russian activities in the Baltic, and gambled on a Russian invasion of Sweden which failed to develop. Townshend's efforts to commend himself to the king, or rather to the Elector of Hanover, proved more constructive and more successful. On the one hand France was successfully discouraged from pursuing her plans for an alliance with Russia; on the other a defensive alliance was negotiated with Prussia. The Treaty of Charlottenburg was the first between the two powers since 1690, and materially improved the security of Hanover at little cost to George I. Against this background it only required the death of the Regent Orleans, and dawning realisation that the affair of the Countess von Platen's proxy dukedom was dead, for George I to abandon Carteret and his works. Early in 1724 Sir Luke Schaub was dismissed and replaced by Horace Walpole. A few weeks later Carteret himself was removed to the Lord Lieutenancy of Ireland, a post where, in the current uproar over the scandal of Wood's halfpence, he could not fail without destroying his own reputation and where he could not succeed without enhancing that of the ministry. Nearly two decades were to

[1] *British Diplomatic Instructions*, iv, p. xvii.

pass before Carteret would once again bring his enormous talents and inadequate will to the foreign affairs of his country.

With the characteristically ruthless destruction of Carteret, Walpole and Townshend were given a clear field both at home and abroad. The mid-twenties were their most brilliant and carefree years. At home there was scarcely an opposition worthy of the name. The Tories were impotent to disturb the stability of Walpole's regime and there was effectively no Whig minority in Parliament. At court under both George I until his death in 1727, and after that his son George II, the ministry was impregnably secure, buttressed in the former case by Townshend's credit with the Duchess of Kendal, in the latter by Walpole's alliance with Queen Caroline. If there was ever a moment in the eighteenth century when ministers were relatively free to pursue their own policies, it was this. As it turned out they did not bring to foreign policy a revolution of the kind associated with a Stanhope or a Pitt. Though both Walpole and Townshend started with doubts about the French alliance, in practice it remained the central plank of their policy in the 1720s. Growing Franco–Spanish accord had initially looked ominous but Britain herself joined with the Bourbon powers in the Treaty of Madrid in 1721 and thereafter there were few obvious signs of stress in the strange new relationship between previously unfriendly powers. Admittedly this relationship was to change subtly. Despite the death of Dubois and Orleans in 1723, the new Regent Bourbon was as dependent on British complaisance as his predecessor. But when Bourbon was dismissed in 1726 and Cardinal Fleury became the director of the young king's affairs, the balance began to shift in favour of Versailles. Even so the alliance held for the time being. Not until the end of the decade were more sinister portents to appear.

In northern Europe, the theatre of so much conflict in the years following the accession of George I, matters were quieter in the 1720s. After the end of the Great Northern War, stocktaking rather than agitation was the order of the day. It was inevitable that British interests would continue to come second to those of Hanover in this area, yet it could hardly be alleged that they were significantly damaged in the process, unless it be in relations with Russia. The

Elector of Hanover's concern with the fate of Schleswig-Holstein, Mecklenburg, and Sweden, continued to dictate an anti-Russian policy, which eventually extended even to the despatch of new squadrons to the Baltic in 1726 and 1727. Whether this was or was not in Britain's interest is matter for debate. Russia might have been a useful ally in continental affairs, as indeed the French court urged; on the other hand it could scarcely be to the advantage of London that the entire balance of power in the Baltic should be tipped decisively towards the Muscovites. As with so many examples of Hanoverian impact on British policy, the prosecution's case is non-proven.

The relative tranquillity of affairs in the north contrived to throw into high relief the stormy aspect of those in the Mediterranean world. In theory the Quadruple Alliance had firmly brought to a close the disagreements between Austria and Spain which had threatened to jeopardise the Utrecht settlement. In practice it did nothing of the kind. The Congress of Cambrai, scheduled to tidy up the loose ends left over by the Quadruple Alliance, was a fiasco even by the standards of the day. For two years between 1722 and 1724 the diplomatic representatives of Europe tested their digestions rather than their skills. A ceaseless round of polite and expensive junketing proceeded while Charles VI withheld the crucial investitures promised for the establishment of Elizabeth Farnese's son, Don Carlos, in the Italian duchies. Not until January 1724 did the Congress officially open, and not until April did it broach discussion of any substantive issues. Even then there emerged irreconcilable differences concerning the precise nature of Charles VI's sovereignty over the duchies, differences which reduced the Congress to total deadlock by October and eventually broke it up. It was in this situation that Spain, dismayed by the recalcitrance of the emperor, and discouraged by the unwillingness of France and Britain to take a stern hand with him, ventured a step which was to transform the diplomatic pattern of Europe. For this not a little of the responsibility lay with France. There the Duke of Bourbon had been subjected to the strain of a severe illness which attacked the young Louis XV and the consequent possibility of a vacancy on the throne which might be filled by Philip V of Spain. In this situation the immediate appearance of an heir was of the utmost importance, and not to be delayed until the Spanish Infanta, betrothed to Louis, was old enough to consummate her marriage. Her ignominious return to Madrid, and the hasty marriage between Louis and Maria Leszczynska, daughter of the French candidate for the Polish throne, was the critical factor in impelling the Spanish court to drastic action. That action took the form of a minor diplomatic revolution. After the ground had been prepared by Ripperda, a Dutch adventurer now in Spanish pay, three treaties were signed at Vienna between Austria and Spain, one of peace, one of trade, and one of alliance. For Madrid the wisdom of this startling new alignment may be doubted. In return for confirmation of the concessions in Italy which Charles VI had already promised under pressure from the Quadruple Alliance, the Spaniards guaranteed the Pragmatic Sanction (providing for the peaceful succession of Charles VI's daughter to the Habsburg dominions), and made extraordinary commercial concessions. However, whatever the prudence of this policy, it was one which had the most dramatic effects in the chancelleries of Europe.

Townshend, who played a more important part in the subsequent diplomatic furore than any other European statesman, took the gravest possible view of the Alliance of Vienna. Within four months of its establishment, he had brought Britain, France and Prussia together in the Alliance of Hanover, signed in September 1725, a manoeuvre which proved the signal for a general post. During the following three years Europe was gradually organised into two great armed camps. Whether Townshend over-reacted at this time is a question not easily resolved. When the administration defended its policy to Parliament, it was able to deploy a number of arguments, of varying appeal. The claim that the Alliance of Vienna posed a significant threat to the Protestant Succession, for example, was difficult to take seriously. No doubt any power hostile to Britain would use the Pretender as a pawn, but it was difficult to see the Emperor and the King of Spain as effective champions of James III, while France was so closely connected with the court of George I. More plausible was the great play made with the danger to British trade. At Vienna, Philip V had given substantial privileges to Austrian subjects, and more particularly to the recently founded

Ostend Company, the licensed imperial competitor of the British, Dutch and French in the West and East Indies. The prospect of intensive Flemish activity in the Spanish empire was not one to be taken lightly at the Hague and in London. Indeed the Maritime Powers had regarded the effective subordination of Belgium to their own commercial interests as one of the most essential elements in the peace settlement after the War of the Spanish Succession. On the other hand, relatively little had been made of the activities of the Ostend Company before 1725 and it may be that ministers exaggerated the company's importance for their own reasons. Certainly they stressed the arguments most acceptable for general consumption; thus in Parliament when their opponents objected that 'the Emperor denied anything prejudicial to England in the Vienna treaty, . . . it was affirmed by Sir R. Walpole he had it from the . . . king's own mouth there was both, in respect to our commerce and the Pretender'.[1]

At bottom however, Townshend's calculations were concerned with the threat posed by the Alliance of Vienna to the peace of Europe. An actual combination between Austria and Spain was a sinister development which not only shattered the Quadruple Alliance but also endangered the balance of power generally. Yet much depended in this argument on debatable points of interpretation. Particularly in retrospect it might be considered that Madrid and Vienna were scarcely natural allies and that the unstable will of Elizabeth Farnese and the temporary and limited interest of Charles VI were not a very secure foundation for future action. However, the ministry in London not only regarded the alliance itself as extremely disturbing, but entertained dark suspicions as to the much discussed secret clauses. In particular the suggestion of a marriage between the Archduchess Maria Theresa and Elizabeth Farnese's eldest son conjured up horrifying possibilities, as Horace Walpole pointed out in the Commons. If the sickly elder son of Philip V did not outlive his father, if the equally delicate young King of France died, and if Charles VI failed to produce a male heir, Don Carlos could be ruler of the three most powerful states on the continent.

---

[1] *The Parliamentary Diary of Sir Edward Knatchbull, 1722–1730* ed. A. N. Newman (Camden 3rd Ser., xclv), p. 98.

To an age ever conscious of the varied fortunes of the ruling dynasties of Europe and well versed in their likely consequences, this was not a mere chimera, but a real possibility.

Nor was Protestant England entirely unaware of the religious implications. Charles VI's aggressively Catholic activities in central Europe revived the spectre of religious warfare at a time when religious issues were still potential dynamite in some quarters. In these circumstances it is not perhaps surprising that Townshend committed himself to a forward policy, nor that the country followed him. From 1726 to 1729, the years of crisis unleashed by the Alliances of Vienna and Hanover, the administration's majority remained perfectly secure, despite the need to raise the land tax to 4/- and place the country on a war footing. Pulteney's small band of opponents to Walpole found little to latch on to in a policy proclaimed to defend trade, religion and the succession, and failed to achieve an effective minority in the Commons, even with Tory support. Nor were they assisted by their intrigues with the Austrian ambassador, Count Palm, who, in attempting to rebut the imputations cast on his master by Walpole and Townshend, made the fatal mistake of dabbling publicly in domestic politics. The letter to George I which he had published in the press savoured of interference in purely British concerns and proved an unexpected bonus to the ministers, who eventually expelled the offending ambassador. Townshend must have felt in these circumstances that the policy of confrontation which he had opted for was a political as well as diplomatic asset.

This is not to say that the Alliance of Hanover had matters all its own way. Not surprisingly its first effect was to drive Spain and Austria even closer together. The additional Treaty of Vienna, signed in November 1725, made firmer arrangements for the betrothal of Austrian Archduchesses and Spanish princes, and ambitious plans for the dismemberment of southern and eastern France. Moreover the Vienna Alliance was quickly joined by Russia in August 1726 and by a bevy of minor German princes thereafter. Even Frederick William I who had so eagerly combined with France and the Maritime Powers at Hanover, was seduced by the emperor in two treaties of October 1726 and December 1728, bartering his guarantee of the Pragmatic Sanction for worthless promises to support his claims to territories on the Rhine. Even so the Hanover Alliance gradually mustered a coalition of equal potential. The formal junction of the Dutch, which occurred in August 1726 was inevitable; that of Sweden, Denmark, Hesse and Brunswick, was obtained with subsidies. By the end of 1727 even Bavaria, which had initially gravitated towards the Viennese camp, had promised benevolent neutrality. Moreover, though France was not over-anxious to unleash a violent confrontation in central Europe, and Britain herself would have found an allied attack on the Austrian Netherlands embarrassing, there was no shortage of sensation elsewhere. Naval demonstrations in the West Indies and off the Spanish coast were countered by preparations for the siege of Gibraltar, and another major conflict seemed inevitable. In the event this 'phoney war' proved sufficient. By the spring of 1727 Charles VI had lost his nerve and left Philip V little choice but to back down. In the Preliminaries of Paris, Austria undertook to forgo its commercial advantages in the Spanish empire, at least for the moment, and to bring its grievances to a new congress. The Spaniards remained recalcitrant for a time but eventually agreed in March 1728 to cease hostilities and join the general negotiations, in the Convention of the Pardo. The policy of confrontation, or so it seemed, had paid off handsomely for the Anglo-French alliance.

In reality Townshend's troubles were just beginning. At the Congress of Soissons, or rather at Paris, since the discussions were effectively conducted there, it became obvious very quickly that the fundamental problem of the years after Utrecht, the disagreement between Vienna and Madrid, had by no means gone away as a result of the Alliance of Vienna. On the contrary, in the spring of 1729 the Emperor not merely repudiated the marriage scheme on which Elizabeth Farnese had set her heart, but refused once again to permit the occupation of Parma and Piacenza on Spain's terms. At home too there were beginning to appear those differences within the ministry which were to transform foreign policy by the early 1730s. The personal connection between Walpole and Townshend was gradually weakening and was not strengthened by the growing stature of the former at every level, at court where it was Walpole not Townshend who had the ear of Queen Caroline, in Parliament where Walpole had made his command of the Commons a quite novel weapon of political supremacy, and even in Norfolk where the new-found wealth of Houghton was challenging the traditional hegemony of Raynham. Nor did the dissolution of the marriage-link between the two men, with the death of Townshend's wife in March 1726, help matters. In terms of policy too Walpole was almost daily finding new reasons for doubting the wisdom of his colleague's strategy. Townshend, like other eighteenth-century Secretaries of State sitting in the House of Lords, was not disposed to take the attitudes of the House of Commons towards the making of foreign policy altogether seriously. Yet increasingly Walpole was finding himself having to defend measures which, though projected by his colleagues, were neither entirely to his own liking nor to that of Parliament.

The general consensus of opinion which had greeted the formation of the Alliance of Hanover with such approval was beginning to sour three years later. This was borne in upon the ministry at the critical moment in the sessions of 1729 and 1730 when it became clear that the Congress of Soissons would settle little and that the expensive war footing on which the country was still placed would have to continue. Naturally enough the administration's Achilles' heel proved its German policy, and in particular its expenditure on mercenaries—always a potential bone of contention. Opposition speakers were not wanting 'to declare the Act of Settlement broken by the continuation of the Hessian troops in the English pay for the defence of Hanover'.[1] In February 1729 the ministers obtained a majority of no less than 207 on this question, but when it was raised again a year later that majority had fallen to 79. Clearly the country gentlemen, on whom in the last analysis the court depended, were becoming restive at the continuance of Townshend's policy. Nor was this the only symptom of discontent. The Anglo–Spanish crisis brought loud protests from City merchants against the hostile activities of the Spaniards in the West Indies. Even at the time, this issue, which was to swell in the course of the following decade and

[1] *Some Materials towards Memoirs of the Reign of King George II by John, Lord Hervey* ed. R. Sedgwick (London 1931), 3 vols., p. 106.

eventually destroy both Walpole and his policies, embarrassed the government not a little in the House of Commons. Though it managed to prevent Parliament demanding strong action in the Caribbean and so endangering the negotiations proceeding across the Channel, it did so only with a majority which eventually fell, in February 1729, to a mere 35. Worst of all, the opposition produced in 1730 a classic 'patriot' issue which seriously alarmed the ministers. Their allegation that the harbour at Dunkirk, contrary to the terms of the Peace of Utrecht, had been put in good order was eventually sloughed off by Walpole but not, as Hervey commented, before 'the whole House was in a flame, and the ministry stronger pushed than they had ever been on any occasion before'.[1] All this clamour was, as even Townshend admitted, evidence that 'this nation will not long bear the present uncertain state of things'.[2] But it was on Walpole that it had the most marked effect. Though he had loyally stood by his colleague's policy, he could hardly avoid the conclusion that that policy could not be sustained indefinitely, and that for the future, if he wished to control the House of Commons, he must also have a larger say in control of foreign policy.

Once Walpole began to formulate his own line in foreign policy, there could be only one conclusion, and that a direct clash with his long-standing friend and comrade. Townshend was committed to a strategy which was based on the assumption that the Emperor was the greatest menace to the peace of Europe and to the interests of Britain. Walpole, under the pressure of his domestic difficulties, could only see that Spain, through her commercial policy, posed an equal threat to his tranquillity. Townshend was convinced that if necessary a firm stance must be maintained to repel the perils which he detected in central Europe, even to the extent of war. Walpole's chief and soon overwhelming concern was to withdraw from a position of confrontation and return to the safe political waters of peace and retrenchment. There could be no compromise. By the spring of 1730 Townshend, in no position to challenge Walpole's

[1] *Some Materials towards Memoirs of the Reign of King George II by John, Lord Hervey* ed. R. Sedgwick (London 1931), 3 vols., p. 116.
[2] *Memoirs of the Life and Administration of Sir Robert Walpole, Earl of Orford* by W. Coxe (London 1798), ii, pp. 638–41.

predominance at court and in the Commons, had resigned, and
within a year a comprehensive revolution in British foreign policy
had been carried through.

The first and most straightforward object of Walpole's policy was a
reconciliation with Spain. Given the fact that Spanish policy was
still primarily directed to the attainment of the Farnese family's
Italian ambitions, it was not particularly difficult to reach agreement
on Anglo-Spanish disputes. William Stanhope was despatched to
Madrid and there negotiated the Treaty of Seville. The treaty,
signed by Spain, France and Britain in November 1729, repeated the
commitment of the Anglo-French alliance to obtain Spain's desires
at Parma and Piacenza, restored the commercial concessions accorded
to British merchants before the war preparations of 1726–27 and
referred the more contentious points to commissioners for settlement. On the surface Seville merely brought relations between
Spain and the other powers back to the position achieved by the
Quadruple Alliance, some ten years before. In fact there was a
significant difference. France and Britain had brought about the
detachment of Madrid from the Viennese alliance by a new and
important concession which provided for occupation of the Italian
duchies not by neutral troops but by Spanish garrisons. To Charles
VI, who indeed occupied the duchies when the Duke of Parma died
in January 1731, this was totally unacceptable and raised the by now
familiar question: would the powers go to war in central Europe to
enforce their solution to the Italian problem? This time however a
new expedient was produced, one which would have been un-
palatable to Townshend, but which fitted Walpole's own objects
perfectly—nothing less than a rapprochement between Vienna and
London, carried out behind the back of Britain's ally across the
Channel. It was not a policy without risks. The negotiations could
hardly be kept secret, and indeed in a sensational journalistic scoop
by the *Craftsman*, soon appeared in the press. Moreover, had they
failed George II would have found himself effectively isolated, with
France furious at her own exclusion, Spain resentful of her continued
failure in Italy, and Austria unsecured. As it turned out however,
the gamble came off. By the Second Treaty of Vienna in March 1731,
Walpole finally brought to a conclusion the great contest initiated in

1725 and went far towards resolving the problems which had beset southern and central Europe ever since the War of the Spanish Succession. The Emperor was brought to make substantial concessions both to Spain and the Maritime Powers. He ceased to argue over the installation of the Spaniards in Parma and Piacenza, suppressed the Ostend Company, and undertook to put an end to all talk of marriage treaties between Austria and any of the great powers. But the price of these concessions was high. The Pragmatic Sanction was guaranteed by the Maritime Powers, and Britain pledged to protecting the rights of Maria Theresa to the Habsburg dominions. Yet this sacrifice, which clearly involved grave commitments in central Europe, seemed worth making. Indeed Walpole had some justification for regarding his handiwork as a magnificent diplomatic *tour de force*, all the more remarkable given his inexperience in international affairs. The endless and damaging disputes about the duchies were over, thanks to Britain, and it was appropriate that the Royal Navy escorted Don Carlos to his new dominions. The cycle of diplomatic crises which had steadily escalated under the direction of Townshend and eventually brought the powers to the brink of war, was broken. Britain, abandoning her armaments, could return to economy and, as Walpole hoped and trusted, domestic harmony.

Even so there was cause for concern in the new Treaty of Vienna. The Anglo-French alliance which had so surprised the courts of Europe when it had been founded by Dubois and Stanhope, was virtually dealt its death blow by Walpole. Though France could not object to its ally's achievement as such, it could hardly be expected to view with complacency a negotiation from which it had been deliberately excluded, and a firm British guarantee for the Habsburg succession. Fleury was not entirely unready to follow the other states of Europe with the paper promises which Charles VI seemed so anxious to secure, but he would not do so without very considerable inducements. In the meantime Walpole's action effectively ended the era of Franco-British cooperation and no doubt speeded the gravitation of the French court towards its Bourbon cousins. Within two years there was to be signed the Treaty of the Escorial, the first of the Family Compacts, which Whigs had fought to make impossible in the War of the Spanish Succession, and which under the pressure of Anglo-French accord had hitherto not materialised. It was scarcely a beneficial development from the British point of view.

Even so it is difficult to condemn Walpole's new policy. For if it was true that he materially hastened the breakdown of Franco-British relations he could reasonably reply that such a breakdown was practically inevitable anyway. The fundamental fact was that the temporary community of interests which had brought the courts of Versailles and St James together was by this time minimal. On the French side in particular it had been the weakness of the dynasty which had dictated a conciliatory attitude. But by 1730 there was no regency desperate to defend its position, and the young Louis XV had, with the birth of a dauphin in 1729, an heir. Moreover the ruling influences which provided the king with a policy were by no means as well-disposed as those of Dubois, Orleans, and Bourbon. Chauvelin, who directed foreign relations from 1727 to 1737, was universally recognised to be a bitter enemy of the British. Even Fleury, the effective first minister, whose real designs lay shrouded behind intrigue and evasion, was scarcely as well inclined as the Walpoles, flattered by his attentions and misled by his sympathy, liked to imagine. It was the Duke of Newcastle who, perhaps surprisingly, saw clearly in this matter. As early as August 1730 he warned Horace Walpole, 'The Cardinal is not dead, but dead to us. Another spirit governs him ... the whole spirit and secret Direction of every measure is in direct opposition to us, as if we were actually broke'.[1]

Even in London pressures were growing which made it increasingly difficult to maintain the Anglo-French entente. Not for long would public or parliamentary opinion readily support it if there was the least opportunity for the opposition to raise a traditional 'patriotic' question. Unfortunately there were several such questions. Typical was that of Dunkirk. Where the rights lay in this matter it is difficult to say, though it would scarcely be surprising if the French were somewhat remiss in carrying out their treaty obligations to render the port useless. Difficulties of inspection and enforcement, even given French goodwill, were considerable. Though Walpole sur-

[1] B. Williams, 'The Foreign Policy of England under Walpole' in *Eng. Hist. Rev.*, xvi (1901), p. 448.

mounted the clamour of 1730 by demonstrating that Fleury was prepared to give reasonable assurances about the demolition of Dunkirk, the airing of the issue inevitably damaged relations between the two countries. Moreover there were potential differences in commercial matters, thanks to competing interests in the Spanish empire, in the Caribbean where the problem of the two countries' respective claims to the Neutral Islands, and particularly St Lucia, were currently causing trouble, and in North America, where French designs on the great American back country could hardly fail to conflict with the expanding energies of the thirteen colonies. It may reasonably be doubted, at least in retrospect, whether it was worth continuing the Townshend policy of combination with France against Austria in order to retain the friendship of an ally which was fast becoming an enemy.

8 Neutrality and Isolation, 1731—42

It did not take long after the Treaty of Vienna for the full implications of Townshend's withdrawal in favour of Walpole to become
clear. To claim that Walpole's foreign policy was fundamentally
pacific would almost be an understatement. Peace was the overriding
object of his ambitions in a way which had rarely been true of other
directors of British foreign policy. At every level Walpole was a
determined advocate of non-aggression. Temperamentally, as his
shrewd and loyal friend Lord Hervey commented, he was 'not one
of those projecting systematical great geniuses who are always
thinking in theory';[1] political inactivity was a state for which he
ever and paradoxically strove. He also had a natural distrust for
commitments to others which stemmed partly from fear of the
consequences, partly from inexperience in international politics.
Long before he had effectively taken charge of foreign policy, in
1723, he had made a remark which would serve well as a comment
on his strategy in the 1730s. 'My politics', he had explained to
George I, 'are to keep free from all engagements as long as I possibly
can'.[2] But this was not a mindless desire for withdrawal and insularity.
On the contrary, Walpole had a perfectly clear conception of the
purpose of his policy. Peace would chime with all his domestic
objectives; under it trade would prosper and taxation languish.
Merchants whose pockets were full would be as disinclined to rock
the ship of state as would country gentlemen whose rent rolls were
unencumbered. Above all while Britain was at peace the Hanoverian

[1] *Some Materials towards Memoirs of the Reign of King George II by John, Lord
Hervey* ed. R. Sedgwick (London 1931), 3 vols., p. 19.
[2] *Memoirs of the Life and Administration of Sir Robert Walpole, Earl of Orford* by
W. Coxe (London 1798), ii, p. 263.

succession, that delicate plant which desperately needed time to grow strong and put down roots at St James, would be safe. No wartime enemy of Britain's was likely to forgo the potential advantages to be derived from support for the Pretender, and Walpole's prediction that 'if there was a war, the King's crown would be fought for on this land',[1] was to be amply fulfilled during the War of the Austrian Succession in 1745.

Walpole's attachment to the policy of peace at all costs is all the more striking when it is remembered what difficulties he had to cope with in order to carry it through. Neither the king nor queen entirely shared his horror of war, and the interests of Hanover were too important at the court of George II for the electoral stakes in European power politics to be neglected. Not even Walpole's own subordinates were entirely of a mind with him. Admittedly Harrington, who had received his peerage for his (insignificant) part in negotiating the Treaty of Seville, and who replaced Townshend as one of the secretaries of state, was a nonentity, and an entirely complaisant one at that. But Newcastle, the other secretary since Carteret's ejection, was not altogether deaf to the cries of those who demanded a positive role for Britain in the affairs of Europe, and with his friends and followers, was indeed to become something of a nuisance by the end of the decade. Moreover Walpole had to cope in the 1730s with a political opposition which was much more powerful and threatening than it had been during the years of Townshend's ascendancy in foreign affairs. The growing cooperation between rebellious Whigs of the Pulteney and Carteret ilk, and the Tories, the alarming domestic crisis associated with Walpole's excise scheme of 1733, the general election of 1734 in the wake of that crisis, the increasingly bad relations between the court and the rising star of Frederick Prince of Wales, all these helped to create a large and dangerous opposition, led by powerful aristocrats like Chesterfield and Cobham as well as by brilliant politicians like Pulteney and Pitt. Opposition in Parliament was rarely disinclined to attack the foreign politics of the court, and that of the 1730s was not exceptional in this respect. The very term associated with the political platform of opposition—'patriotism'—was one which

[1] *Walpoliana* by P. Yorke, 2nd Earl of Hardwicke (London 1781), p. 7.

usggested something more positive and aggressive than Walpole's peace. Yet against these forces Walpole fought steadily and until 1739 with remarkable success, on behalf of non-intervention and neutrality.

The outstanding personal success of Walpole's policy was George II's neutrality in the War of the Polish Succession. Had either the king or queen, or even the other ministers, had the decisive say in the making of foreign policy, Britain would almost certainly have been dragged into that as into most other continental wars in the eighteenth century. It was entirely due to Walpole that she was not. His argument had much to commend it. From the British viewpoint neither the ostensible nor the real issue in the War of the Polish Succession was of central importance. In Poland, where in October 1733 the French candidate for the vacant Polish throne, Stanislas Leszczynski, was deposed in favour of the Austro-Russian candidate, Augustus of Saxony, there was no very vital principle at stake for the west. The French themselves, who declared war in October in their attempt to restore Leczczynski, chose to interpret their obligations to him loosely. They made little effort to save Danzig, the last enclave of his supporters, which fell in the summer of 1734, and indeed seemed principally anxious to avoid giving either Britain or Holland any cause for concern in the Baltic. Even in Italy and on the Rhine, the main theatres of war, Walpole found it possible to claim that the danger to British interests was slight, though his position here was more difficult. Spain, France, Sardinia and Bavaria launched their assault on the Habsburg dominions, technically because it was alleged that Austria's massing of troops in Silesia during the Polish crisis and the pressure which Vienna brought to bear at Warsaw directly challenged their joint interests. In fact the war which broke out in the autumn of 1733 was a cynical and self-interested attempt to dismember Charles VI's empire.

In this situation it might have been supposed that the court of St James, which was committed to join in the defence of Austria against any aggressor by the Second Treaty of Vienna, and which after all had been ready to go to war with Spain in 1718–19 and 1726–27 to foil Bourbon designs on Italy, would not hesitate to join in the fray. Yet Walpole, with the broad support of Parliament, refused to accept either the legal or moral obligation to fight. On both counts it is difficult in retrospect to treat this view seriously. The notion that Austrian diplomatic pressure on the Poles made Vienna the aggressor in the war with the Bourbon powers was not a convincing one, and the emperor had considerable justification for his view that his ally had reneged on treaty obligations. On the other hand Walpole's belief that in terms of expediency Britain could only lose by intervention in Italy or Germany, was a more plausible one. His anxiety to stay clear of continental entanglements cut the ground from beneath the opposition's feet at Westminster and seemed to suggest a perfectly defensible policy. Walpole's celebrated boast to the queen, in the first year of the war—'Madam, there are fifty thousand men slain this year in Europe, and not one Englishman'[1]— was precisely of a kind to appeal to eighteenth-century public opinion, obsessed as it was with the dangers of interfering in continental, and especially German, politics. No less attractive was his assertion that Britain would actually gain by abstention. While Bourbon and Habsburg bled each other white, his countrymen could conserve their energies and keep their own counsel, with a view to seizing the initiative on the Continent later. 'If I can keep this nation out of the war a year longer,' Walpole insisted in 1734, 'I know it is impossible but England must give law to all Europe'.[2] Against such claims not even an opposition swollen by the excise crisis could expect to make much progress.

With hindsight however, Walpole's policy is less easily defended. For example, the predictions which he made and which formed the essential premises of his strategy turned out to be incorrect. There was no protracted and bloody trial of strength among the continental giants. In the event, the Austrians were no match for the coalition ranged against them. Both in Italy and in the west Charles VI proved quite incapable of coping with the onslaught and by October 1735, in the light of the Maritime Powers' reiterated refusal to come to his aid, he was ready to make terms. Though they were not reduced to a definitive treaty until November 1738, when the Third Treaty of Vienna was signed, they represented a substantial defeat for the

[1] *Walpoliana* by P. Yorke, 2nd Earl of Hardwicke (London 1781), p. 361.
[2] ibid.

emperor. Spain abandoned her claims on behalf of Don Carlos to Parma and Piacenza in return for the infinitely more valuable Naples and Sicily, won by conquest during the war. Sardinia was thrown some scraps in the Austrian Milanese, and France in return for guaranteeing the Pragmatic Sanction obtained the duchy of Lorraine, in the short run to compensate Louis XV's father-in-law for his Polish disappointment, ultimately for herself. The prince thus unseated, Francis of Lorraine, was established in Tuscany. This was scarcely the scenario Walpole had planned. Nor was his own diplomacy the brilliant success he had projected. Though he had seen himself as the lordly giver of peace to an exhausted and war-torn Europe, his actual role in the peace was humiliatingly irrelevant. The offer of mediation which Britain and Holland together made came as an insult to Charles VI, who had expected more substantial forms of assistance. On the other side though Fleury professed interest in the good intentions of the Maritime Powers, it quickly became clear in the ensuing discussions at the Hague, that he saw them merely as a means of duping the Dutch and the British into protracted and meaningless talks, while the fate of Europe was settled elsewhere. Peace Walpole undoubtedly had preserved for his country; but it was scarcely peace with either honour or glory.

Even so it does not follow that Walpole's policy of non-intervention was entirely the wrong one. Admittedly the obvious retrospective arguments have much in common with those of Walpole's opponents at the time. Many saw British neutrality in the War of the Polish Succession not merely as dereliction of duty on the part of Whitehall, but actually as dangerously self-defeating. The reasoning employed was not particularly new but it was none the less powerful for all that. Essentially it depended on the old bogey of Gallic hegemony. Both George II and Queen Caroline, for example, were subjected to constant pressure by the Hanoverian minister in London on this subject. 'Hatolf set forth in the most formidable colours the growing power of France and the House of Bourbon,' Hervey recorded in his memoirs. 'He said all the reasons that induced this country to engage in King William's and Queen Anne's war ought to operate much stronger now, as France was more powerful and in better circumstances, and that, this nation having so cheerfully come into those wars, he could not conceive why Sir Robert Walpole should imagine people would reason so differently now'.[1] This argument, which was put in 1734 when the prospects were far from clear, was buttressed by the pattern of the war which followed and by the treaty of peace. By 1738 France, which in the 1720s had at times seemed positively a satellite of Britain, enjoyed a position of ascendancy on the Continent, justifying Frederick II of Prussia's description, 'the arbiter of Europe'.[2] In the war itself, at relatively little cost, she had secured Lorraine, one of the most substantial accessions to French territory in recent times, strengthened her allies, and forced the Habsburgs to an ignominious peace. Thereafter she was to make new diplomatic gains in the Baltic, especially in Sweden, and in the Balkans, where in 1739 she was to mediate a peace between Vienna and the Porte which largely nullified the Austrian achievement of 1699 and 1718. Well might Harrington in January 1739 refer to the 'great ascendent which the crown of France has already gained, and that much greater one which, as appears by all her actions, she is now aspiring to'.[3] Still later events were to add point to this implied condemnation of Walpole's policy. Had Britain fought in 1733, it could be argued, France and Spain would have been checked, Austria strengthened and the War of the Austrian Succession which finally broke out on Charles VI's death in 1740, averted. This was certainly the view of Newcastle, an actor in the drama of both wars, who looked back in 1752 and claimed that a full-scale war in 1733 would have made the war of the 1740s unnecessary. Yet it may equally be doubted whether the doctrine of a stitch in time is always applicable to international affairs. An expensive and lengthy war in the mid-thirties, in a cause which did not directly affect either Britain or even Hanover, would not necessarily have made further conflict on the death of Charles VI impossible. On the other hand it would certainly have created damaging divisions at home where neither Parliament nor public would readily have appreciated the need to intervene in what

[1] *Walpoliana* by P. Yorke, 2nd Earl of Hardwicke (London 1781), p. 343.
[2] Sir R. Lodge, 'English Neutrality in the War of the Polish Succession' in *Trans. Roy. Hist. Soc.*, 4th Ser., xlv (1931), p. 166.
[3] *British Diplomatic Instructions, 1689–1789* (Camden Soc.), iii, p. 119.

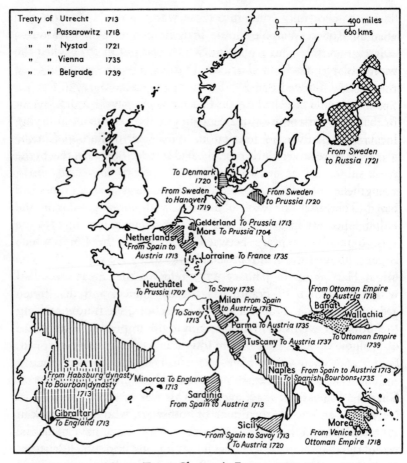

Map 2. Treaty Changes in Europe, 1713–40

seemed a largely continental concern, and where a Jacobite invasion in 1735 might have been very much more dangerous than the one which actually occurred ten years later. Walpole paid the price for his peace, in the form of French diplomatic predominance and a weakened Austria, but it may have been a price worth paying.

It was in a quite different theatre that contemporaries in England severely criticised Walpole for his pacific disposition. Relations with Spain were at least as important as those with France for much of the eighteenth century, and in the late 1730s they became peculiarly so.

There were naturally many matters of dispute. Spain had not abandoned her resentment at the loss of Gibraltar, and its recovery was ever a cardinal point at Madrid. Almost as serious and much more volatile was the constant disagreement over the frontiers of the recently founded British colony of Georgia and Spanish Florida. Spaniards could not view the establishment of a new British province in that area with equanimity, and the provocative activities of her local representatives, not to say those of the new British settlers, were a source of incessant bickering and diplomatic friction in the 1730s. Most important of all however was the problem of illegal trade. British trade with Spanish America was of course long-standing and had been regulated by a series of treaties beginning in 1667 and culminating in the great concessions made in and after the Peace of Utrecht. Unfortunately no amount of treaties could effectively prevent the occurrence of regrettable clashes between Englishmen who sought to expand their trade, and Spaniards intent on restricting it. For most of the problems, the responsibility of the institution officially charged with the management of British trade in the Spanish empire was slight. The South Sea Company, with its official status, its anxiety to preserve its own privileges, the presence on its board of a formally appointed Spanish representative, was not heavily involved in contraband trade, though some of its directors were apt to adopt different standards for their private and unofficial activities. The real difficulty lay with the interlopers, British subjects who without the shadow of legal right to do so, dealt in clandestine trade between Spanish America on the one hand and Jamaica, Barbados or New England on the other. The Spanish authorities in Madrid and on the spot could hardly acquiesce in the massive contraband involved, and those who were employed to enforce their wishes, often little more than licensed pirates, were not overscrupulous in their methods. At moments of international tension as in 1718 or 1727, the consequence was inevitably violent conflict, and even in times of relative tranquillity disagreeable incidents were not unknown. Certainly in the late 1720s there had been considerable discontent among merchant interests in Britain which were affected by Spanish measures to enforce the right of search and confiscation. However, the Treaty of Seville had laid down a procedure for dealing with the various claims for damages, and to some extent the commission consequently set up had done a good deal to settle differences. Moreover, in the mid-thirties the imperial authorities in Madrid took considerable care to avoid incurring British hostility. The need to prevent George II intervening in the War of the Polish Succession against the Bourbon powers, and subsequently to enlist Britain's moral support for Spain's Italian demands, imposed a notable restraint on the activities of law enforcement officials in South America. However, by 1737 these pressures were less evident, and Spanish governors were finding it increasingly difficult to ignore the activities of illegal traders. Even so the Spanish court displayed no great anxiety to provoke an international crisis, and in the face of British protests at allegedly illegal seizures and 'depredations' proved surprisingly conciliatory. Unfortunately forces were building up in England which were to make it impossible even for a conciliatory attitude on both sides to do more than delay a violent confrontation.

The extraordinary passion which arose over the question of Spanish depredations in the late 1730s was and remains a remarkable phenomenon. It was difficult to claim, after all, that the illegal trade with Spanish America was so vital to the economy as to justify all-out war. On the contrary, even within the narrow context of purely Anglo-Spanish trade, the damage likely to be done by war to legitimate trade in the empire and direct trade with mainlaind Spain, far outweighed the benefits which could be expected to materialise. For the interloping merchants however, it happened that the political climate of the last years of Walpole's regime was peculiarly favourable to an agitation of their grievances. The influence of commercial interests in general was always a potent one, and governments, including Walpole's, were extraordinarily sensitive to the pressures they brought to bear. In the 1730s ministers negotiated a most advantageous treaty with Russia to expand the trade of the Russia Company, constantly sought to improve commercial relations with Austria, and brought all their diplomatic weight to bear against the challenge represented by the Swedish East India Company, as earlier they had reacted to that of the Ostend Company. Parliament and the press were still more anxious to please the businessmen.

In the absence of ideological issues or emotional prejudices, economic interest, especially in a mercantilist age, was enormously powerful. To one civil servant indeed the growing impudence of the merchants seemed outrageous. 'These gentlemen,' he remarked of the agitation over Spanish depredations in 1731, 'upon this have assumed a quite different air from what I have formerly known. They used in times past to come Cap in Hand to the Office praying for Relief, now the second word is *You shall hear of it in another Place*, meaning in Parliament. All this must be endured, and now in our turn we must bow and cringe to them'.[1]

Moreover the existence of a large and talented parliamentary opposition considerably augmented the capacity of the business lobby to force government into disagreeable measures. Men like Carteret and the Elder Pitt played the commercial card with impressive skill. Though Pitt has in historical retrospect been given most of the credit for putting the trader's viewpoint, it was in fact the achievement of the opposition in general. Typical was the kind of speech which Carteret would turn on in the House of Lords at a moment's notice. 'This nation has hitherto maintained her independency by maintaining her commerce, but if either is weakened the other must fall. . . . It is by commerce, my Lords, that she has hitherto been enabled to stand her ground against all the open and secret attacks of the enemies of her religion, liberties and constitution'.[2] Such words fell on receptive ears. A public opinion which was increasingly resentful of Walpole and his work, which had largely forgotten the less attractive aspects of major wars, and which was always ready to draw on its almost inexhaustible fund of instant xenophobia, positively lapped up the horror stories which an eager press and Parliament provided it with. Curiously enough the actual incidents which became public property when the House of Commons investigated matters had occurred years before, largely in the period 1729–31. Whether it was Jenkins of the *Rebecca*, whose ear had fallen victim to the inhumanity of Spanish coastguards, or King of the *Robert*, whose crew were tortured by

[1] H. W. V. Temperley, 'The Causes of the War of Jenkins' Ear, 1739' in *Trans. Roy. Hist. Soc.*, 3rd Ser., iii (1909), p. 222.
[2] *Carteret* by W. B. Pemberton (London 1936), p. 166.

'having lighted matches tied between their fingers, and their thumbs put in hand vices and screws',[1] the story was nearly a decade old, yet none the less sensational for that.

The administration was inevitably carried along by the tide which flowed in 1738. To Spain went demands for reparations, claims of free navigation and trade in American waters, and denials of the Spanish right of search. Parliament, in one of its periodic outbursts of patriotism, had to be humoured, and a naval squadron under Admiral Haddock sent to the Mediterranean to maintain a menacing presence. But behind the scenes Walpole fought as hard as he fought for his own political life to preserve the peace. Thanks largely to the basic willingness of the Spanish court to make concessions, to the good offices of the Spanish representative in London, Geraldino, and to Walpole's desperate anxiety to find a formula which would save faces and keep the peace all round, a settlement was by no means impossible. Yet the prospects were shattered by vested interests, in an episode which demonstrates the limits imposed on the making of British foreign policy when matters of national moment were involved. A convention which was negotiated in September 1738 and by which Spain would have paid the sum of £95,000 in settlement of agreed damages in return for the South Sea Company's honouring of its unquestioned debts to the King of Spain (£68,000) had to be dropped, because the Company would not cooperate without having its own grievances concerning the suspension of its priveleges in 1718 and 1727 satisfied. The same obstacle nullified the famous Convention of the Pardo, settled on similar lines in January 1739. Though it was ratified there was no hope of its execution while the South Sea Company refused to pay its own debts. Moreover, any chance that Spain would none the less fulfil its side of the bargain was destroyed when public clamour compelled the ministry to countermand its orders for the recall of Haddock's squadron from Spanish waters. 'This was a precaution', Walpole desperately sought to explain to Geraldino, 'which they felt to be absolutely necessary in face of the unpopularity against them which had been stirred up

[1] *Trade and Peace with Old Spain, 1667-1750* by J. O. McLachlan (Cambridge 1940), p. 107.

in the public by the influence of their opponents'.[1] It would have taken a very submissive gesture from Madrid to appease the British public in its mood of 1739, and Philip V's was not a court which went in for submissive gestures. So the policy of Walpole, a policy launched by a novice in international affairs, and yet one which was in many ways more coherent, more sensible and more fundamentally in Britain's interest than that of most eighteenth-century ministers, was demolished by the vested interest of minority commercial lobbies, and the ill-informed prejudice of an enraged public.

Had Walpole retired in 1739 it would at least be possible to see him as ignobly defeated in defence of a noble policy. Regrettably he remained in power to demonstrate that war was as beyond his abilities as it was against his inclinations. Many of those who had clamoured for war in 1738 and 1739 had regarded the Spanish empire as a fruit ripe for the plucking. In fact it proved a surprisingly difficult proposition when the moment came to test this belief. Apart from the initial success of capturing Porto Bello in November 1739, the war in the West Indies was a total failure. In 1741–42, the years of really sustained campaigning, the expeditions launched against Cartagena, against Cuba, and against Panama, were humiliating fiascos. By the end of 1742 British forces had been withdrawn and the struggle in the Caribbean effectively abandoned. In historical perspective the War of Jenkins' Ear can be seen as something of a landmark, the true beginning of that total commitment to the pursuit of empire which was to dominate the middle years of the century, which was to be epitomised in the achievement of the Elder Pitt, and which was to raise British power and prestige in the affairs of the international community to unprecedented heights. But to contemporaries it seemed a costly exercise in incompetence and inadequacy.

However, by the time the government had been compelled to abandon operations in the West Indies, weightier matters were in agitation nearer home. The international crisis which so many had expected for so long finally burst when Charles VI died in October 1740. The conflagration which this spark ignited threatened to destroy the existing political geography of Europe and engulfed

[1] ibid., p. 120.

Britain as it engulfed the continental states. This was not inevitable, but it was always on the cards. That one or other of the powers which had guaranteed the Pragmatic Sanction would be overcome with greed when the Habsburg dominions actually fell to a defenceless young woman, was scarcely unpredictable. In the end Prussia, France, Spain and Bavaria all succumbed to the temptation, varying only in the alacrity with which they did so. The Italian ambitions of Spain were well established. But Prussia's aspirations under the new king, Frederick II, were more novel, involving as they did the rape of Silesia, arguably Austria's most valuable province. The objectives of France were less specific but still more striking. In fact the plan entertained by Belleisle and the war party was a most dramatic one. The dream which had entranced French ministers for so long at last seemed capable of realisation. The Habsburg dominions would be dismembered and reduced to a powerless rump, the Holy Roman Empire would be entrusted to a puppet prince such as the Elector of Bavaria, and France would be free to meddle not merely in Germany, but beyond. The launching of French regiments across central Europe and deep into Austria's heartland, was delayed only long enough for Fleury to be brought around to these large ambitions, and for Frederick II's brutal invasion of Silesia to create a climate in which French intervention would seem relatively inoffensive to the international community.

In the face of this unlimited challenge to England's traditional if recently alienated ally, Walpole's diplomacy, though largely dictated for him by circumstance, was less than an unqualified success. His attempt to reconcile Prussia and Austria, sensible in its intention of uniting the German powers against the Bourbons, was yet foredoomed to failure by the bitterness created between Vienna and Berlin by the Silesian dispute. After that there was little to do but assist the Austrians in their agony. There was no difficulty about raising subsidies for the defence of Austria and the payment of Danish and Hanoverian troops, thanks to the sympathy entertained in Britain for the plight of the young Maria Theresa, beleaguered as she was by a host of cynical enemies. Even so, little comfort could be derived from the continental situation. By 1742 Charles Albert of Bavaria had been elected Holy Roman Emperor, against the competition of Maria Theresa's husband, French armies had smashed their way across Europe, and Vienna was unoccupied only because the invaders preferred to make for Prague. Thanks partly to the offices of the British diplomat, Lord Hyndford, Frederick II had been brought to suspend hostilities with Austria at Klein Schnellendorf in October 1741, but only for long enough to regroup his forces and rethink his strategy. Above all, so far as English ministers were concerned, George II had disgraced himself and his adopted country by negotiating a convention of neutrality as Elector of Hanover, a convention which involved casting his vote in the imperial diet for Charles Albert, the puppet of Louis XV, and which protected his beloved electorate from the attentions of Bourbon troops. When Walpole was compelled to retire in February 1742, weakened by a general election in which more and more of his friends seemed ready to desert to the opposition, advised even by his closest associates to retire in the face of a general loss of confidence in his ability to run the affairs of the nation during the war, and finally defeated in a series of divisions in the House of Commons, the position was bleak indeed.

Yet there was a bright side to the international situation in which Britain found herself enmeshed in 1742. Superficially she had declined sadly since her triumphant emergence as a great power during the age of Marlborough, to the humiliating neutrality of the War of the Polish Succession, to the appeasement and isolation of the late 1730s, to the desperate crisis of 1742. Yet the rule of Walpole had done much to strengthen a country which could so easily have been demoralised by a continuing dispute over the succession, which without political stability might have failed to seize the commercial initiative from the Dutch and the French, and which might have become fatally bogged down in the morass of continental politics. Moreover the War of the Austrian Succession which seemed such a fatal distraction, albeit a necessary one, from the business of teaching Spain a lesson, had its advantages. Indeed in retrospect it may be argued that it represented one of the critical turning points in Anglo-French rivalry. Before joining in the war in 1741 France had been steadily moving towards a confrontation with Britain overseas. The Family Compact of 1733 had been strengthened by a marriage settlement in 1739 between Don Philip, the second son of Elizabeth Farnese, and a French princess, while the two courts had generally grown much closer in the 1730s. Fleury had made vague overtures to Walpole for a renewal of the Anglo-French alliance, after the disgrace and dismissal of the anglophobe Chauvelin in 1737, yet little had come of them. Above all, once the War of Jenkins' Ear broke out, there seemed every likelihood that France and Spain would join forces in the Americas to sweep British imperialism to a disastrous and comprehensive defeat. In fact in 1740 there was a noticeable heightening of tension between London and Paris with rumours of a French onslaught on British possessions in the West Indies. This was not idle talk; indeed in that year naval squadrons left Brest and Toulon on what seemed to observers a deliberately hostile manoeuvre. In this situation the full peril of Britain's plight was obvious at least to some. Horace Walpole anticipated a fatal confrontation between the navies of the great powers, followed by an invasion which would utterly destroy his country. 'If there is no diversion by a land war upon the Continent,' he remarked, 'and we have no security against invasion from France besides our own strength; . . . I am afraid that by next spring or summer, the seat of the war will be in this island'.[1] From this deadly prospect Britain was saved not by her own strength but by the death of Charles VI and the subsequent events in Germany which lured the French into continental distractions and began that era of renewed Bourbon intervention in central Europe that was to culminate in the disasters of the Seven Years' War. It was no coincidence that the French naval units sent to reinforce their allies in the West Indies returned late in 1740, and remained at home the following year. 'Nothing but a diversion upon the Continent can save us' the ministers in London had forecast.[2] The War of the Austrian Succession, for all its grim beginning, provided just such a diversion.

---

[1] *French Foreign Policy during the Administration of Cardinal Fleury, 1726–1743* by A. M. Wilson (London 1936), p. 324.
[2] ibid.

9 Conflicting Strategies, 1742–54

During the two years following Walpole's fall, foreign policy lay almost exclusively in the hands of Lord Carteret, who as Secretary of State for the North and George II's great favourite in this period, monopolised the confidence of the crown. Eventually the Pelham brothers, employing the weight in Parliament which they inherited from Walpole and which Carteret was imprudent enough to leave unchallenged, were to dent and destroy this paramountcy. But from 1742 until at least the end of 1744 Carteret's hegemony was complete. Ironically in those two years he came to acquire an unpopularity, indeed infamy, which even outdid that of his great enemy Walpole. Spanish depredations and the Convention of the Pardo paled into insignificance by comparison with Carteret's reputation as the slave of Hanover. For this the rantings of the Elder Pitt, now a politician of real weight and one who sought office with growing desperation, were to a great extent responsible. Pitt publicly denounced Carteret in 1744 as 'an English minister without an English heart . . . a Hanoverian troop minister . . . a flagitious taskmaster . . . a desperate rhodomontading minister whose little finger had for six months pressed heavier on the nation than the loins of a ministry which had continued for years'.[1]

That Carteret should have laid himself open to these accusations, wild though they were, was ironic not merely because he had posed as an aggressive patriot in the years of Walpole's ascendancy. He had, after all, appeared to feel a genuine concern for Britain's responsibilities outside Hanover. 'Look to America, my lord,' he had urged Newcastle in 1740; 'Europe will take care of itself'.[2] However,

---

[1] *Carteret* by W. B. Pemberton (London 1936), p. 247.
[2] *Some Materials towards Memoirs of the Reign of King George II by John, Lord Hervey* ed. R. Sedgwick (London 1931), 3 vols., p. 940.

by the time Carteret found himself in power matters had changed considerably. For one thing, once confronted with George II and the need to maintain his political interests with a king for whom the electorate of Hanover was an object of overriding concern, any minister might find himself paying more attention to German politics than he would personally wish. Moreover Carteret was nothing if not a diplomat and once plunged into the intricacies of continental politics, as he had not been since the early 1720s, he was carried away by his own instinctive preferences, dormant for so long. Above all, Carteret had one perfectly respectable reason for his policies in power. He could and did claim that the entry of France into the war (albeit without a formal declaration of hostilities between Louis XV and George II until 1744) quite transformed Britain's priorities. Carteret saw not merely France, but France in her capacity as a European power, as the overwhelming threat to his country's interests. 'I will always traverse the view of France in place and out of place, for France will ruin this country if it can,' he insisted.[1] It was in pursuance of this enmity, one which most informed and impartial Englishmen were at any rate initially prepared to accept as crucial, that Carteret designed his foreign policy.

At first indeed Carteret seemed to bring nothing but prosperity to his country's fortunes. In the course of 1742 and 1743 he played in continental diplomacy a central role, one which was not to be paralleled again until the advent of Castlereagh. His primary aim was to build up a coalition against France which would challenge comparison with those organised in the reign of Louis XIV and which would overcome the petty (as he saw them) disputes of German rulers. The first step was to detach Prussia from the French alliance by a more enduring version of the Convention of Klein Schnellendorf. The result, in the Preliminaries of Breslau, subsequently converted into the Treaty of Berlin, was something of a triumph. For the sake of allied unity, Maria Theresa was brought to recognise Frederick II's annexation of Silesia, while the Prussians withdrew from active participation in the war, and before the end of 1742 concluded in the Treaty of Westminster an alliance with Britain. So great a defection could not but be damaging to the

[1] *Carteret* by W. B. Pemberton (London 1936), p. 209.

cause of France and the new emperor, and by mid-summer 1743 the armies of Austria had pushed back the French forces and occupied the Bavarian homelands of Charles VII. So grave was the plight of the emperor that he even approached Carteret with a view to deserting his Bourbon allies himself. The result, the Project of Hanau, was stillborn; how seriously Carteret regarded it is not easily assessed, since opposition at home to subsidising the emperor and the impracticability of obtaining Austrian approval of this *volte-face*, made its successful conclusion impossible. Even so it was striking testimony to the disintegration of the anti-Habsburg coalition during the Careteret era.

More significant still was Carteret's greatest triumph of all, as he saw it. The Treaty of Worms, signed after protracted negotiations in September 1743, secured the cooperation of Sardinia in the defence of Northern Italy against the Gallispans, the joint armies which Paris and Madrid had launched at the under-belly of Habsburg power. With the encouragement of territorial concessions by Vienna, and financial *douceurs* from London, Charles Emmanuel III of Sardinia committed himself to the cause of Maria Theresa. Quite apart from such apparent master-strokes of diplomacy, events went well for Carteret in 1742 and 1743. The neutrality of Hanover, that stain on George II's character, had been repudiated long since, and electoral interests had been propitiated by the employment of Hanoverian and Hessian troops to form a continental army with which to challenge the betrayers of the Pragmatic Sanction in the west. Though the Dutch were something less than enthusiastic to participate, the result was the appearance in the field of a substantial Pragmatic Army which even under the personal command of George II achieved victory at Dettingen in mid-1743. It was not a great triumph but taken with the disasters for France and Charles VII further east and Carteret's alliances, it was sufficiently striking. Carteret could be forgiven for pluming himself on the transformation which he had worked in European power politics, and ignoring the brickbats of those who attacked him in Parliament as the servant of Hanover.

However, there was another side to this picture. For one thing Carteret showed a thorough and most imprudent disregard for the

political priorities of power at court and in the cabinet. His lofty
attitude towards the mechanics of power, which was heightened by
his majestic progresses around Europe with George II, negotiating
with the crowned heads of state, was not well received at home.
'What is it to me who is a judge or who a bishop?' he asked. 'It is my
business to make Kings and Emperors and maintain the balance of
Europe'.[1] Yet those who remained in London, more concerned with
making judges and bishops, were to destroy his power. Though the
Pelhams had to tread carefully in view of George II's plain preference
for Carteret, they steadily moved against him. When Wilmington,
the puppet First Lord of the Treasury, died in July 1743, it was
Henry Pelham who succeeded him, not Carteret's ally Lord Bath,
the William Pulteney of earlier days. And when Carteret's more
contentious measures came before the cabinet, notably his guarantees
of continued aid to Maria Theresa as part of the Austrian price for
Vienna's concessions to Sardinia, it was Pelham and Newcastle who
intervened to slap him down. Finally it was they who in November
1744 presented George II with an ultimatum which involved getting
rid of Carteret altogether and broadening the ministry with recruits
from the opposition benches. Carteret, quite incapable of forming a
durable alternative administration himself, resigned, and though it
took another palace coup in February 1746 to destroy his standing with
the king completely, his power was at an end. In 1744 as in 1724
Carteret demonstrated that a brilliant statesman was no match under
the British system for a well-organised caucus politician.

The ultimate condemnation of Carteret is not that he proved
wanting as a politician however. More important is the fact that in
the last analysis his elaborate diplomatic strategy failed too, and it
failed not primarily because of ill fortune but because built into it
were a succession of false premises and complete miscalculations,
which must seriously detract from Carteret's reputation as a statesman. The essential fact was that Carteret declined to accept that it
was no longer possible to create a coalition against France which
would enjoy the unity of more ancient alliances. The Prussians for
example, were perfectly content to make peace with Vienna and an
alliance with London; but they were not at all prepared to stand by

[1] *Carteret* by W. B. Pemberton (London 1936), p. 264.

and watch while Austria grew steadily stronger and the European balance of power was tilted in her favour. Frederick II was increasingly dismayed by Britain's refusal to rescue Charles VII from the retribution of Maria Theresa, and alarmed at the re-establishment of Austrian power in Italy, foreshadowed in the Treaty of Worms. Frederick was never one to wait upon events, and by the spring of 1744 he had organised the League of Frankfurt to resist the revival of Habsburg power; in the summer he followed his diplomacy up with an invasion of Bohemia. One of Carteret's primary aims, the detachment of Prussia from the list of Austria's enemies, was thus foiled and not least by his own over-sophisticated and excessively elaborate manoeuvrings. Less perhaps Carteret's own responsibility but equally sinister was the regrouping of the Bourbon powers. The disasters which had beset French arms in Germany together with the Treaty of Worms, which boded ill for the Gallispans in Italy, far from disposing Paris and Madrid to peace, had the reverse effect; a new Family Compact, designed for all out war against Britain, offensives in the Low Countries and in Italy, all these developments did not exactly suggest that Carteret's system had done a great deal to humble the power of the Bourbon courts. Finally, and arguably most dangerous of all, Carteret had done much in the course of erecting his diplomatic system to damage the main plank on which it rested, the alliance between Habsburg and Hanover. Many of the sacrifices which had been made to propitiate Prussia and Sardinia had come from Vienna rather than from London, and even the Sardinian subsidy, for example, had been docked from Parliament's contribution to the coffers of Maria Theresa. Nor were territorial cessions in Lombardy, the effective loss of Silesia, and demands gratuitously to restore Bavaria to its rightful owners, to the taste of the Austrians. In the end the latter gave way to their one real ally on most points, as indeed they had to, but they did it with the worst possible grace. In Vienna there was even ominous talk of abandoning Britain and seeking alliance with France. Of the many statesmen who played their part in bringing about the great Diplomatic Revolution of the mid-eighteenth century, Carteret was by no means the least.

At the time of Carteret's fall the arguments for making peace were considerable on every side. His boasted system had by no means yielded the promised benefits for George II, yet neither was the Bourbon cause achieving the objects which had lured Spain and France into the continental war. The death of Charles VII in January 1745 removed the ostensible leader of the opposition to Maria Theresa and the most obvious challenge to the Pragmatic Sanction, while military deadlock in central Europe suggested the possibility of negotiation. That this did not ensue owed not a little to the coming to power in France of D'Argenson, who nurtured aggressive schemes in the Low Countries and elsewhere, which for a while at least prospered. In Flanders the armies of Marshal Saxe proved devastatingly successful; in particular the battle of Fontenoy in May 1745 opened the way to control of Belgium and brought within the grasp of Louis XV that prize which had escaped even his great-grandfather. By February 1746 Brussels itself was in French hands. Moreover at Bassignano in northern Italy the Gallispans defeated the Sardinians, while in Germany Frederick II inflicted demoralising blows on the Austrians, and forced them to make peace in the Treaty of Dresden. Above all, Walpole's prediction that a war with France would eventually breed a rebellion in the British Isles came to fruition. The 'Forty-Five' was ultimately crushed at Culloden in April 1746, but not before it had demonstrated the dreadful fragility of the Hanoverian establishment and diverted English eyes and arms from the Continent.

Yet in this gloomy situation there was one chink of light. In June 1745 William Pepperell, with a force of New England militiamen and the aid of British naval forces, besieged and captured Louisburg, the fortress on Cape Breton which guarded the St Lawrence and French North America. It was an event of the utmost importance in several respects. For one thing, in the long run the taking of Louisburg brought home to a British public opinion, which had scarcely been aware that North America existed, the enormous potentialities for the imperial enterprise in Canada. For half a century British imperialism had been encouraged to find an outlet in the West Indies and South America, either in the form of commercial expansion, or even of colonisation. The War of Jenkins' Ear represented the high point of this delusion; Carteret himself, for example, had even predicted that 'We shall take from Spain some countries in America, and we shall keep them in spite of the whole world'.[1] But the combination of failure in this theatre in the early years of the war, together with the brilliant and unexpected success of the New Englanders at Cape Breton, notably hastened that transference of interest and attention to North America which was such a feature of the period. No less significant was the strategic debate which the capture of Louisburg initiated or rather renewed. The traditional dispute over the old Tory strategy of 'blue-water', a war on the high seas and in the colonies, had long been overshadowed, despite such incidents as the Anglo-Spanish War of 1739, by the need to safeguard Britain's position on the Continent and particularly the monarchy's interests in Hanover. But a spectacular success in North America played into the hands of those like Bedford and Pitt, who demanded an end to the expensive and largely fruitless expenditure in Europe and the opening of a new front overseas. For the moment this demand was sidestepped. It was a measure of the Pelham regime's political skill that it was able in February 1746 both to head off a new attempt by Carteret to form a ministry, and force Pitt and his friends into government. Pitt had infuriated the king by his repeated and insolent attacks on the employment at British expense of Hanoverian troops, and was accepted as a junior minister by George II only with the greatest reluctance. Part of the package negotiated on this occasion, one which was to ensure the parliamentary success of the administration for nearly a decade, was a promise to launch an expedition against Canada on the lines attempted in 1711. In the event this pledge was not fulfilled, and for the moment Pitt and his clan were content with the places they had won, proving remarkably pliant in office. None the less the grand debate over strategy, once revived, was not to die down for long.

Even in the short run the news of Louisburg's capture had far-reaching effects. For example, it significantly retarded the prospect of peace and killed the hopes of those in the administration, like Henry Pelham and Lord Harrington, who sought a speedy escape from the war. Chesterfield's observation was typically acute. 'One almost insurmountable difficulty I foresee in any negotiation with

[1] *War and Trade in the West Indies* by R. Pares (Oxford 1936), p. 66.

France is our new acquisition of Cape Breton, which is become the darling object of the whole nation; it is ten times more popular than ever Gibraltar was, and people are laying in their claims, and protesting already against the restitution of it upon any account. But, on the other hand, I foresee the impossibility of keeping it'.[1] Nothing is stronger testimony to the underlying influence on British eighteenth-century foreign policy of that undefined but potent force, public opinion, than the positive embarrassment felt by the ministry at the taking of Cape Breton. 'Our people', Pelham himself observed, 'are so mad upon it that it requires more spirit and conduct to get the better of, than I doubt our present Government are masters of'.[2] On the one hand, France would not make peace as things stood without recovering the key to Canada; on the other hand, British public opinion would not tolerate its restoration. It is not too much to say that the remaining three years of war were entirely dictated by the desperate need of Newcastle and his reluctant colleagues to find some way out of this dilemma.

With hindsight it is easy enough to identify the solution. A really serious onslaught on Canada, such as was later launched in the Seven Years' War, would have forced France into concessions sufficient to appease opinion at home. But at the time there were many obstacles; such an onslaught needed time, and the ministry had little of that commodity after six years of debilitating and fruitless warfare. Even in the Seven Years' War it was to take several major campaigning seasons to seize Quebec; moreover the French navy was not eliminated as an effective force until 1747, and little could be achieved in the colonies in the meantime. In addition the French were very much on the offensive in Flanders, despite their reverses in central Europe, and it was understandable that the British government should look to turn the tide there. Unfortunately little solace was to be found in that theatre. The armies of Saxe moved inexorably through the Low Countries, defeating the allied resistance under Cumberland and in July 1747 were poised to take Maestricht, the key to the Dutch Netherlands. The latter, of which

[1] *Studies in Eighteenth-century Diplomacy, 1740–1748* by Sir R. Lodge (London 1930), p. 134.
[2] ibid.

great hopes were entertained after an Orangist coup masterminded from London in 1747, failed to imitate the exploits of their ancestors against Louis XIV, and moved equally inexorably, if with some havering, towards peace. Newcastle placed much reliance on a subsidy treaty with the Russians, which would have brought Russian troops clear across Europe to the rescue of the Low Countries, but this manoeuvre was not entirely without its dangers, and in any case came too late to be useful. The defeat of the Gallispans in Italy in 1746 raised similar hopes which were only to be dashed when an offensive movement against the south-eastern borders of France was baulked in 1747.

Negotiations, formally begun at Breda in August 1746 and continued at Aix-la-Chapelle in 1747, were only partly serious as the combatants waited for decisive news from the battlefields. Even at the bargaining table, however, the Pelhams struggled for an advantage which would compel the French to yield Louisburg. The accession of Ferdinand VI to the Spanish throne in 1746, given the somewhat francophobe sentiments of the new king and his advisers, seemed to offer a real possibility of dividing the Family Compact, and isolating France. Sandwich, Newcastle's negotiator at Breda, strove to exploit this opportunity, but in vain. Even if the commercial differences, which had after all provoked war between Spain and Britain, could be compromised, even if some settlement could be reached with Austria in Italy, George II would have had to surrender Gibraltar to win over Madrid at this stage. Like Stanhope before him, and Pitt and Shelburne after him, Newcastle was prepared to contemplate such a sacrifice, but ultimately declined to carry it through. In the end it was the domestic situation which enabled the ministry to escape from its predicament. A trick general election, called early in 1747, gave the court a chance to secure its parliamentary majority before peace negotiations grew serious. With seven years before the next elections, it was possible to view unpopularity rather more objectively. Moreover with Pitt and his friends firmly in place and not anxious to leave it again quickly, the most obvious leaders of popular opposition were effectively muzzled. Their rear thus protected, and without hope of turning back the French tide on the Continent, the ministers gave way and agreed to restore Cape

Breton in return for French evacuation of Belgium. In October 1748 the Treaty of Aix-la-Chapelle was signed and Europe was at peace again for the first time in nearly a decade.

The Peace of Aix-la-Chapelle lives in history as one of those great stalemates, like the Peace of Amiens later, or the Peace of Ryswick earlier, which made a new war inevitable. Not even at the time was it thought that a settlement which resored the position between France and Britain to that before the formal declarations of war in 1744 would endure. There were naturally many arguments on both sides. The French were apt to imagine that they had been unduly generous in restoring the Austrian Netherlands after a sequence of military successes unprecedented since the days of Louis XIV, and their conquest of Madras in India, where the French East India Company had seemed to have the whip hand over its rivals. Yet Louis XV had not made peace out of charity. The victories of Anson and Hawke in 1747 had virtually destroyed the French threat to British supremacy on the high seas, the Family Compact had been reduced to a shambles, Canada was at risk and Louisburg actually in enemy hands. Worst of all, in 1747 France suffered a disastrous famine and a serious fiscal crisis. In these circumstances there were those in Britain who might have argued for a continuance of warfare such as would bring about precisely those successes which were later achieved in the Seven Years' War. On the other hand, in 1748 Britain was practically isolated, the Dutch about to desert, and the Austrians increasingly ill-disposed towards their ancient allies, while on the Continent the military position steadily worsened. With arguments as nicely poised as these, the diplomatic stalemate was a fair reflection of the underlying situation. The fortunes of war could have tilted the balance either way, but on both sides there was too much war-weariness and too little inspiration to lead either to take extravagant risks.

None the less, the Peace of Aix-la-Chapelle had extensive consequences. It finally settled largely in favour of Madrid, or rather the Farnese family, the territorial disputes in Italy, and it confirmed for the moment at least Prussia's retention of Silesia. But so far as France and Britain were concerned it also threatened the entire diplomatic structure on which their strategies rested. For France the continuance of the Family Compact was exceedingly doubtful. Spain had not yet swung decisively to the camp of George II but neither had the Spanish court been pleased by a peace foisted on it from Aix, giving it few of the aims with which it had begun the war in 1739 and 1740. Equally important for Britain, the 'old system' was near to breakdown; the Austrians who still schemed to recover Silesia, were profoundly disillusioned with British conduct during the war itself and the peace negotiations which terminated it. The Dutch were by now universally recognised as broken reeds, Russia was demanding a high price for cooperation against the Bourbons, and the Prussians were watchfully detached. When the statesmen of Europe turned from warfare to diplomacy in 1748, there was much to play for, and much to lose.

The chance to create some advantage for the court of George II out of this shifting and unstable diplomatic pattern lay largely in the hands of Newcastle. It was customary for one of the secretaries to take the lead in foreign affairs, but such was Newcastle's political power, backed by his brother's mastery of the Commons, and such his extreme jealousy of competition, that Henry Pelham himself, the First Lord of the Treasury, and Lord Hardwicke, Lord Chancellor and close adviser to the Pelhams, were effectively the only brakes on Newcastle. A series of fellow secretaries of state were first caressed and then crushed before, in June 1751, Newcastle found in Holderness a colleague sufficiently sycophantic to abide him and his ways. Yet as Chesterfield remarked on his resignation in February 1748, 'The Duke of Newcastle has taken my department; in truth he had it before'.[1] For a decade, from 1746 to 1756, Newcastle was not merely the major influence on the making of foreign policy, but its prime initiator. This was not necessarily the disaster frequently suggested. Newcastle had a clear head for analysis and more industry than most foreign ministers of the period. Unfortunately in pursuing his objectives, he was inclined to lose all sense of proportion, and policies which had something to commend them if followed with caution and flexibility were often pushed to the point at which they were at best wasted effort and at worst positively counter-productive.

[1] *Studies in Eighteenth-century Diplomacy, 1740–1748* by Sir R. Lodge (London 1930), p. 307.

In this respect his strategy in the years which followed the peace of 1748 was entirely typical of the man.

Newcastle was well aware that his priority was to prepare for the conflict which could not be long suspended overseas. Disputes between France and Britain, particularly over the so-called Neutral Islands in the Caribbean, over the status of the North American back country, potentially Britain's gateway to the West and France's link between Louisiana and Quebec, though old enough themselves, broke out with new and irrepressible force after 1748, and even if the renewal of the Austro-Prussian conflict were held off it was obviously only a matter of time before a new Anglo-French war. Newcastle saw too the essential need to protect Britain's European interests, by creating an alliance on the Continent capable of holding the armies of Louis XV in the Low Countries and in Germany. Given Prussia's refusal to cooperate with Austria, given Russia's awkwardness and remoteness, given Spain's continuing neutrality, he also saw that much depended on the 'old system', by now somewhat more than fragile. Unfortunately as repeated approaches to the court of Maria Theresa revealed, all was not well between Vienna and London, and strong evidence of the good intentions of the Hanoverian monarchy would have to be produced if the Habsburg alliance was to be preserved. All these facts were clear enough, and within limits the logical structure in which they were employed was unobjectionable. Newcastle placed great faith upon what he termed 'the old unalterable system for England';[1] characteristically he exaggerated its attractions, much to Henry Pelham's 'concern to see you run so fast into declaring that you will do nothing without the Court of Vienna'.[2] Yet at the time there were few obvious alternatives, and a very obvious and pressing need to do something. What was regrettable was that reasoning from such safe premises, Newcastle, as only he could do, succeeded in producing an utterly hare-brained scheme.

Who first conceived the imperial election scheme is not altogether clear, though the strongest candidate is not Newcastle himself, but Sir Charles Hanbury Williams, a talented if irresponsible

[1] *Studies in Eighteenth-century Diplomacy, 1740–1748* by Sir R. Lodge (London 1930), p. 392.   [2] ibid., p. 396.

M.P. who took to diplomacy for the sake of his purse. What matters is that Newcastle took it over and made it his own. The principles of the scheme were clear enough and indeed simple. The last continental war, it was reasoned, had been engendered by the death of the Emperor Charles VI and the dispute over the Austrian succession. In addition the election of Charles VII of Bavaria to the imperial throne had been a constant source of friction, making peace impossible before his death and the agreed institution of Maria Theresa's husband, Francis of Lorraine, as emperor. However, the death of Francis II seemed itself a less than distant event, which threatened once again to plunge Europe into war, unless his son Joseph succeeded to the empire. From this anxiety stemmed a variety of arguments. Was not the formal election of Joseph as King of the Romans, the virtually certain heir to the empire, the means to ensure his succession? Would not a union of the German princes to bring about this happy event give the French court cause for caution in contemplating a new German war, as well as ensuring a ready supply of mercenary troops for Britain's use if the temptation to meddle proved irresistible to Louis XV and his ministers? Would not a grateful Austria, sure of the imperial succession, rush to congratulate her erstwhile ally and join so powerful a German federation? And would not such a scheme make possible the establishment of subsidy treaties with the German powers, treaties which were essential to Britain in the event of war, but which if adopted merely on the grounds of the need to protect Hanover, would prove utterly unacceptable to Parliament and the public in peacetime? And would not the success of the scheme redound much to the credit of George II abroad and still more to that of the Pelhams at home?

These arguments had a facile attractiveness which appealed strongly to Newcastle. Yet many of them were distinctly insecure. The election itself was a complex and tricky business. There were those in the empire, and France and its allies naturally encouraged such voices, who believed that the election of a King of the Romans required an 'eminent' majority, that is two-thirds of the college of electors, and not as Newcastle imagined, a simple majority. Again it was difficult to prove that such an election was an essential procedure, when one of its main functions was to convince those at home that

Hanover was not at the bottom of the subsidy policy. Most problematic of all was the matter of the subsidy policy itself. The German electors were old hands at negotiating for French or British largesse and not disposed to make things easy. Moreover Henry Pelham, conscious of the politically sensitive issues involved, was reluctant in the extreme to agree to peacetime subsidies, and was eventually brought to agree to a maximum of one. The result was a protracted and ultimately futile series of negotiations, though admittedly the initial moves were surprisingly successful. The votes of the electors of Hanover, Bohemia, Mainz and Trier, were all effectively in Austro-British hands. Those of Cologne and Bavaria (a striking triumph in view of Bavaria's traditional pro-French stance) were gained by treaty in 1750, Cologne being bought by Hanover and the United Provinces, Bavaria by Britain. However, Cologne seceded almost as soon as joining the new system, and although Saxony was brought in by the autumn of 1751, the difficulties increased rather than diminished. France and Prussia organised a strong opposition lobby in Germany, the Elector Palatine proved an impossibly slippery customer, and, surely the crowning evidence of Newcastle's folly, Austria herself lost interest. Indeed it was the most damning feature of Newcastle's scheme that it ended by endangering the very objectives which it was meant to attain. Austria declined to proceed further unless the French could be brought to cooperate, so averting the possibility of a humiliating failure in the college of electors, and as Newcastle fecklessly confessed in 1752 'there is reason to fear that the acquiescence of France in the election is to depend upon the adjusting of our American disputes'.[1] Fortunately not even Newcastle was prepared to make concessions of such a nature and the election scheme eventually fizzled out in ignominious failure. Not everyone has condemned the election scheme;[2] yet in retrospect it is difficult to see it as anything but a waste of time and effort. As a small and tentative manoeuvre in the direction of pulling together the 'old system' it might have merited at least a trial, as wise Hardwicke, for example, asserted; but as the major diplomatic objective of a great power it was an absurdity.

---

[1] *British Diplomatic Instructions, 1689–1789* (Camden Soc.), vii, p. 25.

[2] R. Browning, 'The Duke of Newcastle and the Imperial Election Plan, 1749–1754' in *Journal of British Studies*, vii (1967–68), pp. 28–47.

PART 4

The Lure
of Empire 1754–83

10 The Struggle for Empire, 1754–63

1754 was a landmark both in domestic and foreign politics. At home the death of Henry Pelham began an era of instability which was not truly to end until the establishment of the North regime in the early 1770s and which was only partially interrupted by the outwardly tranquil and inwardly disturbed administration of Newcastle and Pitt between 1757 and 1761. Though the Newcastle administration, with Newcastle himself replacing Pelham at the Treasury, was to last until the autumn of 1756, it was constantly threatened by the activities, alternately in government and opposition, of the young men who hoped to succeed to Pelham's position, Henry Fox and Pitt. None the less, for the moment Newcastle remained securely in control of foreign affairs. His renewed tenure of power was marked by two sensational developments, the outbreak of arguably the most important of all wars between France and Britain, and the Diplomatic Revolution. The former was perhaps unavoidable. At least for half a century Anglo-French disputes in the North American back country had created problems for the ministers at home. However not until the 1750s, with growing pressure on the west from the English seaboard, and increasing French anxiety to complete a great chain of forts from New Orleans to Montreal, so securing the Indian trade and penning in the coastal fringe of British settlement, did they escalate to truly crisis proportions. But once this happened neither government was capable of restraining its agents on the ground or ignoring the provocations of the enemy. The spring of 1754, for example, saw pitched battle and the defeat of a Virginian force on the Ohio, and it was obvious that war could not be delayed for long. Yet it was left to London to assume the responsibility for beginning hostilities.

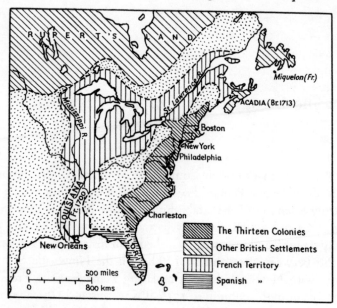

The Thirteen Colonies

Other British Settlements

French Territory

Spanish   „

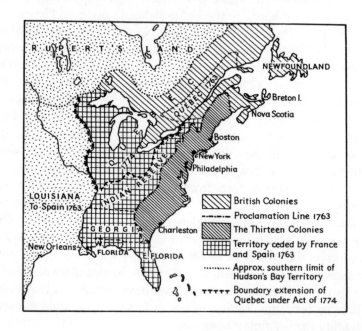

British Colonies

—·—·— Proclamation Line 1763

The Thirteen Colonies

Territory ceded by France and Spain 1763

·········· Approx. southern limit of Hudson's Bay Territory

ⴶⴶⴶⴶ Boundary extension of Quebec under Act of 1774

Maps 3a, b & c. The Struggle for Empire in North America, 1756–83

The despatch of an expedition under General Braddock across the Atlantic was perfectly defensible in the context of the undeclared North American war. What was less acceptable in terms of public morality was the order issued to Admiral Boscawen in 1755 to prevent French naval forces and reinforcements reaching Quebec with much needed supplies. Unfortunately the result was the worst of both worlds. Boscawen succeeded in taking the *Lys* and *Alcide*, two French vessels, but missed the main fleet completely, action sufficient to put George II hopelessly in the wrong with the international community, but quite inadequate to justify the risks involved. As it turned out it was the failure to prevent reinforcements reaching Canada which was crucial. International morals in the eighteenth century were not of the loftiest, and while France had a sympathetic audience abroad, she was doubtless relieved primarily to see her forces successfully ensconced in the St Lawrence. Much more damaging was the great onslaught launched on French commercial shipping in 1755. Dutch and Spanish merchantmen were almost as gratuitously attacked as French, and by the spring of 1756 it was scarcely surprising that France retaliated with an expedition against Minorca, or that both sides were on the brink of declaring war. Unfortunately for the ministers in London, the war to which they had so completely committed themselves, began disastrously. Newcastle himself was scarcely to blame for the humiliating destruction of Braddock's force in America or for Byng's fatal inability to save Minorca. But at home politics were in hopeless disarray as Newcastle fought to maintain control of a House of Commons in which he did not sit, a cabinet in which his supremacy was challenged by Henry Fox, and a policy which was dominated by the influence of the king's son, the Duke of Cumberland. It was inconceivable that he could remain in office after the disgraceful loss of Minorca, nor was it surprising that he was unable to form a new administration of his own during the following year. The loss of Minorca was regarded as the worst disaster to befall British arms since the Dutch had sailed up the Medway in 1667, and not even the Pelham machine could weather its effects.

If Newcastle was less the author than the victim of failure in war, he had more to do, albeit unwittingly, with the making of the greatest diplomatic revolution in recent European history. Admittedly in retrospect it is easy to portray the diplomatic realignment of 1756–57 as an inevitable consequence of earlier events. The fundamental fact was that the traditional community of interest which had long existed between Austria and the Maritime Powers had been shattered by Frederick II's invasion of Silesia in 1740. While France was the principal threat to Vienna's interests in Germany, in the Low Countries, in Spain and in Italy, the 'old system' was perfectly natural. But once Prussia had become Austria's primary enemy, there was little in common between the ancient allies. Almost the sole concern of Maria Theresa was to obtain auxiliaries with which to resist the rising power of Frederick II. Yet the main continental interest of George II was to protect Hanover and hold the French at bay in Europe while they were defeated in the colonies and on the high seas. This was not sufficient to maintain the Anglo-Austrian alliance, and indeed it is difficult to see what could have kept the two powers together by 1756. However, London was appallingly slow to grasp the nature of the change taking place, though repeated attempts to negotiate with Vienna, for example about trading problems in Belgium and the Mediterranean, should have given cause for disquiet. Not until 1755 when Britain directly demanded Maria Theresa's aid against France in accordance with treaty obligations and found that she would not cooperate without a firm reciprocal commitment against Prussia, did it become clear just how far the disintegration of the 'old system' had set in. Beside Austria's desertion, that of the United Provinces, which now sought to avert a new continental war at virtually any cost, was a trivial matter.

Yet if the collapse of the London–Vienna axis was clearly on the cards by 1755, it did not automatically follow that there would be a major international regrouping in consequence. After all it was far from certain that Austria would be able to obtain from France the aid which the British would not supply. Louis XV had no more interest in employing French arms against Prussia than George II. Viennese ministers, and in particular Kaunitz, the ambassador to the court of Versailles and eventually Maria Theresa's principal adviser in foreign affairs, had already been angling for a complete reversal of the ancient Habsburg–Bourbon enmity with little success. It was Newcastle's unintentional achievement to transform this situation by throwing France into the arms of Austria. Yet the action by which he did so had a perfectly logical basis, for the refusal of Vienna to provide its traditional backing left the ministers of George II no alternative but to seek reinsurance for the protection of Hanover in other quarters. Russia was one obvious possibility. Ever since the defeat of the francophile party at St Petersburg in 1741, and more especially since the alliance between the two empresses Elizabeth of Russia and Maria Theresa of Austria in 1746, the Russians had been open to British overtures. Though relations had cooled somewhat after disputes relating to the subsidy treaty of 1746 and Britain's failure to utilise the troops then hired for use in the Low Countries, relatively little difficulty was experienced in obtaining a new subsidy agreement in 1755. The essential link between the two powers was hostility towards Prussia. Russo–Prussian enmity, a continuing phenomenon in the first half of the eighteenth century, was at its height in the 1750s, and Anglo–Prussian relations were poisoned by the basic fact that Frederick II, as Louis XV's principal German ally, was bound to represent a threat to the security of Hanover. But if the alliance was a natural and satisfactory one, Newcastle did not altogether comprehend its true basis, for he set about using it in a manner which conflicted with the spirit if not the letter of the new treaty. From the British point of view, if it was a sensible tactic to pressurise Prussia with a Russian alliance, it was doubtless still more so to draw off Prussian enmity altogether by making Frederick II an ally. And the very fact that Britain had been so successful with the Tsarina was quite sufficient to alarm the Prussian monarch. Hyndford, Carteret's ambassador, had long before remarked that Frederick 'is more in fear of Russia than he is of God',[1] and the Convention of Westminster, by which the king guaranteed the neutrality of Germany and consequently the safety of Hanover, was signed in January 1756, within a few months of the Anglo-Russian treaty. Thereafter Prussian miscalculation dictated the course of the diplomatic revolution. It was Frederick's failure to explain this Anglo-Prussian convention to his French allies which drove them into the First Treaty of Versailles, a purely defensive alliance with Austria, and subsequently Russia, yet none the less a crucial break in the ancient pattern of Bourbon–Habsburg rivalry. It was also Frederick who by his lunatic invasion of Saxony in the summer of 1756, on the slightest evidence of Russian conspiracy, and with scant regard for the susceptibilities of either his allies or European public opinion, pushed France into the Second Treaty of Versailles. This pact, signed in May 1757, was almost unbelievably to commit the armies and resources of Louis XV to the recovery of Silesia, with disastrous consequences for French interests around the world. Yet it was actually Newcastle who by his diplomatic manoeuvres at St Petersburg and Berlin had created the basis for this momentous reversal of alliances.

However, by the time of the definitive Franco-Austrian alliances, Newcastle himself had experienced a spell in the political wilderness for the first time since his youth. Though he eventually returned to office twelve months after the fall of Minorca, he returned not as

[1] *Great Britain and Prussia in the Eighteenth Century* by Sir R. Lodge (Oxford 1923), p. 48.

effective foreign minister, but as First Lord of the Treasury and virtually fund-raiser to the Elder Pitt. Pitt himself achieved office by a judicious combination of palace intrigue and public posturing. His first ministry, which lasted only a matter of months in the winter of 1756–57, lacked Pelhamite support in the Commons and George II's countenance in the closet. But in the following summer both were finally secured to provide the basis for an uneasy broad-bottom ministry. The Pitt–Newcastle Coalition, and especially Pitt's own role in it, is justly celebrated as perhaps the greatest of all Britain's wartime administrations. Its achievement was decisively to humble the might of France, and destroy the primary sources of French imperial power in North America, in the West Indies, in Africa, and even in Asia, a feat which few Englishmen would earlier have dreamed possible. Generations of historians have been disposed to interpret these dazzling successes in terms of the genius of one man. Yet it is not easy in retrospect to analyse the nature of Pitt's contribution to victory. In his basic strategy of striking at French naval and colonial power while diverting Bourbon forces in Europe, there was nothing very novel. Those who had long stressed the need for continental alliances were not a little amused to see Pitt championing subsidy treaties with Prussia and even defending the deployment of British troops in Germany. Pitt admittedly succeeded in turning the political liability of intervention on the Continent into a positive asset. Frederick II became the Protestant Hero and Pitt himself boasted of having conquered North America in Germany. Yet Newcastle's order of priorities had not been obviously different. For example, his criticism of a thoroughgoing blue-water strategy in 1749 was entirely in line with Pitt's policy in the Seven Years' War. 'A naval force', Newcastle had told Hardwicke, 'tho' carried never so high, unsupported with even the *appearance* of a force upon the Continent will be of little use. . . . France will outdo us at sea, when they have nothing to fear by land. . . . I have always maintained that our marine should protect our alliances upon the Continent; and they, by diverting the expense of France, enable us to maintain our superiority at sea'.[1] Pitt had many talents which earned him the

[1] D. B. Horn, 'The Cabinet Controversy on Subsidy Treaties in Time of Peace, 1749–50' in *Eng. Hist. Rev.*, xlv (1930), p. 464.

stature Newcastle could never hope to obtain – confidence so great
as to inspire an extraordinary degree of trust and even adoration in
others, oratory so effective as completely to dominate the House of
Commons, and above all, Pitt's most distinctive contribution in
these years, political courage of the highest order at a time when that
quality was notably lacking among his rival politicians. But so far as
the war was concerned, Pitt's success was the result of persevering
with an established and unsensational strategy. Of original ideas,
Pitt had few, and as more able thinkers like Edmund Burke per-
ceived,[1] was in this respect something of a charlatan.

Between 1757 and 1760 diplomacy was to a great extent overshadowed by the war. While the fate of the western world lay in the
hands of the generals and admirals, diplomats were largely con-
strained to stand by and observe, to negotiate the details by which
Britain's involvement on the Continent was conducted, and otherwise to await the moment when the making of peace would restore
the initiative to them. There was but a single exception to this,
though that an important one, in the matter of relations with the
Spanish court. That Spain's role in the world conflict could be
decisive was realised by all parties. Newcastle had laboured in the
years following the Peace of Aix-la-Chapelle both to settle the
ancient animosities which lay between Madrid and London, and to
draw Spain from the Family Compact. Thanks to the relatively
favourable disposition of Ferdinand VI and his ministers some
progress had been made, notably with Keene's treaty of 1750, a
treaty which by formally abolishing the old South Sea Company
trade eliminated a major cause of acrimony, and which also did much
to restore commerce between the two countries to its ancient
footing. Though it was less easy to come to broader political agreement, Anglo-Spanish relations in the eighteenth century were
probably never better than while Benjamin Keene was ambassador
at Madrid in the early 1750s. Like Newcastle, Pitt also understood
the potential value of a Spanish alliance, and was even ready to
barter Gibraltar to obtain it in 1757, when it was far from clear that
victory overseas against France could be procured without the aid

[1] *The Correspondence of Edmund Burke* ed. T. W. Copeland (Cambridge 1958–),
i, pp. 251–52.

of Ferdinand. Though these negotiations fell through, they were a measure of the importance rightly attached to the attitude of Madrid in the epic conflict in the making between Britain and France.

That importance was not diminished by the death of Ferdinand VI and accession of Charles III in 1759. However, unlike Ferdinand the new king had no predisposition in favour of the British; on the contrary as King of the Two Sicilies he had conceived a marked distaste for the court of George II as a result of the Royal Navy's Mediterranean activities during the War of the Austrian Succession. Moreover traditional disputes between the two countries were once again flaring up. Conflicts in the logwood settlements of central America were creating problems, while the British campaign against neutral shipping was having a particularly deleterious effect, despite the authentic anxiety of the ministers in London to avoid provoking Madrid. Most important of all however, was the astonishing prosperity of British arms in the Seven Years' War, at any rate after the misfortunes of the years 1755–57 in North America and the Mediterranean. The extraordinary and quite unexpected one-sidedness of the hostilities between France and Britain was naturally cause for concern at the court of Charles III. A power which could take Senegal, Louisburg, Goree, Guadeloupe and Quebec with the apparently impudent ease already achieved by the autumn of 1759, was suddenly a much greater menace to the integrity of the Spanish empire than hitherto. In these circumstances some kind of confrontation was little more than a matter of time, and indeed at the height of the Seven Years' War something of a race developed between the mounting irritation of Spain, the growing exhaustion of France, and the increasing impatience of Britain. In this situation Pitt's attitude, once so friendly towards Spain, became one of single-minded hostility. In response, Spanish tactics such as the pressing of claims to a share in the Newfoundland fishery, and interference in the Anglo-French peace initiatives attempted in 1761, were not exactly conciliatory. By October 1761 Pitt was prepared to resign unless war with Spain was declared at once. The cabinet was horrified at the prospect of a further extension of the war with all its financial implications, and under the guidance of the new king George III and his favourite Lord Bute, preferred to wait and see something of Spain's ultimate intentions before resorting to violence. Yet in retrospect it is difficult to deny the validity of Pitt's arguments as to the necessity for a pre-emptive strike against the Spaniards, plundering their treasure fleets from the New World and launching a devastating attack on their navy before it was ready to take the initiative. Though the evidence available in London at the time was not conclusive, Charles III had already, in August 1761, signed the third Family Compact, by which he was committed to come to the assistance of his cousin by the following spring. As a result the cabinet's pusillanimity sacrificed the advantages envisaged by Pitt's policy without the commensurate gain of significantly postponing war. By January 1762 the ministry, left in the hands of Newcastle and Bute, had in any case been compelled to recall the British ambassador and commence hostilities.

There were those who believed that Pitt resigned in 1761 not because his colleagues refused to accept the immediate necessity for war against Spain, but in order to disassociate himself from the process, which must inevitably soon follow, of making a peace, and possibly an unpopular one. This consideration may not have been entirely absent from so devious a political mentality as Pitt's, yet it is difficult to accept that this was his primary motive. More even than most of his fellow politicians, Pitt's concern was power, and it was becoming increasingly clear in the changed political climate created by the accession of the young George III in 1760, that he would have to share his power. 'I will be responsible for nothing that I do not direct', he once remarked,[1] and there is no reason to suggest that he did not see the Spanish issue as a clear instance of such divergence between power and responsibility. George III and Bute did not set out systematically to destroy either Pitt or Newcastle, but it was not unwise of Pitt to resign in October 1761; within a few months, Newcastle himself, that most incorrigible of politicians and most tenacious of ministers, had joined him in opposition.

This is not to endorse Pitt's subsequent political conduct, let alone his bitter attack on the peace eventually negotiated by his successors. On the contrary, the question of who was right on the matter of the

[1] *William Pitt, Earl of Chatham* by B. Tunstall (London 1938), p. 305.

peace, Pitt who denounced it in the Commons or Bute who actually negotiated it, is a nice as well as important one. The peace negotiation itself was not the most protracted of affairs. There had been overtures, admittedly insincere, in 1759, informal negotiations subsequently at the Hague, and serious discussions between Pitt and the French envoy Bussy in London in 1761. The latter had been marked by disagreement over the fate of the fisheries and eventually broke down not least because the French insisted on dragging in the grievances of Spain, to the undisguised fury of Pitt. Even so British inflexibility and French hopes of reviving military fortunes made an immediate peace unlikely. But by 1762 when Bute launched new negotiations with the despatch of the Duke of Bedford to Paris as plenipotentiary, the auguries were better. The British had had a further year of war and a further year of the huge bills associated with it; the French had additionally lost Belle Isle, Martinique, St Lucia and a string of minor colonial possessions, and could plainly not stand the strain of war, even under the leadership of the new minister, Choiseul, for much longer. On 3 November 1762 the Preliminaries of Fontainebleau were signed and on 10 February 1763, after some modifications, the full Peace of Paris was concluded. In the meantime the parliamentary opposition, now featuring both Pitt and Newcastle so recently in office together, had violently castigated the terms, though to little effect at the time; subsequently however the peace of 1763 was to join that of 1713 in the Whig catalogue of Tory sins, with enduring consequences for its historical reputation.

The merits of the peace were judged on two quite different issues, the moral and political wisdom of casting off from the alliance of Prussia, and the alleged sell-out in the terms negotiated with the House of Bourbon. The former involves complicated but none the less manageable arguments. Bute was charged by the champions of Frederick II with improperly terminating the Prussian subsidy of £600,000 which Newcastle had begun and Pitt continued throughout the war, and launching a separate negotiation with France which was intended to leave the Prussians in the lurch. More specifically Bute was said to have sounded the Austrians with a view to treacherously aiding them against Frederick, to have urged the Russian ambassador to join in a conspiracy against the Prussians, and to have whipped up Danish opposition to them. Above all, in the peace treaty itself not only did he desert Frederick, but in stipulating the evacuation by French troops of Prussian territories on the Rhine, the relevant clause was so worded as to permit the Habsburg allies of France to reoccupy the lands involved. Yet these charges were not well founded. There was no clear requirement for Britain to continue her annual subsidies unless she chose to renew the treaties in question, and Bute, impressed by Prussia's lucky recovery from a calamitous situation in 1762 thanks to a change of regime and policy at St Petersburg, and dismayed by the apparent readiness of the novel Russo-Prussian alliance to carry the war to new heights, was entitled to consider that sufficient British treasure had been poured into Frederick's coffers. The Prussians were to lose nothing when they eventually made peace with Austria at Hubertusburg in February 1763, and they could hardly claim to have been decisively weakened by the new policy in Whitehall. The more specific allegations of treachery are scarcely worth dismissing, consisting largely as they did of the fabrications of Russian and Prussian propaganda.[1]

As for the substantive issue of desertion, there was no obligation for Bute to make peace only when Frederick was ready to approve one. Moreover there are certain ironies in the case. It was curious that Pitt, once the bitter opponent of British meddling in Germany, should have denounced the new court for apparently taking his earlier words at their face value. It was still more bizarre to talk of morality in connection with Frederick II, a monarch who was accustomed to break faith with little compunction himself, and who did not make a habit of abiding by commitments longer than they remained to his advantage. This is not to say that there was not a case for retaining the friendship of Prussia. Bute may not have behaved badly by Frederick, but he had scarcely acted in a way likely to retain his amity, and it made more sense to argue about the prudence of this course than its moral validity. In fact the Newcastle Whigs, who resigned from the ministry chiefly on this issue in 1762

[1] F. Spencer, 'The Anglo-Prussian Breach of 1762: An Historical Revision' in *History*, xli (1956), and W. L. Dorn, 'Frederick the Great and Lord Bute' in *Journal of Mod. Hist.*, i (1929), pp. 529–60.

as Pitt had resigned over Spain in 1761, had some substance for their view that the abandonment of the Prussian alliance and the resulting forfeiture of a possible Russian alliance were matters of the utmost gravity. As will be seen, the isolation which Bute created at this time was to bring in its train serious and arguably disastrous problems for Britain in the following years. Yet it is not altogether easy to accept even this line. If isolation was so damaging (which is not certain), it does not follow that a different course of action in 1762 would have averted it. The great aim of Frederick II in the 1760s was to secure and retain the alliance of Russia; his success in so doing did not in any way depend on Britain's attitude. Moreover once he had achieved this object, British alliance had little appeal or significance for him, as his rebuff even of Pitt's overtures in 1766 was to demonstrate. Isolation was primarily a legacy of Britain's fortunes in the Seven Years' War; it was perhaps aggravated but it was not manufactured by Bute's actions in 1762.

Much more compelling, at least with hindsight, is the opposition's case against the actual terms of the Peace of Paris. It was the consistent refrain both of Pitt and Newcastle that Bute and George III threw away the most impressive gains of the Seven Year's War and bartered Britain's future security in return for advantages which were not worth having. The charge must be taken seriously, though parts of it can be dismissed out of hand. For example, the ministry's opponents could not reasonably object to the retention of Canada at the cost of restoring the Caribbean island of Guadeloupe to France. Some of Pitt's conquests had to be given up unless the war were to continue for ever, and though there was a brisk debate in the press about the respective merits of Guadeloupe, a wealthy sugar island which would arguably have made the imperial economy unbalanced, or alternatively have given Britain the hegemony of the West Indies, and Canada whose fur trade and vast potential might or might not be an asset to the North American empire, few politicians were aware of a real choice. The nation's moral commitment to the American conflict during the war, and the need to guarantee the future security of the thirteen colonies, made the annexation of Canada inevitable. Similarly the exchange of Minorca for Belle Isle was unexceptionable, and indeed the expedition against Belle Isle had

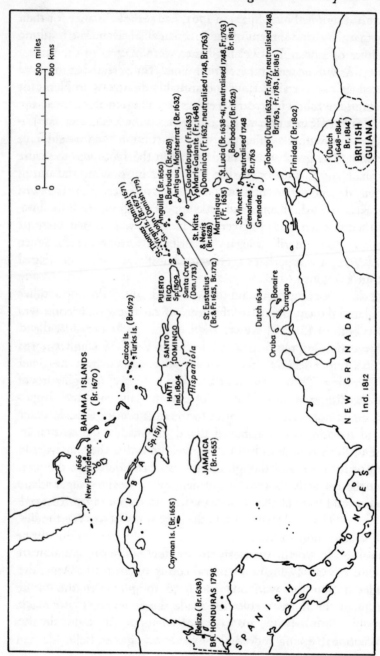

Map 4. The West Indies in the Eighteenth Century

been planned with this end in view by Pitt himself. Nor was it easy to carp at the striking gains made in India as a result of Clive's handiwork.

But the burden of Pitt's protest was that a number of fatal concessions had been made, concessions which he saw as 'the seeds of a future war. The peace was insecure, because it restored the enemy to her former greatness'.[1] In particular, St Lucia and Martinique, both captured late in the war, were returned to Louis XV in compensation for the acquisition of the American hinterland clear to the Mississippi, with the navigation of that river and the remaining 'neutral islands' of Grenada, St Vincent, Dominica and Tobago. In West Africa, Senegal was retained but the French preserved a foothold there by regaining Goree. Havana, that magnificent prize of August 1762, news of which had actually arrived during the peace negotiations, was restored to Spain in return for what was alleged to be a most inadequate equivalent in the form of Florida and some minor concessions concerning the logwood settlements and other Spanish grievances. The still more recent conquest of Manila was restored without any equivalent at all. Above all the Newfoundland fisheries, with which Pitt, that most traditional of thinkers, was obsessed, were not reserved exclusively for the British but remained partially open to their French rivals. For all these charges there was something to be said, and certainly it is possible to criticise Bute's handling of the negotiations; in particular it may be asked whether he, and more especially Bedford who was totally committed to peace at any price, could not have made much better use of the taking of Martinique, Havana and Manila than they did. However, it is important to recognise that the devastating demands which Pitt loudly proclaimed from the opposition benches and which incidentally did not correspond well with such few utterances as he had made on the subject of the peace terms while actually in office, would have lengthened the war considerably. On the question of retaining a foothold in the Newfoundland fishery for instance, the French were quite inflexible, as indeed they were on that of recovering Martinique. There were areas where they were prepared to make concessions; witness their surrender as to the detailed terms for the

[1] *Parliamentary History of England* ed. W. Cobbett, xv, p. 1270.

maintenance of French trade in India after the effective establishment
of British dominance through the East India Company, and their
readiness to cede Louisiana to Spain in return for obtaining Spanish
accession to the peace terms. But on the substantive conditions urged
on the ministers and on Parliament by Pitt and his comrades, they
would not have budged without further strategic reverses.

Shifted to this ground, the whole question becomes a highly
speculative one, with powerful objections on both sides of the
argument. Bedford and his kind insisted that if a Carthaginian peace
were to be the object, the result would be to make such bitter enemies of Britain's rivals in the international community as surely to
bring nemesis at some later date. Yet history was to invalidate this
claim. French desires for revenge were not diminished by Britain's
so-called generosity in 1763, nor was the humbling of British power
at Versailles in 1783 the less for Bute's foresight twenty years earlier.
On the other hand, indefinite warfare to wipe the French empire off
the face of the map was scarcely practicable. Ultimately the decisive
argument in defence of the strategy of Bute was the fact that it was
overwhelmingly endorsed by the nation at large. Admittedly Bute
and his master had been quick to see the desirability of ending a war
whose laurels graced Pitt's rather than their brows. The dispute at the
very beginning of the reign when Bute's version of the king's first
Proclamation referred to a 'bloody and expensive war' where Pitt
insisted on 'expensive, but just and necessary war' was symptomatic
of their anxiety to depreciate the achievements of the previous reign
and its statesmen.[1] Yet in the last analysis they had the nation behind
them. The peace preliminaries were not obtained in Parliament by
the corrupt manoeuvres of the hireling Henry Fox, whatever the
allegations of his opponents, and if the City of London fulminated
against the making of peace, it was not typical in doing so. Though
the British as a nation were apt to enter war unthinkingly, they had
little taste for prolonged and unnecessary warfare. The arguments
marshalled in 1760 by Israel Mauduit's *Considerations on the Present
German War*, one of the most influential pamphlets in the history of
British diplomacy, expressed by no means inaccurately the consensus
of opinion emerging among the propertied classes at this time.

[1] *The Life of William Pitt, Earl of Chatham* by B. Williams (London 1913), ii, p. 64.

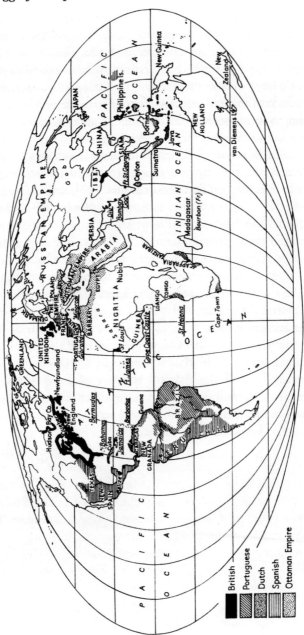

Map 5. The World at the Peace of Paris, 1763

British
Portuguese
Dutch
Spanish
Ottoman Empire

The war had after all been won; whatever the details, and few country gentlemen could bring themselves to study them, the peace must be the most brilliant not merely in decades but in centuries. The acquisition of a vast empire was not to be devalued by the sour grapes of a knot of discontented and factious politicians, even if the latter included the architect of victory. There seemed little point in continuing a war to bolster the fortunes of the now secure Frederick II or to grind France still further into the ground. Above all the cost was becoming intolerable; Britain's capacity to support warfare on a formidable scale was probably much greater than most contemporaries realised, but it could not be exploited without the cooperation of the taxpayer and investor. In 1754-55 the budget, as Mauduit pointed out, had been £4 million; by 1761 it was £19½ million. Most of the increase was financed by loans, but new taxes were continually being mortgaged to pay the interest charges and both taxation and borrowing seemed to be reaching their limits. In 1761, on the brink of war with Spain, Newcastle had been deeply perturbed by the increasing gloom and pessimism among the government's financier friends in the city,[1] and the spectre of national bankruptcy which was so often to the fore in the minds of eighteenth-century Englishmen, was particularly prominent by 1763. When George III made peace he had the grateful support of a loyal nation; the vapourings of opposition politicians, whether sincere or not, were ultimately ineffectual because they were completely out of tune with the country's fundamental attitude.

[1] *War and Trade in the West Indies* by R. Pares (Oxford 1936), p. 582.

11 Impotence and Isolation, 1763–76

Whatever the criticisms made of the Peace of Paris in England, to the outside world it seemed to raise Britain to a new pinnacle of power and prestige. The fall in the country's standing which followed was therefore all the more dramatic. Between the end of the Seven Years' War and the outbreak of the War of American Independence, the respect for George III's government in the international community declined disastrously, as his ministers drifted without any apparent grasp of policy, and above all without allies. Historians have been tempted to describe the period as one of 'splendid isolation'.[1] Yet the parallel with the diplomatic posture of the Victorians is scarcely helpful, for there was little that was splendid about Britain's isolation under George III. Disregard and almost contempt for the British voice in European affairs grew rapidly after 1763 and in the American war it was to turn almost to disbelief at the nadir to which Britain's fortunes sank. Admittedly, continental judgements were much affected by the adverse domestic factors which did so much to weaken British foreign policy in the 1760s. The political instability which formed so prominent an item in European critiques of Britain in the eighteenth century, not always with justification, could scarcely be seen as a negligible handicap. Thanks to the difficulty which George III experienced in finding a ministry which would simultaneously suit himself and Parliament, foreign affairs did not remain long in the hands of any one, let alone any one competent, minister. Between 1763 and 1775 there were seven changes in the southern secretaryship, eight in the northern, and five in the premiership itself. Nor were the men who shuffled through these offices with dismaying rapidity, among the most effective of

[1] *Splendid Isolation, 1763–1780* by M. Roberts (Reading 1970).

eighteenth-century foreign ministers. At best they were only moderately capable, like Suffolk or Rochford, at worst they were indolent like Grafton, and unreliable like Richmond. Continental observers were apt to overrate the effects of this weakness on foreign policy, but they were not entirely negligible.

Equally damaging to the development of a coherent and consistent policy abroad was the distracting violence of the major issues at home. The series of divisive political problems which developed in the sixties, especially those associated with John Wilkes at home and the stirrings of revolt in the colonies, did not encourage statesmen to concentrate on Britain's interests in Europe. 'Little attention', the *Annual Register* lamented in 1771, 'either had, or could for some time past have been given to our foreign interests'.[1] Foreigners were amazed by the spectacle of a nation so appallingly divided almost within months of its greatest triumph for centuries. Again, at least in the case of domestic political disagreements if not in that of colonial problems, appearances were in part deceiving. Opposition politicking, ministerial paralysis in the face of parliamentary or popular sentiment, these were not new and not necessarily disastrous phenomena. What mattered was that they contributed both to foreign disrespect for Britain and to that demoralisation which set in at home. Britain was not fatally weakened as such by the constitutional disputes of the early years of George III's reign, but she was affected by the very pessimism of the times. Horace Walpole's observation that 'We are no longer great in any way' was not a considered verdict based on a careful analysis of the international situation,[2] but it did reflect the contemporary loss of morale as a result of the turn events were taking at home.

The basic problem of the post-war years was not difficult to diagnose and certainly the politicians were not short of possible answers. Britain's isolation was complete and obvious, in a way it had not been for decades. The 'old system', its perennial standby, was in ruins. Austria had cut loose with the Diplomatic Revolution, and even the United Provinces, so long the faithful if reluctant satellite

[1] M. Roberts, 'Great Britain and the Swedish Revolution, 1772–73' in *Hist. Jnl.*, vii (1964), p. 42.

[2] *Horace Walpole's Correspondence* ed. W. S. Lewis (London 1937–), vii, p. 250.

of the British, had cast off in the Seven Years' War. There were those who sought a reversal of these developments. George III himself, who characteristically described his 'political creed' as 'formed on the system of King William',[1] and who in this as in much else out-whigged his Whig critics, felt that the priority should be to detach Vienna from its recent union with Madrid and Paris; during the Grenville Ministry of 1763 to 1765 there was indeed something like a serious attempt to revive the Habsburg connection. However, this, even if it had been wise, was not on the cards. Austria had learned to doubt the value of Britain's alliances and it would have needed more inducements than were currently on offer to lure her back to the fold. By 1765 even Lord Sandwich, the strongest advocate of a return to the 'old system', was forced to admit defeat. There were of course alternatives. Understandably in the light of the great debates of 1762 and 1763 opposition politicians strongly favoured a revival of the Prussian alliance. So-called Whigs whose fathers had placed their faith in the 'old system' were by this time champions of the plunderer of Silesia, most of them for little other reason than that Bute and George III had so completely committed themselves to the contrary view. This school was none the less given its chance in the mid-sixties. When the ministerial cycle brought even the old opponents of Bute to power, under Rockingham in 1765 and Chatham in 1766, a positive attempt to recreate the alliance of the Seven Years' War was made. These ministers had nourished the belief that Frederick's enmity was a purely personal one, to Bute himself, and that as soon as old friends were at the helm, he would see no difficulty in renewing good relations. Frederick himself, out of desire to stir up the political brew in England, had indeed fostered this impression. In the event however, it turned out to be totally incorrect. This was not because of any lack of enthusiasm in England. Though George III himself disliked the initiative and even objected that a Prussian treaty would involve 'ramming Austria deeper with France and kindling a new War by unnecessary alliances', he was prepared to give his ministers their head in foreign policy.[2] First

[1] *The Correspondence of King George the Third, 1760–1783* ed. Sir J. Fortescue (London 1927–28), ii, p. 204.
[2] ibid., i, pp. 124–25.

Rockingham in the summer of 1765, then Chatham in that of 1766, made confident overtures to Berlin. Yet Frederick would have nothing to do with his old allies. Though he made the customary remarks about the inconsistency of British policy and the damage which the great betrayal of 1762 had done to Anglo-Prussian relations, his true reasons for rejecting the approaches were clear enough. Prussia had no conceivable interest at this time in alliance with Britain. In the east, where her interests were largely involved, she was safely covered by the permanent alliance which Peter III had foreshadowed, and which Catherine II finally negotiated in 1764. Russian enmity, the one prospect which had always terrified Frederick and indeed pushed him into his costly mistakes of 1756 and 1757, was safely a thing of the past. A western power could add little to this vital security. As Frederick II himself remarked, 'If there is another war, it will probably be between France and England; there is no point at all in allying with them or involving ourselves. What do Cod and Cape Breton signify to us?'[1]

With neither of the two great Germanic powers responsive to their wooing, there was or at any rate seemed only one option remaining to British ministers, alliance with Russia herself. Unfortunately, though Russian amity often appeared desirable in the eighteenth century it proved surprisingly elusive, despite the good intentions of both sides. London was clear that the Russian alliance would be valuable, both to oppose French interests in the Baltic, in Eastern Europe and in the Mediterranean, and to provide concrete help in central Europe. Equally Russia under Catherine, as under other rulers, saw Britain as a useful potential ally in the same areas. Both governments were fundamentally hostile to the Bourbons in a way which was not true of the other great powers. Unfortunately however there turned out to be crucial differences of emphasis in their respective policies. In particular the Russians were not prepared to commit themselves to supplying military aid to George III unless they received adequate compensations from him. In the long negotiations between the two courts, more or less continuous in the 1760s and 1770s, regardless of the political complexion of successive

[1] F. Spencer, 'The Anglo-Prussian Breach of 1762: An Historical Revision' in *History*, xli (1956), p. 101.

ministries, the actual bone of contention varied. On some occasions Russia demanded financial assistance in Sweden or in Poland, at other times, and this became the vital issue, she insisted on the celebrated Turkish clause, providing for British cooperation against the Porte. But the ministers of George III had little enthusiasm for committing their master to intervention in the increasingly likely event of a new Russo-Turkish war. A decade or two later they might have had doubts about the wisdom of increasing Russian influence in the Eastern Mediterranean; at this time their principal anxiety seems to have concerned the possibility of involvement in a prolonged and expensive side-show, unconnected with British interests. In any event the result was deadlock, and relations between the two courts slowly but steadily cooled. All that Britain obtained to its advantage from these years of endless bargaining was the renewal in 1766 of the commercial treaty which dated back to 1734; for their part the Russians were gratified to receive effective British countenance of the fleet which they sent to the Mediterranean prior to a remarkable naval victory over the Turks at Chesme in 1770. However, as the Russo-Turkish war of 1768–74 wore on it became increasingly clear that Britain's ministers were more and more determined to evade the Turkish clause. By the beginning of the War of American Independence the alliance for which they were one day to offer even Minorca was out of the question.

Apart from these various and equally unrewarding possibilities, there was a further avenue of escape from isolation, though an exceedingly adventurous one. The notion of alliance with France herself, though almost unthinkable to most Englishmen, actually had much to recommend it. Traditionally British power had been exerted to preserve the balance on the Continent by opposing the designs of France, its most dangerous enemy. Those who so eagerly advocated a Prussian or Russian alliance had not changed their view of this apparently fundamental priority in British foreign policy. The Elder Pitt, now Earl of Chatham, for example, one of the few statesmen whose prestige was such that he might have espoused an unpopular French alliance, still fulminated against the menace of the Bourbons and expatiated on the need to construct a 'northern system' against their alliance of the south. Chatham had not had a new or original thought about strategy in years; indeed he had achieved his successes in the 1750s largely by doing the obvious with enormous vigour and confidence, and by the mid-sixties had little but prejudice to sustain his reputation. Minds less encumbered with dead wood had begun to see that France was not necessarily the principal threat to European security. On the contrary the mid-century had made it increasingly obvious that the eastern monarchies and in particular the two new boys among the great powers, Prussia and Russia, had almost eclipsed the Bourbons and Habsburgs in continental affairs. Thus David Hume observed with surprise that 'the two most civilised nations, the English and French, should be on the decline; and the barbarians, the Goths and Vandals of Germany and Russia, should be rising in power and renown'.[1] In this situation and against the background of the 'swing to the east', there was at least a case for radically reviewing Anglo-French relations. Nor was this entirely ruled out on the French side of the channel. Though Choiseul, the dominant minister in the 1760s, plotted steadily for revenge after the Seven Years' War, there was a faction at the French court which was not wholly averse to a realignment in favour of the traditional enemy. Moreover, after the fall of Choiseul in 1770, his successor D'Aiguillon unquestionably worked for a dramatic revision of the usual policy, while on the British side George III was capable of seeing the logic involved. 'If Britain and France would with temper examine their respective situations,' he remarked in 1772 at the height of this rethinking process, 'the antient animosity would appear absurd'.[2]

Unfortunately the opportunities for such a complete change of approach were few. In the 1760s, Grenville, Rockingham and Chatham were all intent on proving their impeccably anti-Bourbon credentials by pursuing with vigour the minor disputes which existed between the subjects of George III and the Family Compact after 1763. There were, for example, a number of fairly trivial problems arising from the varying interpretations of particular

---

[1] *British Public Opinion and the First Partition of Poland* by D. B. Horn (London 1945), pp. 18–19.

[2] *The Correspondence of King George the Third, 1760–1783* ed. Sir J. Fortescue (London 1927–28), ii, pp. 428–29.

points in the Peace of Paris. Dunkirk and its fortifications, that traditional grievance especially beloved of the 'patriot' politicians; the Manila Ransom, compensation which Spain owed Britain in return for the restoration of an unplundered capital of the Philippines in 1763; the Canada Bills, notes of credit which the French court had granted its subjects in Quebec and which had passed into the hands of British merchants; the Newfoundland fisheries, ever the cause of Anglo-French bickering; even compensation for the maintenance of prisoners of war, all these issues were taken up with spirit by successive ministries with differing degrees of success. In most there was at least some justification for the sense of grievance felt in London, but none of them, as a realist like the Duke of Cumberland pointed out, were 'worth going to war for'.[1] Yet it was not surprising that by the late 1760s the belligerence always just below the surface in Anglo-French relations was near to breaking out with its ancient force. Not all the blame was on the British side. French action in annexing the island of Corsica, legally a Genoese possession, was a flagrant provocation. But like the acquisition of Lorraine thirty years before, it went without serious protest from Britain. An attempt to whip up a public campaign in favour of Paoli and the Corsican patriots made some impact, but ministers had other matters on their minds than Mediterranean adventures.

Much more sinister was the crisis which burst in 1770. The Falkland Islands dispute resembled the other great Anglo-Spanish incidents of the eighteenth century. It stemmed equally from the arrogant and absurd extravagance of Spanish claims to territory in the New World, and from the mindless warmongering which overtook the English when confronted even with trivial insults. Spain's claim to these almost valueless islands had profited considerably by French abandonment of their own pretensions in 1766. However the British, who were not blind to the advantages of planting a flag on the route to the Pacific, chose to reinforce their own claims in 1769. The result was forcible expulsion from Port Egmont by the governor of Buenos Aires, which when news of it reached England caused a domestic and diplomatic furore of violent propor-

[1] *Memoirs of the Reign of King George III* by Horace Walpole, ed. G. F. R. Barker (London 1894), ii, p. 161.

tions. There was the inevitable outcry in London, the equally inevitable cold response from Madrid. By the summer of 1770 the powers were on the verge of war, with Britain arming its navy and Spain no less ready for combat. All hinged on the attitude of France, and there Choiseul thought he had found the ideal opportunity to obtain revenge for his humiliation in the Seven Years' War. Fortunately other factors intervened. In the British cabinet, North the Prime Minister, and Rochford, the Secretary of State involved, were desperately anxious for peace. Despite the public outcry, and despite the resignation of Lord Weymouth, who as the other Secretary of State considered that his colleagues were insufficiently firm, North was ready to make concessions, albeit secret ones, which effectively pledged British evacuation of the Falklands within a short time. However, the decisive development was a revolution in French politics. In December 1770 Choiseul succumbed to one of those palace upheavals which plagued Versailles even more than St James, and Louis XV personally wrote to his cousin in Madrid: 'My minister would have war, but I will not'.[1] Without French assistance, Charles III was helpless and the crisis naturally fizzled out. The Spanish authorities publicly disavowed the action of their agents in South America, as well as promising reparation for the damage done. For their part North and his colleagues, after allowing the storm to die down, were to withdraw British forces, though without prejudice to the long-term question of legal ownership. A wild campaign by Chatham and his colleagues, cynically designed to whip up an anti-Spanish fever comparable to that of 1739, was ultimately unsuccessful, as it became clear that at any rate in public Britain's honour was untarnished.

Though it came nearer to causing war than any other episode since 1763, the Falkland Islands crisis preceded an improvement in the prospects of an Anglo-French *entente*. For one thing it brought to the fore a convinced champion of rapprochement in the Duc d'Aiguillon. Moreover in the following two or three years the international community was given clearer evidence than ever that the enemies of European security might be located in the east and

[1] M. C. Morison, 'The Duc de Choiseul and the Invasion of England, 1768–1770' in *Trans. Roy. Hist. Soc.*, 3rd Ser., iv (1910), p. 105.

north rather than in the south and west. The first partition of Poland, a cynical act of international piracy by Austria, Prussia and Russia, clearly signalised, if any further indication were needed, that the eastern powers menaced both the general interest of Europe and the particular liberties of the lesser powers in a new and sinister manner. The moral too was evident; only a new grouping of the western powers could offset the tilting of the balance to the east. Those who urged the public to abandon ancient animosities in order to save the liberties of the Poles, stressed that 'that doctrine must be weak indeed that pretends we must always be in opposition to France, because we have often taken a part against her. [It is] ridiculous to say that any state is our natural enemy, because we have been at war or because we are rivals'.[1] However, there was little by way of response to such appeals. On the whole British opinion was more concerned by the Prussian threat posed to commercial interests in Danzig than by the danger to the continental balance of power. Moreover almost simultaneously with the Polish partition a parallel crisis in Sweden was actually exacerbating Anglo-French relations. The revolution in Sweden which took place in August 1772 brought to an end the era of oligarchal rule in Stockholm and re-established the monarchy, under Gustavus III, as something more than the cipher it had been ever since the death of Charles XII. At the same time it registered a major diplomatic triumph for France and a damaging defeat for Russia and to some extent for Britain. At the height of the ensuing crisis in the spring of 1773 various possibilities emerged; a war between Russian and Sweden with the former intervening to oust Gustavus, a war between Russia and France in the Eastern Mediterranean with the latter endeavouring to embroil the Russians further with the Porte, and even a war between France and Britain. Relations between the government of George III and Louis XV could indeed have developed in either of two quite different ways. Alliance with France against Russia was not inconceivable; D'Aiguillon worked actively for it and ministers in London did not entirely discountenance the notion, at any rate in their discussions with French diplomats. Alernatively, French naval activity in the Baltic

[1] *British Public Opinion and the First Partition of Poland* by D. B. Horn (London 1945), p. 65.

or the Mediterranean might precipitate open warfare between the
two countries. The outcome was however somewhat inconclusive.
Russia decided against intervention in Sweden; France, impressed
by British warnings, backed down, and war was averted. Unfortunately so was that alliance which might have emerged from this
period of review and reappraisal. Though George III and his servants considered the idea of an Anglo-French rapprochement
seriously, they ultimately had not the courage to undertake it.
The fundamental fact was that public opinion in England would
have been intolerably alienated by an alliance such as Stanhope had
negotiated nearly sixty years before. As Rochford himself pointed
out, if an alliance was agreed with the French, the House of Commons
would 'demand the head of the Chancellor who sealed it, and the
minister who had signed it'.[1]

In the decade which followed the Peace of Paris, British statesmen
had contemplated almost every possibility in their anxiety to escape
from the isolation which was the legacy of the war. All had failed
them in one way or another. Yet it is at least worth asking whether
the premises upon which they based their policies were justified.
Somewhat ironically Pitt had established it as a maxim of British
foreign policy that a continental connection was necessary not
merely to preserve the balance of power in Europe but in order to
assert British interests overseas. In their desperation to live up to this
requirement, politicians became increasingly irrational. In particular
the Russian alliance, the one alignment which seemed really practicable as well as useful, was vastly overrated. 'The empire of Russia',
one British diplomat, Sir Joseph Yorke remarked, 'is absolutely
necessary for us either in peace or war'.[2] Yet it is difficult to believe
that in the extremity to which Britain was to be reduced in the War
of American Independence the Russian alliance would have been of
much assistance. Only if France and Spain launched a continental
war in which Germany in general and Hanover in particular became
enmeshed, would an ally on the European mainland be an asset to
the cause of George III.

[1] M. Roberts, 'Great Britain and the Swedish Revolution, 1772–73' in *Hist. Jnl.*,
v (1964), p. 29.
[2] H. Butterfield, 'British Foreign Policy, 1762–5' in *Hist. Jnl.*, vi (1963), p. 136.

That this would indeed happen was more or less assumed in England in the 1760s. Paradoxically in view of their traditionally passionate opposition to 'Hanoverianism', Englishmen had now grown accustomed to expect a full-scale European conflict whenever their interests became entangled with those of the Bourbons. War with Spain over the right of search in the Caribbean had ended in participation in the War of the Austrian Succession. War with France in the North American back country and on the high seas had similarly led to involvement in the Seven Years' War. Yet these precedents were fatally misleading. In each case they had been the result of circumstances which were no longer applicable at all. For example, the conflict between Prussia and Austria which had produced the decisive Prussian strikes against Silesia in 1740 and Saxony in 1756, was not necessarily to be repeated. Nothing was likely to put Vienna and Berlin on friendly terms for some considerable time, but neither did it follow that Prussia, intent on licking her wounds and consolidating her conquests, and Austria, concerned to develop her interests in new directions, would wilfully resort to war in the near future. Still more important the link between British interests on the one hand and the continental situation on the other had depended on the unwitting collaboration of Louis XV. The two great wars of the mid-eighteenth century had been characterised by French readiness to continue the ancient policy of meddling in German affairs. On each occasion this had been against the advice of those at Versailles who had had more concern for French interests in the colonies than on the Continent. However, in future such voices were to be listened to. Not only was there no guarantee that France would divide her forces and severely hinder her overseas war effort by a diversion in Germany again; on the contrary after the Seven Years' War, unbeknown to British ministers, the court of Louis XV was determined not to repeat the errors of earlier years. Choiseul in the 1760s and eventually Vergennes in the 1770s were to base French foreign policy and strategy on one central premise. For the future continental adventures must be avoided, the tempting lure of Hanover must be ignored and British power must be confronted not where it was apparently and most deceptively vulnerable, in Germany, but where it had its source overseas. Against this background the British preoccupation with the continental balance of power was at best irrelevant and at worst profoundly damaging.

There were after all alternative strategies. In particular it was of the first importance to prepare for an all out overseas war, unaccompanied by continental diversions, by ensuring that the Royal Navy was capable of preserving that mastery of American, Mediterranean, Indian and home waters which it had won in the last stages of the War of the Austrian Succession, and in the middle phase of the Seven Years' War. Something like the two-power naval standard beloved of Victorians was essential in the reign of George III if the combined forces of the Bourbon monarchies were to be crushed without the benefit of continental diversions. Ministers in London were not unaware of the importance of the navy. Indeed the one alliance for which they were notionally prepared to give a peacetime subsidy was that with 'such a foreign Power, whose Fleet joined to ours may still maintain the Superiority against all the endeavours of the united force of the House of Bourbon'.[1] Unfortunately, in default of such an alliance, they were not always successful in finding the money to maintain the Royal Navy itself at a high pitch. In the aftermath of the Seven Years' War the stress was understandably on economy, and the navy suffered its share of budgetary reductions. Even after 1770 when the vigorous and somewhat maligned Sandwich took over at the Admiralty the pressures exerted by the Treasury were formidable. North, like Grenville, and the other Chancellors of the 1760s was insistent that 'great peace establishments will . . . prove our ruin',[2] and Sandwich's efforts to maintain and modernise the obsolescent navy which he inherited from previous First Lords had to be unremitting. Unfortunately when the moment of trial came in the late 1770s they proved insufficient, and Sandwich's boast in 1777 that 'our navy is more than a match for that of the whole House of Bourbon', proved sadly mistaken.[3] However, by this time questions of naval standards and continental alliances had succumbed to a much more important

[1] *The First Rockingham Administration, 1765-1766* by P. Langford (Oxford 1973), p. 90.
[2] *The War for America, 1775-1783* by P. Mackesy (London 1964).
[3] ibid., p. 175.

issue, one which was dramatically to affect British foreign policy—that of imperial authority in North America.

From 1774 indeed, the pattern of diplomacy in western Europe was determined largely by the rebellion of Britain's American colonies. Technically George III did not issue a proclamation of rebellion until the end of August 1775, while the colonies themselves ventured a declaration of independence only in July 1776. However, this paper warfare had been preceded by armed conflict in the spring of 1775, at Lexington, Concord and Bunker Hill. Moreover at least as early as March 1774 when Lord North's ministry definitely decided on a policy of coercion in response to the Boston Tea Party, European opinion was well aware that events on the other side of the Atlantic might produce a sudden and spectacular change in the delicate balance of international power. Nor was it difficult to foresee the nature of that change. It was common knowledge, indeed common sense, that the Bourbon powers would seek to exploit the internal strains of the British empire to regain ground lost in the Seven Years' War. As early as February 1765 Choiseul had designed his diplomatic strategy with precisely such an eventuality in view. 'Only the revolution which will occur some day in America, though we shall probably not see it, will put England back to that state of weakness in which Europe will have no more to fear of her'.[1] Surprisingly soon, as it turned out, his successors were granted the opportunity for which Choiseul had planned.

In retrospect it is easy to condemn Lord North and his colleagues for their foolishness in gratuitously presenting their enemies with a crucial advantage. Yet it is easier to criticise British policy than to suggest a constructive alternative. The struggle against America was not after all a piece of ill-considered folly; to argue that Whitehall should have concentrated on conciliating rather than coercing the thirteen colonies and thus remained free to face the Bourbon threat is quite to misunderstand the significance for the mother country of the American rebellion. In the first place it was axiomatic that the colonies were themselves essential elements in the empire's

---

[1] E. S. Corwin, 'The French Objective in the American Revolution' in *Am. Hist. Rev.*, xxi (1915–16), p. 53.

international power and prestige. America's function was to enable Britain, not inherently the greatest of European powers, to rank herself with and even above France. The French minister in London in 1767, Durand, put the position with perfect clarity. 'England herself has discovered with surprise that they are the sources of the power which she enjoys and that these great objects of power and ambition draw in their wake the balance of power in Europe'.[1] However, if the American colonies were an essential part of the fabric of British power, they were so only as long as they could be readily controlled from London. Whether they were regarded primarily as suppliers of raw materials, or as markets for home manufactures, or as reserves of naval and military manpower, their proper subordination to the authorities at home was vital. To the minds of all but a few Englishmen, a colony which in the last analysis could make all its own decisions was a source of weakness rather than strength. Though taxation provided the issue over which mother country and colonies clashed, and inspired the flow of debate on either side of the Atlantic, the central issue was simply and solely the authority of the imperial government. It was for this reason that Chatham's repeated attacks on official policy, his contention that taxation could be yielded and yet the power of the imperial parliament retained, his pleas to face the foreign rather than the colonial enemy, were so utterly unacceptable. If the colonies would not obey Parliament in paying imperial taxes, there was no guarantee that they would do so in the manifold regulations and restrictions which were held to be vital to the functioning of the imperial economy in peace and in war, or so the ministerial view alleged. It was all the more necessary then to solve the problem once and for all, by reining in the dangerously self-willed colonists before the next contest between Britain and her European rivals. 'We must get the Colonies into order before we engage with our Neighbours,' declared George III himself.[2]

Given this basic commitment on the part of Britain to the cause of

[1] E. S. Corwin, 'The French Objective in the American Revolution' in *Am Hist. Rev.*, xxi (1915–16), pp. 53–54.

[2] *The Correspondence of King George the Third, 1760–1873* ed. Sir J. Fortescue (London 1927–28), ii, p. 372.

subduing the colonies, there remained only one major question so far as policy in Europe was concerned. Should the Bourbon powers be permitted to aid the rebel colonies, albeit clandestinely at first, or should the arena of conflict be widened at once by a surprise attack on France such as had been launched, with scant regard to moral decency, in 1755? Frederick II, the veteran of more than one 'pre-emptive strike', felt that Britain would have done well to emulate his example, admittedly with the advantage of hindsight. 'If she wanted to make war on her colonies,' he wrote in 1782, 'she ought at once to have laid up the French navy and bottled up her shipyards, which was very possible in the beginning'.[1] Though Frederick underestimated the difficulties of imposing an effective blockade on France, this was a possibility which had not escaped Whitehall. Indeed Rochford actually pointed out to the French ambassador the potential advantages to Britain of a savage and sudden assault on the helpless French fisheries in Newfoundland, and the temporarily vulnerable French West Indies. On the other hand, there were strong arguments against a precipitate plunge into warfare on such a scale. It was considered for example, that France was not in a position to take full advantage of Britain's predicament; the state of French finances left much to be desired and there were substantial pressures on the new king, Louis XVI, to adopt a policy of retrenchment. 'There is reason to believe', Suffolk felt able to assure his envoys, 'that œconomy will now be a leading principle in the French cabinet'.[2] This was in May 1774, long before Turgot was defeated in his attempts to impose such a policy. Yet even after Turgot's fall, as late as December 1776, the British cabinet believed that financial stringency would force France to adopt a cautious role. Equally reassuring for the North ministry, but still more fallacious, was the belief that Vergennes, Louis XVI's foreign minister, rather resembled a Fleury than a Choiseul. Rochford called him a 'man of business integrity and of no enterprizing disposition . . . more disposed to the continuance of peace and more likely to carry on an amicable correspondence with us than any of the others who were talked of for

[1] *American Independence through Prussian Eyes* by M. Brown, jun., (Durham, N.C., 1959), p. 17.
[2] *British Diplomatic Instructions, 1689–1789* (Camden Soc.), v, p. 230.

that employment'.[1] In reality Vergennes, if more subtle than Choiseul, was animated by the same ideas and guided by the same
strategy. More than anyone else he was to be the architect of
Britain's downfall in America.

Despite these miscalculations, Whitehall was probably justified in
its decision not to seize the initiative against France. The dangers of
a full-scale war, isolated as Britain was, were colossal. Moreover
Vergennes himself could hardly rush into alliance with the rebellious
colonies. Premature French interference in North America might
well be just the factor to reunite mother country and colonies
against the Family Compact and bring back Chatham, the scourge
of the Bourbons, to lead the British empire to new victories. Nor
could a speedy military conclusion to the American rebellion be
ruled out, and no French minister would readily commit his master
to a major conflict with Britain unless the Americans first demonstrated their capability in the field. In short, the ministers in London
relied on a reasonably quick victory in the colonies both to quash
the rebellion and deter France from intervention, a policy which
was initially vindicated by events. Though France was supplying
aid to the colonies from May 1776 she only did so unofficially through
the agency of Beaumarchais, and her progress towards a fuller
commitment in favour of the rebels was significantly delayed by
information from North America. Thus in the summer of 1776 the
report of Howe's capture of New York led Vergennes to draw back
from the brink, and a year later news of the loss of Ticonderoga to
Burgoyne had a similar effect. Only if Britain lost a major battle
would France be drawn openly into the struggle, and when that
happened it was not British diplomacy, but British generalship,
which was to blame.

[1] *British Diplomatic Instructions, 1689–1789* (Camden Soc.), vii, p. 142.

12 Imperial Disaster, 1776–83

In the early years of the American war, while Clinton, Carleton, Howe and Burgoyne were frittering away the advantages their own arms had gained, the principal role of their colleagues in the diplomatic service was that of support for the war effort. As ever, manpower was a chronic problem. The customary treaties with minor German powers were made and resulted in the despatch across the Atlantic of nearly thirty thousand troops in the course of the war. Even in this area, however, there were major disappointments. Russia, after appearing in August 1775 to encourage a request for an army of twenty thousand, declined to be treated on a footing with petty German princes by accepting a subsidy. In addition the Dutch effectively rejected a suggestion that the ancient 'Scotch Brigade', long in the service of the States-General, should be loaned to Britain. The Secretaries of State were left to draw consolation from a few crumbs of success. It was encouraging that the ill-judged attempt by Congress to open diplomatic relations with the European powers proved generally a humiliating failure. Paper victories were also gained in the efforts which British diplomats made to restrict or eliminate trade between the rebel colonies and the Continent. Holland and Denmark were bullied into compliant gestures, though in practice their respective islands in the Caribbean thrived on clandestine trade with the Americans. Even France, while Vergennes bided his time, was brought to renounce, at least nominally, her scandalous complacency with regard to the activities of American privateers. Finally, the quality of British intelligence proved high, especially that controlled directly by diplomats. Their better-known exploits, ranging from the suborning of Edward Bancroft, the secretary to the American mission in Paris, to the impudent plundering of Arthur Lee's official papers by Hugh Elliot, the British envoy in Berlin, were the work of a secret service which kept ministers and diplomats well primed with information. But these were matters of essentially secondary significance. In the early years of the American War all parties were waiting for news from the other side of the Atlantic. Thus the diplomats of Europe awaited the report which would either send them scurrying to congratulate His Britannic Majesty on his success in subduing his treacherous subjects beyond the seas, or alternatively remould the existing pattern of European relations. When it came, in December 1777, it told them that Burgoyne had surrendered at Saratoga on 15 October.

Saratoga was not by any standards a great battle. Technically it was not even a British defeat, though it represented the loss of some five thousand men, a force difficult if not impossible to replace. Yet its psychological and diplomatic importance was monumental. It entailed, for example, a dramatic change of policy by Britain; the military evacuation of all but New York and Rhode Island, the switch from a strategy designed to strangle New England to one intended to play to the strength of loyalism in the south, the despatch of a peace mission under Carlisle, and ultimately a strategic shift to the West India theatre, all followed logically from the consequences of Saratoga. But no less important was the series of diplomatic defeats for Britain in which French historians have understandably seen a remarkable triumph for Vergennes. That France would now formally ally with the Americans was a foregone conclusion. It may be doubted whether the faint possibility of an Anglo-American rapprochement which Franklin held over Vergennes' head and which was given some colour by a semi-official British overture to the American negotiators, was needed to cement the alliance. In any event two treaties were signed in February 1778, one of amity and trade, one of alliance. French and British ambassadors were recalled in March, and while there was no immediate declaration of war as such, a naval engagement between HMS *Arethusa* and the *Belle Poule* in June signalised the commencement of hostilities.

In theory at least the British government had more room for manoeuvre with France's partner in the Family Compact. Spain was notoriously ill-disposed towards the American rebels. Her own vested

interest on the American continent was much too great to permit
any but the coldest attitude towards Congress, as the complete
failure of John Jay's mission to the Spanish court between 1780 and
1782 was to demonstrate. None the less, the price of Spanish
neutrality in the shape of Gibraltar, was high, and neither George III
nor his ministers were ready to pay it. Once it had become clear that
Spain would not obtain Gibraltar by diplomacy alone, a further
widening of the war was inevitable. In April 1779 the Spanish court
issued an ultimatum to Britain offering its mediation on intentionally
unacceptable conditions, and simultaneously signed, in the Convention of Aranjuez, an offensive alliance with France, though not
one which guaranteed the independence of America. On 21 June
1779 war was declared and preparations for the invasion of England,
long since conceived, moved into their final stages. Informal negotiations were reopened between Spain and Britain in 1780 but again
they foundered on the rock of Gibraltar. According to Vergennes,
Spanish defection at this stage would inevitably have involved
American defeat. Even so it would not have been easy for the
British government to give away Gibraltar. Neither Parliament nor
the public would readily have sanctioned such a sacrifice at a time
when the British cause in America was in any case far from lost.

That France and Spain would align themselves against Britain was
doubtless unavoidable. More galling and also unexpected was the
failure of the North administration to enlist the aid or even the
benevolent neutrality of Russia. No less than four attempts to
negotiate an alliance were made between January 1778 and February
1781, as the cabinet frantically sought an escape from the isolation
which it had inherited. Extraordinary concessions were contemplated during these years. The refusal to assist Russia in her
Turkish ambitions, which had wrecked the efforts of successive
ministers in the 1760s to obtain a Russian pact, was now jettisoned.
Even more remarkably Minorca was offered as an outright cession
to obtain the hoped-for prize. Sandwich, who brought a reluctant
cabinet and a still more reluctant George III to accept this sacrifice,
even believed that if Russia proved hostile, 'we shall never again
figure as a leading power in Europe, but think ourselves happy if we
can drag on for some years a contemptible existence as a commercial

state'.[1] That even this astonishing offer was rejected was bad enough; still worse was the bombshell which Russia exploded in the spring of 1780, the declaration of armed neutrality. That declaration and the subsequent adherence to it of every major neutral power in Europe represented the low point of British diplomatic standing, certainly in the late eighteenth century and arguably in the century as a whole.

The basic issues in the armed neutrality arose out of the vexed question of neutral rights at sea, one in which Britain had a particularly important stake. The right of combatants to search and confiscate shipping on the high seas was one which had a long and confused legal history. To a great extent it depended on a diffuse mass of tradition which could be interpreted in a number of conflicting ways; in addition there were between some of the powers specific treaties which regulated the matter in a more definitive way. Such contention as arose centred on two questions of substance, the right of neutral ships to carry goods belonging to combatants, and the precise nature of contraband, the goods which on any reading were confiscable. On both issues it was natural that Britain, whose survival in war depended on her ability to deny supplies to her enemies, should seek to reduce the rights of neutral carriers to an absolute minimum, though ironically her own position in the previous century as a mercantile power with an interest in carrying goods at all times to all places, had left her with a legacy of inconvenient treaties. Particularly in the American War it was made clear by Whitehall that naval stores from the Baltic, which France and Spain depended on for the effectiveness of their fleets, and which the neutral powers felt perfectly entitled to transport for them, would be treated as contraband. The ministers in London had hoped for support from Catherine II in this matter and indeed initially expected the declaration of armed neutrality to be directed against the Spanish rather than the British navy. In fact the declaration, when it was released in March 1780, made it clear that Russia was prepared to use force to protect neutral carriers of naval stores to the enemies of George III, and the accession in due course of all the other major powers—Sweden and Denmark in 1780, Holland, Prussia and Austria in 1781 and even Portugal and the Two Sicilies

---

[1] *The War for America, 1775–1783* by P. Mackesy (London 1964), pp. 383–4.

eventually—made the armed neutrality too grave a matter for neglect. Though the British staunchly resisted the principles of maritime law enshrined in the declaration, in practice they could not flaunt the views of the powers involved; strong protests, particularly by Russia and Prussia, against the conduct of naval commanders, generally produced compensation in full.

The impact of the armed neutrality was not limited to the activities of the Admiralty; it also brought about the addition of the Dutch to Britain's enemies. Though the United Provinces were technically allies of Britain, and indeed by treaty required to come to her aid if requested, their position for most of the American War had been that of malevolent neutrals. French influence at the Hague, which grew steadily in this period at the expense of the pro-British stadholder, William V, together with the enormous value to the Dutch of illegal trade with the rebel Americans, naturally played their part. The States-General had of course made placatory gestures in response to complaints about the flagrantly illegal commerce conducted between Europe and the thirteen colonies through St Eustatius, the Dutch free port in the West Indies. However, the entry of the Bourbon powers into the war and the imminence of the armed neutrality put a new complexion on affairs. The Dutch were the principal carriers of Baltic goods to France, and despite the daunting opposition of their British allies were fatally attracted by the lure of commercial gain. In the circumstances war with Britain was unavoidable; it was however hastened by the declaration of armed neutrality. Once the United Provinces had declared their adherence, the other signatories would have been bound to resist by force a British attack on Dutch shipping. Speed was therefore of the essence. Aided by the fortuitous capture in September 1780 of papers which could be represented as evidence of a firm alliance between the Dutch and the American rebels, the cabinet was able to conceal, at least to the satisfaction of diplomatic consciences, the real nature of the issue, and force the States-General into an unwinnable war. In November 1780 Sir Joseph Yorke, the British envoy in Holland, delivered his government's final ultimatum requiring the States-General to perform their ancient treaty obligations and come to the aid of Britain. War ensued at once and just before the Dutch formally joined the armed neutrality, in time to prevent an open conflict between its supporters and George III.

To continental eyes the plight of Britain in the years following Saratoga presented an extraordinary spectacle. At war with France, Spain and Holland, marooned by the hostile neutrality of almost every power of any significance, the subjects of George III seemed destined for a catastrophe even more spectacular than their triumph barely a decade earlier. To the French in particular it appeared that their ancient rival had been comprehensively routed at least on the field of diplomatic battle; at every point Vergennes had foiled Lord North and his colleagues. Yet in retrospect it is possible to see that some points at least went to the ministers in London. The movement to war with the Dutch for example had been conducted with a combination of skill, speed and cynicism which would have done credit to the French foreign ministry. There was admittedly a case against alienating the Dutch; it could be argued, for instance, that the cost (in the shape of twenty ships of the line which would be added to the combined Bourbon strength) was too high. Less pertinently the parliamentary opposition hotly denounced ministerial perfidy in deserting a traditional ally, an allegation which conveniently ignored the flagrantly pro-French policy of the States-General. Yet the need to deprive the Bourbon fleets of Baltic supplies was vital, and North's cabinet, led by Stormont and Sandwich, acted resolutely and with effect. Again, British diplomacy won a notable victory in Scandinavia. Though Denmark joined the armed neutrality, her action in doing so was effectually nullified by a special convention negotiated between Britain and the Danish court, by which the Danes were permitted unrestricted export of their own produce, in return for abandoning the right to carry naval stores.

Moreover the critics of the North ministry did not find it easy to outline an alternative policy. If isolation had been unavoidable in the years of peace after the Seven Years' War, the War of American Independence did not make it less so. Alliances, especially offensive alliances involving aid against the American rebels on the one hand and the Bourbons on the other, were not there for the taking. Typical was the case of Russia. In the mid-sixties Catherine's court had at least been ready to consider the possibility of an alliance on the right terms; but a decade later with their own mounting interest in the fate of the Turkish empire, with France, Spain and Britain satisfyingly involved overseas, and with Britain's maritime interests constantly causing irritation, it was not surprising that the Russians preferred neutrality and even hostility to amity. In addition there was a feeling in Russia and elsewhere that British pride was due for a fall. Nobody wanted a shattering Bourbon victory but there was much to be said for reducing the weight of British power in the European scales. Thus James Harris, George III's representative at St Petersburg, explained Russian sentiments to his masters. 'The return of England to the situation she was in before the war of 1755 would make her feel the necessity of the friendship and alliance of Russia more than she did after the peace of 1763 confirmed her decisive supremacy at sea, for then she began to show intractability in all her negotiations with us'.[1]

Understandably in this situation some diplomats yearned for the days of the 'old system' when the court of St James had not wanted for allies on the Continent. Stormont, who was effectively in control of foreign policy after the death of Suffolk in 1779, and was at any rate an experienced career diplomat, complained bitterly that 'Since the destruction of that system all our foreign politicks have been nothing more than the little expedients of the day'.[2] Yet there was no way of reviving that system in the circumstances of the American War. This was powerfully demonstrated in the Bavarian crisis of 1778, when, on the Elector of Bavaria's death, the Austrians attempted to obtain a large portion of his territory. The resulting diplomatic confrontation divided Germany into two camps and bore every sign of developing like earlier conflicts in central Europe. It was not fantastic to envisage a situation in which France, Spain, Austria and Turkey would end by fighting Britain, Prussia and Russia, in a major war affecting every theatre. Yet the pattern of earlier wars was broken and it was broken not because Britain no longer had allies on the Continent, but because of the changed attitude of France. Joseph II's plea to Louis XVI for assistance, almost coincident in

[1] *Britain, Russia and the Armed Neutrality of 1780* by I. de Madariaga (London 1962), pp. 108–109.
[2] ibid., p. 197.

time with the signing of the Franco-American treaty, was politely rejected, and after an inconclusive campaign in Bavaria, Russia and France jointly mediated a face-saving peace at Teschen. Nothing could have showed more clearly that Vergennes, like Choiseul, had learned the lesson of the mid-century wars. The Habsburg alliance was to be used to stabilise Germany, not to divide it; the fatal lure of Hanover, once regarded as Britain's hostage to fortune, was ignored, and the power of the British empire was to be destroyed overseas, where it had its source. This time the fate of America would be decided not in Germany, as Pitt had believed it to have been in the Seven Years' War, but across the Atlantic.

If Britain was powerless to do more than make minor modifications to the unpropitious pattern of diplomacy which confronted her, it is also fair comment that her misfortunes were in part illusory. Much though Vergennes prided himself on his triumphs in the chancelleries of Europe, the issue would ultimately be decided on the battlefield. Admittedly the armed neutrality had some effect. Though the neutral powers avoided going to war to defend Holland's freedom of navigation, and so averted a trial of arms with the Royal Navy, the respect which the British cabinet felt bound to pay to this manifestation of organised international opinion, certainly reduced the effectiveness of its economic blockade. Sandwich, for example, blamed 'the subterfuge of neutral colours, and . . . our fear of disgusting the Northern powers' for the succour which the French navy received from the Baltic.[1] Even so it would be easy to exaggerate the impact of the armed neutrality. The fate of Britain ultimately depended on her admirals and her generals, and at the time when Europe seemed to be uniting against her, they appeared to be serving her well. The defeat of the Bourbon invasion attempt of 1779, the relief of Gibraltar, the success of Clinton and Cornwallis in the Carolinas, Rodney's spirited policy in the Caribbean, all did much to offset French successes in the West Indies and keep hopes alive at home. However, when defeat eventually came, it came as a result of the difficulty of fighting on too many fronts, against too many enemies. As George Washington remarked, sea power was the

[1] *Britain, Russia and the Armed Neutrality of 1780* by I. de Madariaga (London 1962), p. 385.

'casting-vote' in the American War.[1] For three years the navy struggled manfully, blundering at times, as off Ushant in 1778 when the Bourbon fleets averted destruction and again when the French Toulon fleet was allowed to reach the western Atlantic, but muddling through. However, the strain proved too much. As Sandwich pointed out, 'England till this time was never engaged in a war with the House of Bourbon thoroughly united, their naval forces unbroken, and having no other war or object to draw off their attention and resources'.[2] Disaster finally struck when as the result of a series of errors by overstretched naval commanders and uncharacteristic enterprise by a French admiral, a British general found himself surrounded by the enemy not only on land but at sea. It was Cornwallis's encirclement and surrender at Yorktown in October 1781 which brought Britain to her knees, and set the courts of Europe buzzing.

Yorktown, like Saratoga, had an impact far beyond its military significance. Though seven thousand troops were lost there remained another thirty thousand in North America, and the British still garrisoned New York, Halifax, Charleston, Savannah and St Augustine. None the less, Yorktown sapped the will to fight on; Lord North's exclamation on hearing of Cornwallis's surrender— 'Oh God! it is all over'—proved very apt.[3] By March 1782 the independent country gentlemen, on whom in the last resort the government had relied for the maintenance of its American policy, had abandoned their support for the continuance of the war and compelled North to leave office. Peace negotiations began almost as soon as a new cabinet, based on the opposition factions, had been formed. Despite Yorktown it was by no means the case that Britain now faced a Carthaginian peace. Though America was to all intents and purposes lost and orders for the evacuation of the last major garrisons on the coast already given, the game had not been thrown up elsewhere. France was in possession of several of the smaller British islands in the Caribbean as well as Minorca, and Spain had overrun West Florida, but this was the extent of Bourbon success.

[1] *The Diplomacy of the American Revolution* by S. F. Bemis (Bloomington 1967), p. 110.
[2] *The War for America, 1775-1783* by P. Mackesy (London 1964), p. 314.
[3] ibid., p. 435.

Admittedly British policy at the negotiations looked as if it were to be gravely damaged by divisions within the cabinet. The acrimonious disputes between Fox, who as the new style Foreign Secretary would be in charge of negotiations with France, Spain and Holland, and Shelburne, who as Colonial Secretary was technically responsible for those with the rebel colonies, threatened to shatter any co-ordinated strategy to the diplomatic battle approaching at Paris. However, by July Shelburne, aided by the death of the nominal head of the cabinet, Lord Rockingham, and by the clear support of George III, had driven his opponent from office and imposed a coherent pattern on policy. Moreover the position of Britain's opponents after Yorktown was far from enviable. The alliance of the rebels with France and Spain was already showing cracks which with ingenuity and effort might be worked into gaping chasms. Congress was concerned first and foremost with independence and exclusively North American problems; in the aggrandisement of the Bourbons the Americans had no real interest. France, on the other hand, was by no means a disinterested onlooker. Vergennes and Louis XVI had fought to weaken Britain, not to erect a mighty new power across the Atlantic, and looked with a jaundiced eye on the ambitions of Congress in Canada and on the Mississippi. Spain was even more concerned to restrict the activities of the American rebels and more-over had ambitions at Gibraltar and in the Gulf of Mexico, which seemed likely to prolong the war and embarrass the French. Above all, the high hopes which Madrid and Versailles entertained of their arms were to be sadly disappointed. Thanks largely to the efforts of the North ministry in its last months, the final points in the war were marked up to Britain. Gibraltar, so vital to the Spaniards, was impregnable against one final and massive attack launched in September 1782. In India the vigorous attempts of Suffren and Bussy to resurrect French power on the Coromandel Coast were foiled. But most important of all, in the West Indies Rodney won the naval victory which Britain had so badly needed since 1778. The Battle of the Saints, in April 1782, was not a very great victory, but it was a sufficient one, and Rodney had some justification for assuring Sandwich 'You may now despise all your enemies'.[1]

[1] *The War for America, 1775–1783* by P. Mackesy (London 1964), p. 459.

Jamaica was saved and the danger of France and Spain sweeping the board in the western Atlantic, as Britain had done in the Seven Years' War, over.

After almost a year of negotiations, mainly in Paris, the peace preliminaries were signed, with the Americans in November 1782, with France and Spain in January 1783. The definitive peace treaties were signed still later in September 1783, though without significant modifications. The Dutch, ignominiously relegated to the role of observers while France and Britain bargained over the fate of their empire, were able to postpone their own settlement only until May 1784. It was inevitable that the peace terms would be contentious in Britain, where national humiliation was something that had to be re-learned after a long period of national arrogance. Even in retro-spect they are capable of varied interpretation. Perhaps understandably American historians have been tempted to see the final settlement as a great triumph for Franklin and his colleagues, a diplomatic lesson administered to the old world by the new.[1] This is a curious view. Independence was achieved on the battlefield, not in the peace negotiations. Though there was much haggling throughout over the precise timing of Britain's recognition of the thirteen colonies as the United States of America, that issue was never in doubt; it had been settled in March 1782. Nor is there much to admire in the activi-ties of Franklin and his colleagues. Thanks to their anxiety, much increased by John Jay's inexperience, to reach an early settlement of the question of independence, they sold a major diplomatic pass in making what amounted to a separate peace with Britain, disobeying the instructions of Congress to work in harness with Vergennes, and dangerously isolating themselves from their French allies. Nor did they make the best of the subordinate points at issue. It is clear that the British cabinet, intent on dividing its enemies, would actually have made much greater concessions, particularly in the matter of Canada's boundaries for example. It was the precipitate action of Jay and his fellow commissioners which enabled Shelburne to make terms well below what the government in London was actually ready to grant. This is not to argue that the terms were not generous to the colonies. On the contrary Shelburne was to fall, and his peace

[1] See, for example, *The Peacemakers* by R. B. Morris (New York 1965).

preliminaries were initially to be rejected by Parliament because to a resentful public opinion in Britain they seemed positively charitable. The boundary of Canada was defined so as gratuitously to renounce the Old North West and give Congress territories which were to become the heart of the prosperous Mid-West in the nineteenth century. Fishing rights were conceded off Newfoundland, old British debts were inadequately secured, and above all the loyalists received only the earnest recommendation of Congress to the States that they should be adequately treated and compensated, a farce which was quickly exposed after the Peace. Yet these terms, in so far as they were to the advantage of the new republic, were scarcely to the credit of America's negotiators. They sprang largely from the attitude and approach of the premier, Lord Shelburne.

Shelburne remains one of the most remarkable and also unfathomable of eighteenth-century statesmen. Nothing was more typical of his liberal concern with new and fashionable argument on the one hand, and his disregard for practical politics and pragmatic calculations on the other, than his policy in the negotiations of 1782-83. He had never favoured the renunciation of sovereignty over the colonies, and was brought to it only with the greatest difficulty. As late as August 1782, for example, he was expressing the fatuous hope that the Americans might accept comparable status in the British empire to that of Ireland.[1] Even when he recognised the need to grant independence, he made it his aim to produce such a settlement that the Anglo-American connection would remain a tangible reality. In his vague schemes, he envisaged common citizenship, reciprocal trading arrangements in accordance with the new ideas of economic pundits, a partnership in the exploitation of the American continent, even ultimately a federal union with Britain. A few thousand square miles in the area of the Great Lakes, a few furs in the Ohio Valley, a few fishing rights off Newfoundland, these were not to be weighed in the balance with such prospects. Nor did he see any point in putting every conceivable pressure on the American negotiators, for example by utilising the hints of Vergennes and Rayneval that France herself would not be averse to cooperating in

[1] *The Founding of the Second British Empire, 1763-1793* by V. T. Harlow (London 1952, 1964), i, p. 267.

order to diminish the aspirations of the Americans. For his progressive schemes Shelburne doubtless deserves much credit; with historians, it is important to be on the side of the future, and Shelburne's stock almost stands higher today than that of the Younger Pitt, who had many of the same ideas but also dealt in realities. Unfortunately for Shelburne contemporaries were more concerned with the present than the future. When the Peace Preliminaries came before the House of Commons they were censured, and with them the ambitious plans for Anglo-American commercial cooperation which had been drawn up. Ultimately there was no choice but to accept the substantive settlement of 1782, but for the moment M.P.s were determined to show their feelings towards Shelburne's handiwork. Neither in Britain nor in America were men ready for his concepts. Shelburne paid for his mistake by losing power. Canadians may even feel they paid for it with the loss of their natural hinterland.

Where his visionary notions had less relevance, as in the negotiations with France and Spain, Shelburne produced a fair and reasonable settlement; indeed even his opponents in the House of Commons found it impossible to criticise it at all effectively. Given the strategic stalemate in most theatres of the war France could not hope to achieve her basic aim of overturning the Peace of Paris, though gains were made. The French share of the Newfoundland fisheries was improved, the British West Indian island of Tobago ceded, the old French possessions on the Senegal restored, and a nominal and insignificant cession in India made. For the rest, captured territories were mutually restored. The British had hoped to make a substantial gain at the expense of Holland, but Vergennes's refusal to join in the partition of the Dutch empire enabled him to resist British demands for all but the minor settlement of Negapatam in India and the right to navigate, though not to trade, in the Dutch East Indies. The greatest difficulty in these negotiations involved Spain rather than France. For the court of Charles III it seemed that Gibraltar was a *sine qua non*. Perhaps surprisingly neither George III nor his ministers objected to a cession on satisfactory terms, though some members of the cabinet, notably Richmond, raised vociferous objections. There was a case for renouncing Gibraltar; neither its strategic nor trading potential had been realised effectively in the preceding eighty years. None the less the arguments were nicely balanced, and whatever its limitations Gibraltar had certainly acquired a place in the public affection. For George III Gibraltar was 'this proud fortress . . . in my opinion source of another war, or at least of a constant lurking enmity'. But for the public it was 'the Golden Image of English Idolatry'.[1] The surrender of Gibraltar would unquestionably have been acutely unpopular, especially after its courageous defence against every enemy assault, and it may have been as well that it did not go through. Various equivalents were considered and eventually Vergennes was able to bring the ministers at Madrid to accept peace without Gibraltar. Instead they received Minorca and the Floridas.

Both sides chose to interpret the peace terms of 1783 as a victory. Rayneval, Vergennes's right-hand man, considered that Britain had been 'plucked like a chicken', while Henry Strachey, one of the British negotiators, described the peace as 'the best that could have been made'.[2] However, some of the more militant at home felt that Britain should have fought on against the Bourbons once America had been detached. It was a nice point whether Britain or France was the more exhausted; on both sides of the Channel the ministers most involved in finding the money, as opposed to those employed in spending it, prophesied national bankruptcy if a further campaign had to be maintained in 1783. Shelburne himself alleged that the Royal Navy was not in a fit state to continue, though it is difficult to believe that he did not exaggerate. In any event it is doubtful whether the game was worth the candle. As it was, the terms of 1783 were scarcely a major setback for Britain apart from the independence of the American colonies. Had it been a question of restoring the French to the position they had held in India in 1755, as Louis XVI's ministers sought, or of surrendering Jamaica and Gibraltar, then a further grim campaign or two might have been possible. But Shelburne was probably right in arguing that there was little point

[1] *Gibraltar in British Diplomacy in the Eighteenth Century* by S. Conn (New Haven 1942), pp. 231, 256.
[2] *The Diplomacy of the American Revolution* by S. F. Bemis (Bloomington 1967), p. 252; *The Founding of the Second British Empire, 1763–1793* by V. T. Harlow (London 1952, 1964), i, p. 297.

in prolonging the strain of world war in order to retake West Florida, Tobago and Minorca, or to seize portions of the Dutch empire.

In retrospect it is possible to see that the Peace of Versailles was nothing like the disaster predicted beforehand and even imagined at the time by some. Many of the assumptions made in the American War were later demonstrated to be false. Not least was this true of the original object of the war, the subordination of America. Lord George Germain had not been alone in his belief that 'we can never continue to exist as a great or powerful nation after we have lost or renounced the sovereignty of America'.[1] This was one thing agreed on both sides of the Atlantic. Thus, Tom Paine had complained that America was 'the make-weight in the scale of British politics'.[2] Yet America's liberation did not in the event destroy Britain as a great power, partly because the imperialism of the mid-eighteenth century had simply exaggerated the benefits of the thirteen colonies, partly because the rise of industrial power in Britain was amply to compensate for the disintegration of the old economic structure of the empire. The real significance of the Treaty of Versailles arguably lay in quite different directions. For example, the peace was essentially a western European matter. The diplomatic proprieties were preserved by permitting Austria and Russia to appear as 'mediators' in the peace treaties, but to all intents and purposes the war and the peace had confirmed that drifting apart of western and eastern powers which had become discernible in the 1760s. For the first time in the eighteenth century a major war had been fought without involving central or eastern Europe, and while the powers of the west had all in some degree been weakened, those of the east seemed more menacing than ever. Again, there had appeared in the negotiations a new and important issue. For the first time the Dutch empire was seriously threatened. Though Holland did not lose either the Cape of Good Hope which France had occupied, nor Ceylon which the British had taken for a while, it was clear that both powers were preparing to take an interest in the fate of the Dutch seaborne empire.

[1] *The War for America, 1775–1783* by P. Mackesy (London 1964), pp. 460–1.
[2] *The Diplomacy of the American Revolution* by S. F. Bemis (Bloomington 1967), p. 12.

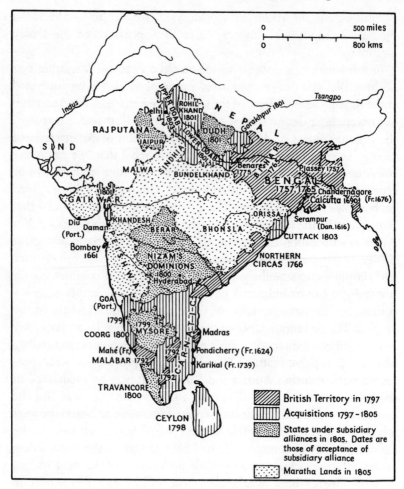

Map 6. The Growth of British Power in India

Finally a particularly intriguing possibility began to appear. Both
Vergennes and Shelburne were thinking, once the fate of the
American colonies was settled, in terms of a major recasting of
Anglo-French relations. That regrouping, involving a new alliance
such as might counter the growing threat from the east, presented
particularly by the unexpected Austro-Russian treaty of 1781, was

not merely a speculative possibility. Not the least significant of the terms stipulated at Versailles was provision for a commercial treaty to be negotiated between the two powers on the lines of the celebrated but abortive proposals of St John seventy years before. In this, it might be thought, lay the germs of a new diplomatic revolution.

PART 5

The Importance
of Europe, 1783–1815

tonight

13 The End of Isolation, 1783–91

By the time the last of the peace treaties, that with the Dutch, had been signed, government was in the hands of the Younger Pitt. Shelburne was destroyed by Parliament, the Fox–North coalition by the king himself, and it remained for the son of Chatham to be tested. Though it was not appreciated at the time Pitt's emergence was to have tremendous consequences, not least in the sphere of foreign policy. Between the news of Yorktown and the completion of the peace settlement, George III had been served by no less than five ministries, and it was understandable that foreign observers should be sceptical about the prospects of a young and untried politician, whose only asset seemed to be his father's reputation and the king's support. Moreover it was generally believed, not altogether unjustly, that the new minister would be amply occupied by his pressing commitments at home, and indeed Pitt himself made no secret of the fact that his primary concern at least initially lay in the direction of financial recovery and retrenchment after an exhausting and damaging war. Even so he was to surprise the chancelleries of Europe. He was to remain Prime Minister for almost the rest of his life, longer than any of his predecessors with the exception of Walpole, and was to bring to British foreign policy a firmness and consistency which it had long wanted. By 1786 he was playing a vital role in the conduct of relations with other states, drafting official despatches, corresponding directly with key envoys abroad and overriding both Foreign Secretary and king. The former, Carmarthen, soon became known to the foreign ministers of other nations as 'Pitt's puppet',[1] and the latter allowed himself to be guided by Pitt's opinion even

[1] *Recueil des Instructions données aux Ambassadeurs et Ministres de France*, xxv–2, ed. P. Vaucher (Paris 1965), p. 552.

against his own better judgement. But Pitt chose his lieutenants well. Despite the deficiencies of Carmarthen, the men who actually carried out the directions of the cabinet were an impressive group. Sir James Harris, a friend of Fox whom Pitt none the less entrusted with the conduct of relations with Holland, was by any standards a brilliant diplomat as well as an experienced one. Though he was not disposed to undervalue himself, neither were others; Talleyrand considered him the ablest British diplomat of the age and certainly his achievement at the Hague was to sustain such a judgement. William Eden, later Lord Auckland, was also plucked from opposition by Pitt, though in his case, that of a prominent leader of the Foxites, the conversion was truly sensational. Whatever his political morality he was to prove a capable diplomat and certainly Britain's most effective commercial negotiator of the period. William Grenville, Pitt's cousin and friend, was no less important. In his role as adviser, as a kind of roving diplomat, despatched for example on special missions to the Hague and Versailles in 1787, and eventually as Carmarthen's successor at the Foreign Office, he was enormously influential. With the aid of such men, Pitt was to rebuild British prestige and power to heights which it had not attained since 1763, though in a manner and by means which might not have been predicted.

It might have been supposed for example, that the new minister would prove eager to build on the foundations laid by Shelburne, his father's friend and his own political mentor. Shelburne had looked to a rosy future in which Britain would live in amiable association with both her transatlantic cousins and her continental neighbours, bound together by the cement of commercial harmony. At least in private he liked to boast that the treaties of peace were dominated by the 'great principle of free trade, which inspires them from end to end'.[1] Pitt himself had introduced the abortive commercial concessions to the former colonies in the House of Commons, and was known to be a disciple of Adam Smith. None the less, in practice he was to prove a realist. This was clearly demonstrated at an early stage in relations with the newly independent American republic.

[1] *The Founding of the Second British Empire, 1763–1793* by V. T. Harlow (London 1952, 1964), 2 vols., i, p. 448.

The preamble to the peace treaty between Britain and the United States made specific provision for the establishment of 'such a beneficial and satisfactory intercourse between the two Countries upon the Ground of reciprocal Advantages and mutual Commerce as may promote and secure to both perpetual Peace and Harmony'.[1] However, in the early years of the Pitt ministry this pious intention was conveniently forgotten. David Hartley, the envoy whom the Fox–North administration had despatched to Paris to negotiate a trade agreement with the American peace commissioners, was recalled, and the persistent demands of John Adams, the first American ambassador in London, for the promised negotiations ignored. It was made brutally clear in a series of Orders-in-Council and statutes that the Americans were to expect nothing which could not be justified entirely on the grounds of imperial interest. Though American raw materials were allowed into Britain, and some American provisions permitted to go to the West Indies and Newfoundland, in each case because they were essential for the purposes of empire, the erstwhile colonists were not permitted to carry on an unrestricted trade in their own ships. Similarly the Navigation Act of 1786 killed any hope that the primacy of the British shipping interest would in any way be allowed to fade into the background. It is not difficult to criticise the measures of the government in this area. Smuggling was so rife in the Caribbean and the enforcement of the British restrictions so difficult that in practice they had limited effect. Moreover they were infinitely damaging to Anglo-American relations. There were of course, other issues; the regrettable failure of the United States to meet their commitments in the peace treaty in connection with mercantile debts and the treatment of loyalists, was sufficient to justify the refusal of Britain either to send an ambassador to the States or to evacuate the forests of the Old North-West. However, British obstinacy over trade severely soured relations between the two countries, and it was not until 1791 with the threat of American counter-measures, and the blandishments of the anglophile Alexander Hamilton in Washington and Gouverneur Morris in London, that the court of George III sent a representative across the Atlantic

[1] *Great Britain and the United States* by H. C. Allen (London 1954), p. 257.

and began to talk seriously, if inconclusively, about commercial agreement. Had the economic issues been settled amicably after the signature of the peace treaties, relations between the former colonies and mother country would surely have been different.

On the other hand it is easy enough to follow the logic of Pitt and his colleagues. For one thing there seemed little point in giving way to American demands on the score of the carrying trade, when it seemed clear that Congress had little pressure to bring to bear. In the 1780s trade between the British and Americans once again soared and as a market for British manufactures the United States seemed even more capacious than the thirteen colonies. France, amply encouraged both by American and French politicians to compete, did so to little effect. The British embassy secretary in Paris, Daniel Hailes, rejoiced that 'Notwithstanding the very heavy load of taxes, and the consequent high rise of the price of all sorts of provisions in England, we still continue to furnish America with every necessary article of life, and at a cheaper rate and of a better kind than the French can possibly do'.[1] In fact the main result of Franco-American amity in the years following the alliance of 1778 was that Americans sold to the French to obtain currency with which to purchase English manufactures. This, for the British, comforting supremacy naturally led government in London to see little danger in the possibility of American opposition. Gouverneur Morris, sent to England in 1790 to make overtures to the ministers, reported back that they 'consider a treaty of commerce with America as being absolutely unnecessary and that they are persuaded they shall derive all benefit from our trade without treaty'.[2] There were in any case other considerations. The American War itself seemed to point to the dangers of commercial conciliation. Readiness to concede independence had been reluctant at best and anti-Americanism, which was rife in these years, could plausibly be expressed in a reversion to the notion of a strong and strictly controlled mercantilist empire from which the rebels must be excluded. If America was to be given

[1] *Despatches from Paris, 1784–1790* ed. O. Browning (London 1909–10. 2 vols.), i, p. 39. See J. Godechot, 'Les relations économiques entre la France et les Etats-Unis de 1778 a 1789' in *French Historical Studies*, i, (1958), pp. 26–39.

[2] *Great Britain and the United States* by H. C. Allen (London 1954), p. 271.

the privileged status she had enjoyed as a colony, how would it be possible to prevent the rest of the empire disintegrating? Moreover national defence was important. The war had been lost largely through failure to maintain naval supremacy; all the more important was it then to ensure an ample supply of trained seamen, nurtured by a reassertion of the ancient Navigation Acts, for any future conflict. Arguments such as these were deployed in their most sophisticated form, for example, by Lord Sheffield in his pamphlet assault on Shelburne's scheme for commercial cooperation of 1783, and by Charles Jenkinson, a strong mercantilist, in his unremitting attention to commercial legislation and negotiation thereafter. But they were also deeply representative of views in and out of Parliament. Even the well-disposed Fox–North ministry had failed to carry through a policy of commercial liberalism with regard to the Americans; it need not be surprising that Pitt declined to do so.

In appearance at least Pitt's ministry was more flexible in trade negotiations with other nations. The 1780s witnessed a remarkable series of negotiations—'the present Rage for Commercial Treaties', Carmarthen called it[1]—not merely with France and Spain, which had both been promised such discussions in the peace treaties of 1783, but with many others, with Portugal, with Russia, with Sweden, with Turkey, with the Austrian Netherlands, with the Two Sicilies. The day of Adam Smith, it might seem, had arrived with the coming to power of Pitt. On closer examination however this appearance turns out to be misleading. For one thing almost all these negotiations were far from fruitful. Protracted bargaining with Spain, Portugal and Russia eventually broke down, as did that with the lesser powers. The initiative only came from London in three cases and in all Whitehall showed a greater concern for a businesslike concentration on British interests than an abstract enthusiasm for a new liberalism in international trade. In one case, that of Russia, there were also aggravating and humiliating circumstances. Twice before, in 1734 and 1766, Britain had reached advantageous trade agreements with Russia, and failure to renew these in 1786 was

[1] *The British Government and Commercial Negotiations with Europe, 1783–1793*, by J. H. Ehrman (Cambridge 1962), p. 185.

rubbed in by the success of France in negotiating a commercial treaty with Russia in 1787. Nor was Pitt's one really successful negotiation all that it seemed. The Eden Treaty with France, signed in the first instance in September 1786, was undoubtedly beneficial, opening the French market as it did to British manufactured goods, without exposing British silks to French competition or sacrificing the Portuguese wine trade to French vineyards. However, the pressure for the treaty had come more from Versailles than from London; indeed Pitt had only been brought to the negotiating table by the threat of French protectionist measures. Though French merchants and manufacturers were later, without much foundation, to blame the treaty for their economic difficulties in 1788 and 1789, it was as much a triumph for Vergennes, who envisaged it partly as a diplomatic and political weapon, and partly as a victory for French agriculture, as for Pitt and Eden. There were other similarly deceptive manoeuvres in these years. The agreement in 1786 with Spain, which went some way towards resolving the traditional hostility of the two powers in central America, was not to lead to a new era of amicable cooperation. The much acclaimed missions to China by Cathcart in 1787 and Macartney in 1792 were largely abortive, thanks to the premature death of Cathcart and the failure of Macartney to make a significant impression in Peking. The appointment of a Consul-General in Egypt turned out scarcely to be worth the money spent on it, while the ambitious negotiations with the Dutch, which aimed at a major adjustment of Anglo–Dutch relations in the Far East and would greatly have benefited British traders there, broke down despite the frantic efforts of Eden to repeat his success in Paris. It would, of course, be a mistake to claim that Pitt's commercial diplomacy was of no consequence at all. There was undoubtedly a readiness with proper safeguards to negotiate on the basis of reciprocity. But there was no great diplomatic and commercial offensive, nor a progressive scheme such as Shelburne might have attempted. In the last analysis Pitt was a hard-headed patriot, not a visionary idealist.

This was also demonstrated in the first of the major diplomatic crises with which Pitt had to deal, in the United Provinces; the outcome of that crisis was an international triumph such as Britain had not experienced at least since the 1750s, and the emergence of the English court from two decades of isolation. It was all the more welcome in that it followed what seemed to be a series of substantial victories for Versailles. French recovery after the disasters of the Seven Years' War, thrown into relief by Britain's loss of her American colonies, seemed to have been confirmed and strengthened in a number of ways. France and the United Provinces, or rather the States-General, had moved ever closer since the Anglo-Dutch war of 1780 and by November 1785 a full scale alliance had taken place; Holland, so long the friend of England, had at last been seduced by the allurements of the French. Moreover Vergennes adroitly contrived to prevent the tension currently developing between his Austrian ally, Joseph II, and his Dutch friends, producing open war, without alienating either. Joseph's attempts to open the Scheldt and to exchange the Austrian Netherlands for Bavaria, both totally unacceptable to the Hague, were foiled and Austro-Dutch disputes adjusted with the mediation of France in a treaty of November 1785. British attempts, such as they were, to fish in these troubled waters were utterly unsuccessful, and the stage seemed set for the complete triumph in the United Provinces of the puppets of France, the total humiliation of the House of Orange, traditionally the foundation of the British interest at the Hague, and the permanent accession of Holland to the French camp.

Yet within two years the situation had been completely reversed. In September 1787 Frederick William II of Prussia, brother of the Princess of Orange, and the British government, jointly intervened in Holland to establish William of Orange in power and destroy their enemies. The whole affair was a model of military and diplomatic coordination. For Britain, Sir James Harris at the Hague proved brilliantly effective as a focus for Orangist and anti-French feeling, and as the agent of Anglo-Prussian cooperation. In London Pitt moved carefully and deliberately to an overwhelmingly powerful position, supplying Harris with money and promises, converting a reluctant George III to his way of thinking, and finally mobilising British forces in a dazzling piece of brinkmanship. The French bluff was sternly called. France 'must, as things stand', Pitt declared, 'give up in effect their predominant influence in the Republic, or they must determine to *fight for it*'.[1] The court of Louis XVI wriggled on the hook, but was powerless, trapped by its own divisions and contradictions in dealing with its agents at the Hague, and betrayed by its own absurdity in promising the Dutch aid which it could not afford and did not have. At the critical moment in September 1787, when Prussian troops crossed the Dutch border to crush the internal enemies of the House of Orange, the French claim to have a great force poised for counter-measures at Govet, near the frontier, was exposed as the fraud it was. In Holland the pro-French patriots were smashed and the powers of the Stadholder restored, and in France the government was compelled to sign a declaration disowning the activities of its erstwhile agents and disclaiming any desire to meddle in Dutch affairs. For the French it was a substantial defeat and one which they had quite failed to anticipate. The mortification at Versailles was reflected in the remarks made in the official instructions to the ambassador in London in January 1788. 'The unforeseen conduct of the British Government with regard to the disturbances in the United Provinces has totally destroyed the calculations which were made on the basis of Mr Pitt's character and England's needs, and completely overturned the notions entertained of the principles and policy of that minister'.[2]

Not the least of the consequences of the Dutch crisis was the emergence of Britain from its isolation. The preliminary treaty with Prussia, which with Anglo-Dutch and Prusso-Dutch agreements already signed, constituted the new Triple Alliance, was drawn up at Loo in June 1788, and the definitive alliance in Berlin in the following August. According to Harris, it was only his own adept handling of the anti-British party among the Prussians, and his expert wooing of Frederick William II at a midnight masquerade in Loo, which brought about this alliance. But for his expertise, he boasted, 'we should have been reduced to the *same isolated situation* we stood in some time ago'.[3] In fact the events of 1787 clearly

---

[1] *Ambassadors and Secret Agents* by A. Cobban (London 1954), p. 183.

[2] *Receuil des Instructions données aux Ambassadeurs et Ministres de France*, xxv—2, ed. P. Vaucher (Paris 1965), p. 541.

[3] *Diaries and Correspondence of the First Earl of Malmesbury* ed. 3rd Earl (London 1844, 4 vols.), ii, p. 428.

pointed towards alliance and it is difficult to believe that Prussian compliance was so hard to win. In any event the end of isolation was a momentous landmark for Britain. Ever since 1763 the makers of foreign policy had sought an alliance in Europe on acceptable terms. Pitt's ministry had not differed in this respect. Carmarthen had made overtures not merely to Prussia, but to Austria and Russia almost as soon as taking office. Hopes of Joseph II had been particularly high but had been wrecked by George III's independent action as Elector of Hanover in joining the German league which opposed Joseph's schemes for obtaining Bavaria. Pitt and his colleagues were not consulted in the matter, and frankly considered that the king had 'got into a damned scrape'.[1] The whole episode was a reminder that the ambiguities involved in the King of England's continental and personal possessions had not entirely been dissipated by the accession of a king who 'gloried in the name of Briton'.

Expectations entertained of the new alliance in London were amply fulfilled in the event. From 1788 to 1791 the Triple Alliance played a central role in European diplomacy, and gave to Britain in particular a degree of influence in the affairs of the Continent which it had long lacked. Few alliances work equally to the advantage of each party and it was a striking fact that in the Anglo-Prussian joint actions it was the influence of Whitehall which had the upper hand. There was indeed a significant difference of emphasis in the way London and Berlin regarded their cooperation. Both wished to play a prominent part in the series of crises and emergencies which characterised the late 1780s, but for quite different reasons. Carmarthen saw the two powers as 'contributing by their joint efforts towards the maintenance of the general tranquillity of Europe, and the accommodation of those particular disputes which have unhappily arisen in the Eastern and Northern parts of the continent'.[2] Prussia on the other hand had considerations other than the general good in mind. Thus when Joseph II and his successor Leopold found themselves in difficulties both in the war with Turkey, a war begun by Russo-Turkish friction, and with internal insurgents within the empire, Prussia naturally sought to exploit these embarrassments.

[1] *The Younger Pitt: The Years of Acclaim* by J. H. Ehrman (London 1969), p. 474.
[2] *British Diplomatic Instructions, 1689–1789* (Camden Soc.), vii, p. 303.

In particular when the rebellious Belgian provinces sought independence of the Habsburgs and appealed to the Triple Alliance for assistance, Frederick William favoured intervention in their interest. Yet it was the British view, a view which preferred a weak and semi-autonomous Austrian Netherlands to a fragile and potentially francophile Belgian state, which prevailed. In the matter of the Eastern question, Berlin was still more belligerent. Treaties were made both with the Porte and Poland in 1790 with the clear intention of going to war against Vienna if necessary. Either by war or diplomacy Frederick William was intent on preventing Austrian gains at the expense of Turkey and above all on forcing Leopold to yield up Galicia to the Poles and so enable Poland to surrender Danzig and Thorn to Prussia. With these involved schemes the court of George III had little sympathy. Anything that increased the Prussian stranglehold on the Polish economy or which tended to upset the balance between the Germanic powers was deplored in London. Again, when the moment of truth came at Reichenbach in July 1790 it was the British line which won the day; despite the enormous pressure brought to bear by the Prussian diplomats, the empire of Leopold was preserved, and indeed subsequently strengthened slightly at the cost of the Porte in the Peace of Sistova a year later, much to the chagrin of Frederick William.

The high point of British recovery in the decade following the American War was reached in 1790 with the Nootka Sound crisis. Like the War of Jenkins' Ear and the affair of the Falkland Islands, the Nootka Sound episode was a typical example of the tension which results when a decaying but not dead empire confronts an aggressive and enterprising commercial power. When news filtered through in the early months of 1790 that Spanish officials had uprooted a base engaged in exploiting the growing fur and fish trade of the north Pacific at Nootka Sound, on the grounds that the navigation and settlement of the entire Pacific coast of America were their exclusive preserve, another great dispute was inevitable. Yet the British case was not as strong as many in London liked to imagine. John Meares, the leader of the British expedition involved, paid scant regard to truth in his reports to the government and his publicity in the press; in particular it was not true that what was at risk was an ancient settlement gratuitously torn up by the Spaniards. However, an issue which combined the expansion of British trade and navigation and traditional Hispanophobia, was not one which any ministry could neglect. At the height of the crisis in May Britain was busily engaged in overt preparations for war. The navy was mobilised and a general press ordered; Parliament was asked for a large vote of credit, and a great diplomatic offensive launched. Prussia and the United Provinces were forthcoming with aid under the Triple Alliance, the former with a promise of land forces in the event of war, the latter with ten ships of the line. In France and in the United States Pitt's agents sought to ensure the preservation of neutrality. In the face of Britain's clear readiness to go to war, and Pitt's evident diplomatic superiority, Spain could not hold out for long. Though some of his colleagues were ready to go to war regardless, Floridablanca signed a convention in October, which while allowing for some saving of Spanish face provided redress for the original damage inflicted on Meares' ships and settlement, and effectively gave the British an *entrée* both to the coast from Northern California to Alaska, and to the fisheries of the Pacific and South Seas. Though Pitt and his contemporaries overrated the economic gains involved, the Nootka Sound crisis was striking testimony to the vigour of British diplomacy and the power of the Triple Alliance.

Understandably historians have seen these years as a remarkable recovery for George III and his ministers, years it has been alleged of 'hegemony' in Europe. At the time British diplomats were themselves intoxicated by the power which they suddenly found entrusted to them. Harris talked grandly of negotiating a new Treaty of Westphalia which would give peace and stability to a war-torn Europe. In the north Hugh Elliot, the envoy to Copenhagen, found that British prestige was such that he could mediate peace between Sweden and Denmark, rival the influence of Prussia, and preserve the King of Sweden by scarcely lifting a finger, and all without the actual authority of London. It would be absurd to deny that Britain enjoyed in these years a degree of power and influence on the Continent for which Whitehall had long sought in vain. None the less, there are qualifications to be made. For one thing, the extent of Britain's emergence from gloom and defeat was partly a result of a diplomatic illusion. The depths of defeat and humiliation in and after the American War had been grossly exaggerated, both in Britain and on the Continent. Joseph II for example had hardly been justified in describing the British as a second-rate power. Similarly Frederick II, in informing Carmarthen's envoy at Berlin that Europe was totally dominated and Britain hopelessly hemmed in by a great alliance of France, Spain, Russia and Austria, took no account of the actual differences which lay below the surface between Vienna and Moscow on the one hand, and Paris and Madrid on the other. As has been seen, the terms of the peace of 1783 had been deeply annoying to the court of George III but they did not represent a masive alteration in the balance of power as had, for example, those of the Peace of Utrecht or the Peace of Paris.

If Pitt had a stronger base from which to work than many contemporaries realised, it was also the case that he was substantially assisted by the circumstances which prevailed in the Europe of the late 1780s. The fortuitous death of Frederick II in August 1786, for example, was a great stroke of good fortune for Whitehall. It brought to the throne of Prussia a king whose instability and even stupidity made him a very different proposition from his uncle. It is difficult to believe that Frederick II would have taken the risks involved in the Prussian military intervention in the United Provinces in 1787, or joined in the Triple Alliance, or once that alliance was made, permitted Pitt and his colleagues to dictate the joint policy of the powers. Yet without all these measures on the part of Prussia, Pitt would have been quite incapable of exercising the influence he did. Both in the Dutch crisis and in the Nootka Sound affair the threat of Prussian military action and a continental war was at least as alarming to the Bourbon powers as was the menace of British naval mobilisation. The British did not normally favour a Prussian alliance; indeed throughout the late eighteenth century British diplomats tended, for reasons which are far from obvious, to prefer a return to the old alliance of Austria. In these circumstances the alliance of Prussia was an unexpected and certainly unmerited bonus, a gratuitous piece of fortune which much strengthened the British position.

Equally fortuitous from the British standpoint, yet equally to their advantage, was the temporary collapse of France as a significant diplomatic force during these years. The progressive onset of financial disaster and political disintegration worked greatly to the benefit of Pitt's policy between 1787 and 1791. Vergennes' death alone, which took place early in 1787, deprived French foreign policy of one of its most successful directors in the eighteenth century. Yet even Vergennes could scarcely have sidestepped the troubles of the later 1780s and it may be that his death saved him from humiliation in Holland, humiliation which his successor Montmorin was instead compelled to undergo. The effects of the French political and financial crisis between 1787 and 1789 were manifold. In the Dutch affair for example, the French diplomatic effort was crippled by the political chaos surrounding the summons of the Assembly of the Notables. When William Grenville went to Paris in August 1787 to size up the situation there before Pitt finally committed himself to action in the United Provinces, Pitt noted that 'the extreme disorder of the French finances (which the proceedings of the Notables had disclosed to the world) and the unsettled state of their government since the death of M. de Vergennes made it very improbable that they would hazard a step which might tend to commit them with other powers'.[1] It was at almost the same time that a major diplomatic opportunity was missed elsewhere. In 1787 the French successfully negotiated a commercial treaty with Russia which put Britain's nose more than slightly out of joint. It was reasonable to assume that a full scale alliance would follow, and there is no question that from 1787 to 1789 that alliance was France's for the asking. Yet thanks to the instability and divisions of French government, and in particular to the disagreements between Montmorin and Necker, the chance was missed. The situation was not improved in the year of the Revolution. By October 1789 Eden was predicting that France would be 'very interesting as to its interior, but probably for a long period of little importance with regard to its external, politics'.[2] The sheer disorganisation of the early years of the Revolution hit foreign policy particularly hard because it was one area which clearly remained

---

[1] J. H. Rose, 'The Missions of William Grenville to the Hague and Versailles in 1787' in *Eng. Hist. Rev.*, xxlv (1909), p. 282.

[2] *The Cambridge History of British Foreign Policy, 1783–1919* ed. Sir A. W. Ward and G. P. Gooch (Cambridge 1922), i, p. 190.

within the competence of the monarchy and yet which could not be run effectively without the help of its opponents. In addition there was, at any rate briefly, that idealism which as the British embassy staff in Paris observed, required that 'all ideas of National grandeur, beyond what was to be acquired by trade and commerce, were to be relinquished as being vain and beneath the consideration of a Nation naturally so great and now free'.[1] In the Nootka Sound crisis this combination of factors was enough to shatter the Family Compact as a major diplomatic force. Though Mirabeau talked of war and Pitt was sufficiently anxious to send a mysterious mission to Paris to work for neutrality, there was little chance that France would go to war to save Spain's unrealistic claims in the Pacific. As with the sudden friendliness of Prussia in these years, so with the unexpected collapse of the *ancien régime* in France, Pitt was extraordinarily fortunate and owed not a little of his remarkable success to the unpredicted and unpredictable.

Moreover the Triple Alliance was, whatever its benefits, not a panacea for Britain's problems, as was forcibly borne in upon Pitt in 1791. It was ironic that the greatest of Pitt's diplomatic successes, in the Nootka Sound affair, was quickly succeeded by a failure that clearly demonstrated both the limitations to which the Triple Alliance was subject and the extent to which its success had derived from circumstance. In the spring of 1791, in collaboration with Frederick William, the British cabinet issued an ultimatum to Catherine II, an ultimatum which required her to abandon her claim to the fortress of Ochakov, won from the Turks in December 1788, and to make peace with the Porte on the basis of the *status quo ante bellum*. Pitt acted with the firmness which he had demonstrated in the Dutch and Spanish crises; Parliament was informed and Catherine given clearly to understand that war with the Triple Alliance was inevitable unless she came to terms with Turkey on the basis agreed by the Convention of Reichenbach. Yet this time Pitt was humiliated. Within a matter of weeks the government had been compelled to withdraw its ultimatum and admit that Russia must be allowed to keep Ochakov. The cabinet had split, the Foreign

[1] *Despatches from Paris, 1784–1790* ed. O. Browning (London 1909–10. 2 vols), ii, p. 325.

Secretary had resigned, and the opposition had created a clamour such as Pitt had not previously had to suffer on matters of external policy. Above all, the Triple Alliance had been lastingly damaged by Britain's failure to support Prussia to the hilt, and the Pitt administration had suffered one of its most humiliating defeats.

It is easy to see that Pitt overreached himself. Though he felt that Russian aggrandisement had reached a point at which it must be contained if the European balance of power was not to be upset, and later commentators have not been wanting to point out that in so doing he was anticipating the Victorians, it was difficult for most of his contemporaries to see the point of war. British opinion was traditionally rather pro-Russian, and as Fox, himself a great champion of Catherine II remarked, Russia was 'a power whom we could neither attack, nor be attacked by; and this was the power against whom we were going to war'.[1] Moreover Ochakov and the relatively small amount of territory which went with it scarcely seemed the sticking-point which Pitt, urged on by the influential British envoy at Berlin, Joseph Ewart, desired to make it. According to Pitt and Ewart, it did hold the key to Poland's Black Sea trade route, a matter in which the government was becoming increasingly interested with the failure of Russia to continue its close trading relationship with Britain. Yet expert information, sparse though it was, suggested that this was not altogether so; in particular that which came from Dutch sources through Eden, the British ambassador to the Hague, flatly contradicted Ewart's assertion.

That Pitt was badly mistaken in his judgements in the Ochakov crisis is certainly confirmed by the evidence of the day. Whatever the later enthusiasm of armchair diplomats for his insight in detecting the menace of Russian power to British interests, at the time there can be no question that there would have been little support for a war for Ochakov. In part, of course, Pitt was repeating the tactics of brinkmanship with which he had defeated the French in the Dutch crisis of 1787 and the Spaniards in the Nootka Sound affair of 1790. In 1787 even the parliamentary opposition had been driven to engage themselves in support of Pitt's activities, so vital were the Low Countries considered to Britain's interest. Again in the affair of

[1] *Charles James Fox* by J. W. Derry (London 1972), p. 285.

Nootka Sound, jealousy of Spain and thirst for an empire of trade if not of dominion had raised a great popular force in Pitt's favour. It is worth quoting the description written by a visiting American, John Rutledge, of that jingoism which came over the Commons in the matter of Nootka Sound as it so often came over them where competition with the Bourbon powers overseas was concerned. 'As soon as the house rose I went amongst the members I was acquainted with, afterwards dined in company with others, and in my life I do not remember to have been amongst such insolent bullies. . . . They were all for war, talked much of *Old England* and the *british Lion*, laughed at the Idea of drubbing the Dons, began to calculate the millions of dollars they would be obliged to pay for having insulted the *first power on Earth*, and seemed uneasy lest the Spaniards should be alarmed at the british strength, ask pardon for what they had done, and come immediately to terms'.[1] This, the authentic tone of the British in war mood was totally lacking when the point at issue was a remote fortress in eastern Europe. There were indeed not merely vigorous opposition attacks on Pitt in Parliament, but a strong wave of public feeling, expressed even in the form of constituency instructions to M.P.s. Thus Eden in Holland was informed by a correspondent from London in May 1791, 'I assure you in and out of Parliament (and this is not to be understood as the ignorant account of an interested partisan), there is not a word urged by way of argument for the Russian war. The country throughout have told Mr. Pitt they will not go to war'.[2]

The lessons of the Ochakov crisis are several. In its way it represents the beginning of that Russophobia which was to be so marked a feature of prejudice and policy in the nineteenth century. Dundas was soon prophetically to remark that he was 'as an India minister not wishing the Turkish power in the hands of Russia'.[3] But no minister can force on Parliament and public a policy as remote and

[1] *Flood Tide of Empire: Spain in the Pacific North West, 1543–1819* by W. L. Cook (London 1973), pp. 213–14.

[2] *Journal and Correspondence of William Eden, Baron Auckland, from 1771 to 1814* (London 1861–62), ii, pp. 387–88.

[3] *Britain's Discovery of Russia, 1553–1815* by M. S. Anderson (London 1958) pp. 202–203.

repugnant as was Pitt's in the Ochakov crisis in 1791. When exerted on particular questions, public opinion, even under the unreformed system at its most unrepresentative, exercised a decisive influence. But the crisis also warned of the dangers of recent policy. For long the British had sought a way out of isolation; now they had it they found that there were penalties. For Prussia Britain's reaction in the Ochakov crisis was the last straw, and Harris (now Lord Malmesbury) had no doubt that Pitt indeed made a terrible mistake in climbing down. 'It has broken our continental system and let us down from that high situation in which we stood'.[1] Even so, it would be a mistake to exaggerate this argument. For by 1791 events were taking place on the Continent which were to make the Triple Alliance an irrelevance and create quite a new pattern, a pattern which was to dictate the course of British foreign policy for over two decades and drag the court of St James into a new era of continental entanglements.

[1] *Great Britain and Prussia in the Eighteenth Century* by Sir R. Lodge (Oxford 1923), p. 212.

14 The Impact of Revolution, 1791–1803

'Unquestionably there was never a time in the history of this country, when, from the situation of Europe, we might more reasonably expect fifteen years of peace than at the present moment'.[1] Thus Pitt reassured the House of Commons in February 1792, just one year before Britain was plunged into the revolutionary wars. At the time it seemed a safe enough statement, buttressed as it was by the international impotence which was the French Revolution's first legacy to France, and accompanied as it also was by a firm intention on Pitt's part to have nothing to do with intervention in the internal affairs of the French. Later on Frenchmen sought to depict Pitt and his colleagues as unwavering enemies of the Revolution, seeking initially to subvert it from within and eventually to destroy it from without. Nothing could have been further from the truth. The hysterical outbursts of Burke played no part in the calculations of George III's cabinet, and the notion of hordes of British secret agents at work in Paris during the Revolution was entirely mythical. George III himself was clear that non-intervention was the only possible policy. 'We have honourably not meddled with the internal dissensions of France,' he wrote in October 1790, 'and no object ought to drive us from that honourable ground'.[2] Even two years later when the appalling violence of the summer of 1792 and the full implications of the Revolution for the future of the Bourbon monarchy had begun to emerge, he would still not contemplate interference. 'Undoubtedly,' he told Grenville, 'there is no step that I should not willingly take for the personal safety of the French king and his family that does not draw this country into

[1] *William Pitt and the Great War* by J. H. Rose (London 1911), p. 32.
[2] *Cambridge Modern History*, viii, p. 291.

meddling with the internal disturbances of that ill-fated kingdom'.[1] This basic neutrality, equally pursued both by the king and his ministers remained unshaken in the face of the strongest appeals from more interested parties. Pleas from Calonne on behalf of the émigré princes began as early as December 1789 and were repeated in the following years; yet all were politely rejected. Similarly after the flight to Varennes, when the rulers of Austria and Prussia took a hand, in the Padua and Vienna Circulars, and in the Declaration of Pilnitz, Whitehall maintained its aloof detachment. Even war between the central powers and the Revolution, Brissot's 'war of peoples against Kings', did not shake British policy. Pitt's claim in Parliament when war between Britain and France eventually broke out, that the court of George III 'had most scrupulously observed the strictest neutrality with respect to France', was entirely justified.[2]

This is not to say that concern with events across the Channel was small. On the contrary a revolution in France was bound to affect Britain's interests and indeed eventually led to war. But it was a conflict which reflected Whitehall's concern with the European balance of power, not with the social stability of the *ancien régime*. The war between Austria and Prussia on the one hand and France on the other, was indeed a matter of the utmost concern. When the Prussians were halted in the artillery duel at Valmy, and the Austrians defeated at Jemappes in November 1792, the way lay open to Belgium, now unprotected by the ring of fortresses which had buttressed it against the Bourbons. Beyond Belgium lay Holland and it scarcely required the French decree opening the Scheldt in November to alert Pitt and his colleagues to the dangers. Nothing could be more apt than Canning's comment of 1796. 'Tell me if any statesman that ever lived on being shown that France was mistress of the Netherlands and of Holland . . . would not exclaim at once "then England *must* be at war with her" '.[3] The power which had been ready to go to war merely to counteract French influence at the Hague in 1787 was not likely to stand by while French regiments took up station there. Given the vulnerability of the *ancien*

---

[1] Historical Manuscripts Commission, *Fortescue MSS*, ii, p. 317.

[2] *The War Speeches of William Pitt the Younger* ed. R. Coupland (Oxford, 1940), p. 32.

[3] *George Canning* by P. J. V. Rolo (London 1965), p. 194.

régime in the Low Countries and the boundless energies of the young French republic war was ultimately inevitable, and the government in London had almost certainly recognised that it was so by December 1792. In the subsequent diplomatic wranglings which occupied the month before and after Christmas, in the confused disputes over the precise intentions of the French Assembly, in the clumsy equivocating over the position of the French ambassador, Chauvelin, after the removal and then execution of Louis XVI, it is possible that Pitt could have been more adroit and less stiff. In the last analysis however, the conclusion was inevitable; the French declaration of war against Britain and Holland on 1 February 1793 merely set the seal on decisions already made in effect.

The war which followed, and which was not terminated even temporarily until 1801, was for Britain a war of stalemate. It is natural enough that Pitt should incur much of the blame involved. Even so, caution must be employed in the attribution of responsibility. For Burke, for Wyndham, for Portland, in short for the men who saw the war as a crusade against revolution and a defence of the *ancien régime*, it seemed that Pitt should devote all his efforts to the support of French royalism whether by aiding the émigrés, ever clamorous for action, or by reinforcing the internal enemies of the republic in the Vendee and the Midi. In fact Pitt was not entirely blind to these appeals, as the activities of William Wickham, spymaster-general at Bern, and the expeditions to Toulon in 1793 and Quiberon in 1795 suggest. However, the forces of counter-revolution in France and for that matter outside were hardly such as to instil confidence; in this it is difficult to believe that Pitt's caution was misplaced. A related criticism, which has commended itself powerfully to historians, is more serious. It cannot be denied that Pitt's strategy was one which seemed essentially peripheral. The alleged frittering away of forces which might have crushed the Revolution at the start, a small and useless expedition under the Duke of York in the Low Countries, minor combined operations against Toulon in 1793, Corsica in 1794, and Quiberon in 1795, above all the diversion of substantial forces to the fever-ridden West Indies—'a terrible roundabout road', as Burke called it[1]—all arguably wasted

[1] *The Collected Works of Edmund Burke* (Bohn's edn. London 1853), v, p. 239.

British resources and enabled the French republic to survive the 1790s, to build new roads into Europe and to lay the basis for the Napoleonic empire. Yet there are points worth making in Pitt's defence. For one thing Britain's colonial gains in the West Indies and in the Indian Ocean were not to be despised. The strategy of picking up colonial bargaining counters was not necessarily as relevant in the 1790s as it had been in the 1750s, but it was sufficiently alarming for the new policy makers in France to take it at least as seriously as the old had done. Disturbing as the expensive failure to master Haiti was, the capture of much of the French West Indies and intervention in the Dutch empire was neither a negligible nor useless achievement. Again a maritime strategy was to some extent an unavoidable one for Britain. Pitt pursued it not because he was hopelessly burdened with the strategic legacy bequeathed by his father and deceptively endorsed by the experience of the Seven Years' War, but because as the servant of a naval and colonial power he could scarcely ignore the overseas theatre. The preservation of the navy's lines of supply and communication, the maintenance of imperial bases and lifelines, the acquisition of commercial assets, these, even in a war begun defensively to preserve the balance of power on the European continent, were a natural and indeed inevitable policy. They were as vital to British interests as the great naval successes which not even the most churlish of the government's opponents could denounce—the Glorious First of June in 1794, St Vincent and Camperdown in 1797, the Nile in 1798. If such a strategy bore little direct relevance to the struggle on the Continent, it was none the less unavoidable. As Nelson remarked, 'We English have to regret that we cannot always decide the fate of Empires on the sea'.[1]

On land, admittedly, the picture of Pitt's years in control of the war was a bleak one. Britain's traditional role as a military auxiliary, prepared to subsidise and support her allies but not to lead them on the field of battle, proved disappointing. Yet the responsibility for this state of affairs was more accurately located at Berlin, Vienna and Moscow than in London. The so-called First Coalition, which was actually little more than a loose body of subsidised allies, was

[1] *The War in the Mediterranean, 1803–1810* by P. Mackesy (London 1957), p. 389.

wrecked not by strategic weakness at Whitehall but by the fatal divisions inherent in it from the start. Thus in 1793–94 when Belgium was temporarily cleared thanks largely to the Austrian victory of Neerwinden, and when there was a real opportunity to crush the French republic in its infancy, any hope of effective cooperation was vitiated by affairs in the east. Polish preoccupations, which produced two partitions in as many years, proved an irresistible distraction for the German powers, especially Prussia. Moreover Russia found Turkey as well as Poland a fruitful field of interest compared with the west and confined herself to encouraging the other powers to destroy the revolutionary menace there. The results of allied disagreements were profoundly discouraging. By 1795 both Prussia and Spain had been brought to a shameful peace at Basle, while Holland had been overwhelmed by force of arms. Only Austria remained, and though links between her and Britain were strengthened in 1795, the flood of French successes, spilling over into Italy, forced her to a humiliating peace at Campo Formio in 1797.

It was no fault of Pitt's that the lessons of the First Coalition were not learned by his European partners in time to provide for the success of the second. Though French aggression provided an adequate base for the emergence of a new alliance in opposition, it did not compel a degree of unity sufficient to be capable of victory. Despite a mission to Berlin headed by Grenville's own brother, Thomas, the Prussians remained satisfied with what they had gained in 1795 at Basle, the neutralisation of north Germany. The refusal of Frederick William III to take his part in the coalition represented a grievous blow to the enemies of France. Russia and Austria, thanks to the Mediterranean ambitions of the new Tsar Paul, and the Italian anxieties of the Emperor, proved more forthcoming. Unfortunately Nelson's victory at the Nile, which wrecked French aspirations in Egypt, and Suvaroff's spectacular progress in northern Italy and the Alps, began the War of the Second Coalition with more *éclat* than could be maintained. Britain's latest strategic diversion in Holland was a failure, while the Russians' belief that Austria had been insufficiently cooperative in Switzerland had damaging military effects, driving Tsar Paul into the arms of the French and even provoking the formation of a second armed neutrality of the north. Finally Napoleon's victory at Marengo knocked the heart out of the coalition, reducing the Austrians to a humiliating peace at Lunéville. By 1801 the strategic deadlock which Britain had faced in 1797 was once again complete.

The history of the Second Coalition makes it difficult to lay the blame for its failures at Britain's door. In several respects the Pitt ministry had learned its lesson from the First Coalition. The extreme caution in providing subsidies which had limited the sums paid to George III's allies in 1793 and 1794 and restricted the loans made to Austria in 1794 and 1795, was later considerably modified. In particular the loans had created far more friction than unity and were not repeated in subsequent coalitions. Still more important, Pitt and Grenville had grasped the need for a new and far more effective diplomatic strategy in confronting the French threat. In 1793 they had been content to see the war as essentially similar to those which Britain and France had fought at periodic intervals since the Revolution of 1688. At the time this was understandable enough. Few Englishmen had the prescience of the young Castlereagh, who had declared 'The tranquillity of Europe is at stake and we contend with an opponent whose strength we have no means of measuring. It is the first time that the population and all the wealth of a great kingdom has been concentrated in the field; what may be the result is beyond my perception'.[1] However, by the time the Second Coalition was in the making this recognition that France since the Revolution presented a quite novel force, was more general. Grenville's coalition scheme of 1797–99 was an altogether more serious proposition than the loose amalgam of states which had been the aim of Whitehall in 1793, and envisaged a close union of the major powers, presented with clear strategic aims during the war and a carefully considered settlement for the peace which was to follow it. Both as a concept and a detailed programme it had much in common with the similarly ambitious schemes of Pitt at the outset of the Third Coalition in 1805 and of Castlereagh before the formation of the Fourth in 1813.

[1] *The Foreign Policy of Castlereagh, 1812–1815* by C. K. Webster (London 1931), p. 7.

Unfortunately, clear thinking in London was not in a position to dictate the course of European diplomacy, much though it might assist it. Both the First and Second Coalitions were rendered useless by the differences of the allies. This was not a matter of the selfishness of any individual power—all the allies including Britain were blinkered at one stage or another in this respect, though some more than others—but simply of differing interests which militated against the formation of a unified strategy, let alone its actual execution. Britain had after all entered the war in order to keep Holland out of French clutches; yet none of the other powers had much anxiety on this score. Austria had now lost interest in the Low Countries almost entirely; Prussia, despite its commitment to the Stadholder in 1787, had not been encouraged to maintain that commitment by its experience of the Triple Alliance. Moreover the continental powers had their own particular obsessions. Prussia's primary concern was to digest her gains in Poland and maintain the stability of northern Europe; for this she had fatally weakened the First Coalition, and declined to play any part at all in the second. Austria's concern with southern Germany and northern Italy made her a natural enemy of France, but did not give her common interests with the other states, and indeed tended to make her positively jealous, when as in 1799 the Russians intervened with such spectacular results in Italy and Switzerland. Russia herself had limited enthusiasm for western Europe and intervened there only when, as in 1798, a crazy ruler interpreted his country's interests in the Mediterranean in a novel and eccentric manner. Among the lesser powers Spain was capable of damaging the allies, for example, by joining France in 1795–96, but had little to gain by war. Turkey, the Two Sicilies, Sardinia, Denmark, might have transitory, and in some instances vital interests involved, but in no case did they have more than a local capacity to influence events. This was a patchwork of differing interests and differing objects, of confusion and misunderstanding at worst, and of self-interested and limited cooperation at best. It was hardly the stuff of a successful coalition. Not until all the powers had been humbled by the French would the continent of Europe unite in one common aim—the destruction of France's post-revolutionary energy. In the meantime the British would continue to find themselves fighting at times in lonely and perilous isolation, sustained only by their naval strength.

It was not surprising that Pitt and his colleagues began relatively early to think in terms of a possible compromise peace. Though Burke thundered against those who could not see that 'France is formidable, not only as she is France, but as she is Jacobin France',[1] and would settle only for the re-establishment of the Bourbon monarchy, the ministers were more realistic. The war had been commenced with limited aims and a limited peace was not to be rejected out of hand. However, the first tentative approaches, made in 1795–96, were totally unsuccessful. The Austrians were not at this stage interested and France made negotiation impossible by demanding both her natural frontiers and restitution of all Britain's colonial conquests. A further attempt to discuss terms a year later, towards the end of 1796, proved similarly futile, as the strategic jockeying for position on the Continent continued. While Austria's cause was prospering on the Rhine, Vienna had little enthusiasm for talk of peace, and when Bonaparte began to break the stalemate in Italy Paris similarly lost interest. Moreover the British were not yet prepared to abandon Belgium, long denied the Bourbons, to the republic of France. By 1797 however the picture had changed considerably. In Italy the complete collapse of Austria eventually forced her to terms which while providing the Habsburgs with consolation in the shape of Venetia, expelled them from north-west Italy and the left bank of the Rhine. At the same time the pressures for peace in England grew noticeably stronger. Not only had George III lost his only remaining ally of any consequence, but Franco-Spanish power in the Mediterranean had compelled the Royal Navy to withdraw from that theatre altogether. At home 1797 was the year of the mutinies at the Nore and Spithead, and also of the financial crisis which ended in the abandonment of the gold standard, an emergency measure which would not have been contemplated earlier in the century though it proved less grave now than any might have predicted. While these disasters pushed Pitt closer to peace, the domestic policies of France for once seemed to point to compromise. The politics of the Directory were and remain a murky affair, but

[1] *The Collected Works of Edmund Burke* (Bohn's edn. London 1853), v, p. 164.

royalism, however divided within itself, was growing apparently stronger, and British agents were doing their best to increase its influence. Thus in 1797 both sides were prepared to talk, the British under the pressure of their difficulties at home, the French under that of the growing power of moderation in domestic politics. Malmesbury and the emissaries of the Directory accordingly met at Lille, and for a while it seemed that there might at least be some possibility of agreement. Pitt was now ready to recognise the French acquisition of Belgium and to return all his overseas conquests with the exception of the Cape, plundered from the Dutch, and Trinidad, from the Spaniards. However, domestic politics again intervened. Just as royalist victories in the French election of 1797 had pushed the Directory into negotiations, so the *coup d'état* of 18 Fructidor, by which the rulers of the Directory retaliated and decisively crushed the forces of royalism, utterly wrecked the prospects of peace. The Lille negotiations were abruptly terminated and the Continent returned to confusion. As Grenville pointed out, there was now no hope of an honourable or remotely bearable peace. The only basis for settlement was of the Continent 'abandoned without defence of any kind to these monsters, of the Netherlands, Holland and Italy left in their hands, of Germany revolutionised, and of the little hope we can have of any permanent tranquillity in the midst of this wreck and convulsion of everything around us'.[1]

When the next opportunity for peace came, the scene had changed considerably. The Second Coalition had emerged, had briefly prospered, and had collapsed. Above all, in London Pitt's ministry, which had initially given both the country and its foreign policy one of the stablest and most successful periods of the century, had come to an end. Yet the reason for this change bore little relation to the war. Pitt actually resigned over George III's determined refusal to permit Catholic Emancipation in the wake of the Irish Union. Though there were those who suspected that he stood down solely to throw the odium of an unavoidable peace on his successor, there are no grounds for concluding that the problem was anything but George III's interpretation of his coronation oath and Pitt's commit-

[1] *The Underground War against Revolutionary France* by H. Mitchell (Oxford 1965), p. 218.

ment to an Irish Union accompanied by Catholic toleration. Even so Pitt's resignation did have the effect of throwing onto a new and far less capable minister the complex and awkward negotiations for peace which were bound to follow the collapse of the Second Coalition. Addington, the new Prime Minister, cannot be seen as anything but a mediocrity, even if he hardly earned the savage ridicule of Canning. Many Pittites were prepared to support him, and indeed, in the face of Pitt's own benevolent neutrality towards his successor, serve under him. *The Times* found much to applaud in Addington and there were those who pointed out that whatever his rhetorical superiority, the 'pilot who weathered the storm' had not been the most brilliant of war ministers. 'At the close of every brilliant display,' Sydney Smith remarked, 'an expedition failed or a kingdom fell. God send us a stammerer!'[1] Even so it is difficult to regard the Addington ministry's handling of the peace settlement as other than disastrous. It was not the case, for example, that Britain's bargaining pieces were of such little value as to justify the low demands which the government made at the negotiating table. On the contrary, the War of the Second Coalition had produced a stalemate of the familiar kind, not an ignominious defeat. In some respects indeed the British had rescued a good deal from the débâcle of 1801. At Alexandria the ill-fated French expedition was about to be forced out of Egypt, and at Copenhagen in April 1801 the Danish navy had been crushed before it could be turned against Britain. The armed neutrality, which might have had sinister consequences for British commerce, had been firmly dealt with by the Royal Navy, and on the death of Tsar Paul, the Baltic countries signed a convention with George III's ministers which effectively put an end to it.

Yet Addington and his colleagues conducted affairs as if they had little on their side of the argument to urge in Britain's favour. The Peace Preliminaries of London were badly mismanaged by Lord Hawkesbury, who found himself in a position of responsibility for which he was hardly at this time fitted. He permitted himself to be pressurised into signing the preliminaries on 1 October 1801, just one day before news arrived that the French had surrendered at Alexandria. The actual terms involved practically no concessions by

[1] *Addington* by P. Ziegler (London 1965), p. 111.

France and many by Britain. The only point obtained from Bonaparte was a promise to evacuate southern Italy; French influence
elsewhere, in the Low Countries, on the Rhine, and in northern Italy
was unaffected. For her part Britain returned virtually all her maritime conquests in both the Indies and in the Mediterranean. The
abandonment of Malta, Egypt and above all the Cape, which Pitt
had seen as an essential strategic base for the Royal Navy, seemed
extraordinarily injudicious. Only Trinidad and Ceylon were
retained, neither at the expense of France. The definitive treaty which
was signed at Amiens in March 1802 did not improve matters. The
choice of Lord Cornwallis, a superannuated proconsul, whose sole
concern seemed to be to sign an agreement and return to his country
house in Suffolk as soon as possible, was indefensible. Cornwallis
succeeded in selling virtually every pass that remained. On Malta
he negotiated an agreement which in handing the island to a Nea-
politan garrison would practically have returned it to France whenever she chose to take it. The Cape was to be fully restored to the
Dutch, who, as organised in the Batavian Republic, could not possibly
have prevented Napoleon using it as he wished and when he wished.
None of the points which Whitehall had reserved for discussion, the
question of the payment of Prisoner of War expenses for the preceding years, the matter of commercial relations, the problem of
compensation for the unseated rulers of Holland and Savoy, were
satisfactorily dealt with. It would be difficult to deny Malmesbury's
prediction, well before the event, that the peace negotiated by the
new ministers, would be a 'peace without reflection or consideration'.[1]

Unfortunately, in the months that followed the signing of the
Peace of Amiens, it became clearer still that the government had
been guilty of a major error of judgement. At the time at least it
seemed possible for Britain and France under the Consulate to settle
down to some kind of uneasy *modus vivendi*, if not a stable peace.
Looking back at these years from St Helena Napoleon claimed that
for the war which broke out within barely a year of the treaty, the
British were entirely to blame, and that he had at the time intended
to abandon the martial arts in favour of moral ones. 'At Amiens I

[1] *The War of the Second Coalition, 1798 to 1801* by A. B. Rodger (Oxford 1964),
p. 278.

believed in perfectly good faith, that my future and that of France, was fixed . . . I believe that I should have performed miracles. I would have made the moral conquest of Europe, as I was on the point of achieving it by force of arms'.[1] Had this statement borne any relation to the truth then peace could well have been preserved. But it actually represented as complete a misrepresentation as any to be found in the Napoleonic legend. The fundamental fact was that whereas Britain had seen Amiens as the genuine basis for general peace, Napoleon saw in it merely the terms on which Britain agreed to exclusion from the affairs of Europe and non-intervention in the erection of the new Charlemagne's empire. In his view Amiens in no way prevented him continuing with his great work, and indeed during and after the negotiations his expansionist, basically aggressive policy continued. Overseas he planned recovery of St Domingo and exploitation of Louisiana, just regained from Spain; in India General Decaen would soon be on his way to re-establish the French cause. In the eastern Mediterranean Napoleon was clearly prepared for new adventures, and the Sebastiani report, which was printed in the official French papers in January 1803, and which laid bare French designs on Egypt, was indeed one of the critical factors which convinced London that the leopard had not after all changed his spots. In Europe Napoleon showed himself no less unfettered by the peace. In Switzerland he intervened to settle local political differences and preserve French communications over the Alps. In Italy he set about remodelling the Cisalpine or Ligurian Republic with a view to asserting complete control of the region. In Holland he showed no signs of withdrawing the French troops which remained at Utrecht and Flushing, clearly menacing Britain across the North Sea. In all these ways Napoleon made it crystal clear that for him Amiens was an episode in the construction of a great new western European empire, not the concluding phase of French revolutionary expansion. The misfortune was that thanks to the amateurism of the Addington ministry it had no legal right to complain of most of these actions. As Napoleon himself claimed, the security and independence of the existing states was guaranteed not by the Treaty of Amiens, but by the Treaty of Luneville, a Franco-Austrian

[1] *Napoleon* by F. M. H. Markham (London 1966), p. 108.

agreement to which Britain was not a signatory. It was useless for the British cabinet to insist that it had regarded Amiens and Lunéville as essentially part of the same settlement. And yet it was precisely Napoleon's infringement of Lunéville which was so alarming; it was precisely his intervention in northern Italy, in the eastern Mediterranean, and in Holland that directly threatened vital British interests.

This is not to accuse Addington and his colleagues of mindless appeasement or cowardice. On the contrary, once it became clear that the fate of western Europe was again in the balance the ministry moved towards war with dignity, with courage and even with boldness, catching off guard Napoleon himself, who had imagined that Amiens would give him at least a substantial breathing-space before George III's court recovered its nerve. None the less, it was a measure of the ministry's incompetence that it had placed itself in a position where it could only preserve the country's interests by actions which technically put it in the wrong. The sticking point selected was Malta, a wise choice since that sanctuary was of the utmost importance to the navy's capacity to control the Mediterranean. But in international law the ministers unquestionably infringed their own treaty by insisting on retention of Malta for at least sufficient time to construct a new base on the adjacent small island of Lampedusa. When Napoleon refused to accept this demand, he at least had the satisfaction of going to war again having placed his enemies completely in the wrong. It is ironic that Bonaparte, who was fundamentally the aggressor in this situation, should have had right on his side, or at any rate more right than his opponents, and that Addington, who had sought only an honourable peace and now sought only to protect the liberty of Europe and with it the pacific interests of his country, should have been compelled to appear the perfidious betrayer of treaties. Pitt had claimed to support Addington's peace, but as the country once again prepared for war and as both public and Parliament once again clamoured for his return, he could hardly but derive satisfaction from the incompetence which had characterised his successor's foreign policy.

15   Survival and Settlement, 1803–15

Britain declared war once again on 18 May 1803. Though it is natural to see the eleven or twelve years fighting which followed as merely a continuation of the battles of the 1790s, in reality this was to be quite a different kind of conflict in a number of respects. For example, the war had fundamentally changed from a serious attempt to contained the 'armed opinion' of the French Revolution to a desperate endeavour to resist the union of Europe under a Corsican emperor. Ideology remained an element in the struggle but the new forces were no longer all on one side. The French revolutionaries had promised to raise a war of peoples against kings; ironically in the later stages of the Napoleonic wars there was to be at least an appearance of a war of peoples in defence of kings and against the imperialism of France. So far as Britain in particular was concerned the war also became more and more a grim struggle for survival. During the 1790s there had been dangerous moments, but scarcely more so than the invasion scare of 1779, and Britons tended to be more alarmed by the possibility of revolutionary doctrines crossing the Channel than French troops doing so. A decade later the menace to Britain's existence as an independent power was greater than at any time since the reign of Elizabeth. In 1805 of course the invasion threat was particularly serious; in no sense was it a bluff by Napoleon. Nor did the triumph of Trafalgar dispose of it. Contrary to popular belief, the years which followed 1805 were years of constant strain, years when a minor slip by Collingwood could have cost his country the war, years when Napoleon still planned to challenge the naval strength of his most implacable enemy, years when the strain on the Admiralty's resources were far more severe than was readily admitted. Moreover from 1806 George III's government was compelled to

219

cope with a strategy which had previously been hinted at but never really enforced. The Continental System was a systematic attempt to bring the British economy to its knees; blockade, traditionally the weapon of Whitehall, was turned against its master. As it happened the Continental System failed, but its failure was neither inevitable nor even predictable, and the pressure it placed on economic prosperity and social stability was utterly real.

The symptoms of this heightened strain were manifold. Britain never adopted the policy of the *levée en masse*, the nation in arms. Indeed when measures were initiated, as in Addington's Army of Reserve Act, which actually promised to produce a vast national corps, the propertied classes positively retreated from such a possibility. Even so there was a grim readiness to exploit national resources in a new and significant way. A whole series of schemes to improve home defence were organised. There was a new and intriguing concern with the importance of propaganda, reflected in the increasing status of the press. Public opinion was more than ever vital in the conduct of the war and as the stakes grew higher and the commitment ever more complete, the politicians found themselves increasingly involved in a climate of intense public excitement. Politically the new mix was potent and volatile. As the long years of war, and the changed nature of the struggle with France began to tell, so politics became more and more divisive. In the 1790s Pitt had had matters almost entirely his own way. In Parliament the opposition had never seriously been able to challenge the necessity of war, despite the huge financial and economic cost. Thus in January 1794 Fox had mustered only 59 votes against 297 in the Commons on a peace motion. In 1796 when the situation was at almost its grimmest during this phase of the war, a further initiative raised the opposition vote to a mere 81 against 285. But after the Peace of Amiens and the renewal of war the situation changed dramatically. Ironically Pitt himself was partly to blame by resigning in 1801, and fatally dividing the coalition which he had so ably held together in office. One wing of the Pittite block, that headed by Grenville, moved into opposition; hostile to Addington's peace, infuriated by Pitt's refusal to join in tearing down his successor's ministry, the Grenvilles coalesced with the Foxite Whigs to form a new and much more

formidable opposition party. The Pittites themselves were badly
split in these years, and though temporarily brought together by
Pitt's return to power in 1804 were again shattered by his death in
1806. There was no outstanding heir to Pitt's prestige and power.
The able young men like Castlereagh and Canning fought bitterly,
at one point to the extent of duelling, while the more stolid if less
brilliant leaders—the aged and almost incapable Portland, the
competent if uninspiring Perceval, the sensible but mediocre
Liverpool, struggled to maintain government on an even keel.
Not surprisingly in the bewildering politics of this period there were
bad moments. The opposition grew steadily more defeatist and
pacific, and no element of strategy could be regarded as unconten-
tious. The worst point perhaps occurred in 1809–10. Then the
disastrous Walcheren expedition, the scandal of the Duke of York's
allegedly corrupt activities, the bullion emergency, all conspired to
produce the most desperate of political crises. In one division
on the Walcheren affair the government was actually defeated by
195 votes to 186, and Perceval only emerged from this series of
crises with his administration intact by a judicious mixture of
manoeuvre and concession. To the men responsible for conducting
Britain's war policy, the years which followed the Peace of Amiens
represented a new world of experience after the stable days of the
Younger Pitt's ascendancy.

The renewal of war in May 1803 made the return of Pitt inevitable.
Though the Addington ministry had shown courage if not competence in its final confrontation with Bonaparte, scarcely anyone even
in the cabinet itself expected that it could soldier on for long.
Moreover, though it was the unholy alliance of Foxite Whigs and
Grenvilles which threatened the ministry's command of the Commons, it was Pitt's cautious but none the less clear withdrawal of
confidence from Addington which truly made the administration's
continuance impossible, and it was he who was bound to benefit by
change. Unfortunately Pitt's last two years of power were in the
event happy neither for him nor for his country. His curious
retreat into sphinx-like inscrutability at a time when his young men
longed for positive leadership did not assist his relations with other
politicians; moreover the loss of the Grenvilles and the political

discredit of his closest friend, Dundas, as a result of charges of corruption, sadly embittered Pitt's second ministry.

Abroad, the situation bore a hideous resemblance to the failure of the first two coalitions, and was only partially relieved by the reassertion of British naval supremacy at Trafalgar. The formation of the Third Coalition itself was scarcely a triumph of British diplomacy. Negotiations conducted with the Tsar Alexanders' emissary Novosiltzoff, were marked by inconclusive squabbling over the future status of Malta and the size of British subsidies. When Austria and Russia did eventually join in the struggle against Napoleon, they did so because of the latter's aggression. The proclamation of the kingdom of Italy and the annexation of Genoa in the spring of 1805 were the most clear and unmistakable signs that Bonaparte had no intention of resting content with the *status quo*. Though these actions had the effect of creating a new coalition, they did not operate equally on all powers. Sweden, under the quixotic Gustavus IV, had already joined Britain in the struggle after the execution of the Duc d'Enghien, though this was a marginal rather than major accession. But as in the Second Coalition it was Prussia, whose weight could have been crucial had it been thrown into the scales at this point, that proved reluctant to take part. Pitt tried hard to bring the Prussians in, with a special mission under the former Foreign Secretary, Lord Harrowby, to Berlin. But not for the first time Prussian eyes were incapable of seeing beyond the German horizon, and also not for the first time British hands were tied by the crown's Hanoverian possessions.

Alexander proved embarrassingly ready to sacrifice Hanover to the need to obtain the aid of Prussia, but it was out of the question for the ministers of George III even to contemplate the possibility of ceding the electorate. Napoleon was all too anxious to fish in these waters, and at the critical point in his military confrontation with the forces of the two emperors, succeeded in luring Frederick William with his own promise of Hanover. Those in London were well aware that the attitude of Berlin was decisive at this moment of crisis and even considered offering the prize of the Dutch Netherlands. 'No bribe seems to me too high for Prussia at the moment,' wrote Lord Mulgrave, the Foreign Secretary. 'With that Power it now remains to determine whether Bonaparte is to be Emperor of the Continent of Europe or not'.[1] However, by the time that Prussia began to discern Europe's and her own ultimate interest more clearly, it was too late. Ulm and Austerlitz had removed the Austrians from the war and seriously reduced the Russian threat. Ahead lay the shameful destruction of Prussia's military reputation at Jena and Auerstadt and the Napoleonic settlement with Russia at Tilsit. Pitt had died earlier in January 1806 but even then it was obvious that the Continent lay impotent before Napoleon and that once again Britain would have to face the power of France alone. However, for this Pitt's own responsibility was limited. His diplomacy had failed but it had not lacked vision or logic; no one could have over-come the blinkered selfishness which reigned at Berlin. Admittedly the usual strategic mistakes were made. There was possibly some-thing to be said for the British operations in northern Germany though they achieved nothing, and in southern Italy which pro-duced only a minor victory over the French at Maida. Yet they could not be better than peripheral while Napoleon, as ever the exemplar of Clausewitz's military truisms, concentrated and won at the strategic centre on the Danube. Even so it would be a mistake to place much emphasis on these errors. As before it was the impos-sibly divided interests of the great powers which made Napoleon's military genius decisive. Not until Britain, Russia, Austria and Prussia all placed the defeat of Bonaparte above all other local priorities, or at least postponed the latter until France had been dealt with, would there be a real chance of success.

Pitt's death was the signal for one of the more bizarre ministerial experiments of George III's reign. The new coalition of Grenvilles and Foxites was given the opportunity, in combination with a sprinkling of Pittites, to form a broad-bottomed administration. Unfortunately neither the variety of abilities thus brought forward, nor the presence in the king's cabinet of men who had been in the political wilderness since 1783, was sufficient to make the Ministry of All the Talents a distinguished one. Though defenders of their record have not been wanting, it is difficult to rate them highly.

[1] *The Cambridge History of British Foreign Policy, 1783–1919* ed. Sir A. W. Ward and G. P. Gooch (Cambridge 1922), i, p. 587.

Strategically, they were responsible for a series of disasters, ranging from the ignominious failure of the Buenos Aires expedition, through the regrettable mismanagement of the Dardanelles adventure, to the complete defeat of a new onslaught on Egypt. Nor was Fox, now given his chance to stand forth in government as the pacific friend of the new model France, able to negotiate successfully with Napoleon. When the ministry fell, it did so on the domestic issue of Catholic Emancipation, but it could hardly claim that its going was a grievous blow to British foreign policy. In fact until Castlereagh became Foreign Secretary in 1812 in the infant but eventually stable Liverpool administration, the vacuum left by the removal of Pitt was scarcely filled. Canning's first spell at the Foreign Office in the Portland ministry of 1807–09 was not his most brilliant. Though he acted firmly if cynically to secure the Danish and Portuguese fleets before the disaster of Tilsit could throw the whole of Europe's naval strength into Napoleon's hands, his main achievement during these years was to wreck the ministry of which he was a part, by his ambitious and ruthless persecution of his rival Castlereagh. Castlereagh himself, though an excellent Secretary at War in these years, seriously marred his record with the expensive failure at Walcheren, intended to be Britain's response when the Austrian flame flickered once again before being extinguished at Wagram. It was designed both to cut out the French naval threat which was building at Antwerp, and to relieve pressure on the German theatre. In each respect it failed utterly, causing an embarrassing political crisis as well as damaging the career of Castlereagh who had chosen its obviously inadequate commander, Lord Chatham. In the succeeding ministry of 1809–12, which was headed by Perceval, the Foreign Secretary must rank as one of Britain's worst at any time. Wellesley was guilty of the rankest idleness and incompetence, a misfortune only partially offset by Perceval's common sense.

The years between 1807 and 1812 were in many ways demoralising, so that it was not altogether surprising that defeatist sentiment waxed stronger than ever in England, culminating in the bullion crisis of 1810. Tilsit and Wagram seemed to suggest that there was little to prevent the completion of a vast Napoleonic empire in Europe, while the Continental System made the possibility of Britain's inclusion in it, or at any rate subordination to it, a real one. All hopes of coalition on the Pittite lines temporarily vanished. Instead, the makers of British foreign policy were preoccupied with two major developments which lay outside the mainstream of European politics but which might have considerable bearing on them. The first was the rebellion of Spain in the face of Napoleon's attempt to unseat the Bourbon dynasty in favour of his brother Joseph. When Spanish representatives arrived in London to ask the help of George III in June 1808, it was Canning who led the way in committing the British to a policy of support. 'We shall proceed', his celebrated declaration of policy ran, 'upon the principle that any nation of Europe that starts up with a determination to oppose a power which . . . is the common enemy of all nations, whatever may be the existing political relations of that nation and Great Britain, becomes instantly our essential ally'.[1] There were many, including the king himself, who by no means favoured either this principle or its par-ticular application, and Canning's boldness in espousing this strategy as well as the later perseverance of the Perceval ministry in main-taining it in the difficult times ahead, had much to commend them. The course of the Peninsular War itself was not indeed an easy one. After the instant successes of Baylen and Vimiero there followed a number of less unequivocal assets, beginning with the Convention of Cintra and the Battle of Corunna, and a danger that British forces in the Iberian Peninsula would have to be withdrawn altogether. Moreover the Spaniards interpreted their relationship with London in a way which seemed to lay more emphasis on the direction of British men, money and material to Spain, than on the compensating authority to trade with the Spanish American colonies, which their allies, not altogether unjustly, felt it reasonable to request. None the less there lay ahead a story of substantial if gradual success; Welling-ton was to secure Portugal, to inch his way across the Peninsula, and eventually at the end of 1813 to invade France itself. Unpopular though it was in many quarters the Peninsular War was to play a not in-considerable part in Napoleon's fall and signified to Europe a

[1] *Guineas and Gunpowder: British Foreign Aid in the Wars with France, 1793–1815* by J. M. Sherwig (Cambridge, Mass., 1969), p. 197.

commitment by Britain to continental warfare such as she had not made, at any rate in blood, since Marlborough's war.

The second development of these years, the deterioration and eventually complete breakdown of Anglo-American relations, was scarcely less important. On the face of it this problem was a somewhat surprising one, since the initial effect of the Revolutionary wars had been to bring the two powers closer together. The Jay Treaty of 1794 was admittedly not a great triumph. Though it purported to open the old British West Indian trade to the Americans, it did so on terms which proved completely unacceptable to and indeed unratifiable by the United States; moreover it barely attempted even the pretence of resolving disputes over the vexed question of neutral rights at sea, in which the Americans were rapidly acquiring a strong interest. On the other hand it did finally provide for British evacuation of the old north-western posts, as originally promised in 1783, and it did at least point the way to a solution of some of the lingering differences concerning the territorial boundaries of the United States and Canada. It also signified Britain's readiness, in the light of George III's European embarrassments, to revise its previous attitude towards the ex-colonists, and this was reciprocated by the anglophilia which reigned at any rate in official American circles during the years of Federalist rule at Washington.

Unfortunately these encouraging symptoms were in some ways deceptive. Jefferson's victory in 1801 brought to the fore in America a strain of anglophobia which was not unrepresentative of the standard American view towards the old mother country. Moreover in the context of a very long European war there were underlying difficulties which were bound to ignite ancient animosities. There was, for example, the embarrassing matter of impressment. It was one of the Royal Navy's most essential privileges to search shipping for seamen who were guilty either of evading or deserting service under the white ensign. Inevitably the one-time colonial status of American shipping and seamen, the natural temptation the American merchant navy presented to those Englishmen who sought to escape serving their own country, the enormous difficulty of distinguishing between American and English seamen, especially at a time when neither the law of nations nor the law of Britain provided properly for the definition of nationality after a successful colonial rebellion, all made impressment on the high seas a highly sensitive subject. The most recent authorities allow more justice to the cause of Britain than is traditional. For her the war was one of survival; moreover the licences issued by United States consuls, and purporting to guarantee the *bona fide* American nationality of their holders, were the instruments of corruption and fraud on a large scale. But whatever the rights and wrongs of the matter impressment was bound to create general resentment and particular flashpoints. Scarcely less contentious was the matter of neutral rights. The British practices which had led to the formation of an armed neutrality in 1780 and 1800 were relevant here if only because the Americans, so far as international trade was concerned, had become the most important neutrals of all, quite outclassing the Dutch in this respect. Moreover the legal position was even more complex in this instance; American trading with France in the Seven Years' War had built up a case law about the extent to which it was legitimate to trade with enemy colonies in non-contraband goods, which immeasurably complicated an already intricate issue. Again the legal points are scarcely worth clarifying so far as foreign politics are concerned. Both Britain in the seventeenth century and America in the eighteenth century took a view of this problem which stemmed from their major vested interests as neutral carriers. Equally Britain in the eighteenth century and America in the nineteenth century completely changed their attitudes when their interests were those of major belligerents.

Whether these differences could have been reconciled it is not easy to judge. However if the chance existed it was lost. The critical period was 1806–07 when Napoleon was inaugurating the Continental System in the Berlin and Milan Decrees and Britain was retaliating with her Orders-in-Council. Each side made it virtually impossible for neutrals to trade anywhere in Europe except on its terms. The Royal Navy placed Britain in the stronger position to enforce its view but also made it the more obvious source of grievance. Even so Franco-American war was as likely as Anglo-American, and since the United States could hardly afford to fight both powers at once there was much to be said for embroiling the

Americans with France, even at the cost of British concessions. Unfortunately an attempt to negotiate a treaty in December 1806 foundered thanks partly to the problem of impressment and partly to Jefferson's hostility; similarly the *Chesapeake* incident of June 1807, a direct naval confrontation between the two powers, did nothing to ease tension. None the less the British ambassador in Washington brought affairs almost to an accommodation, and was ultimately disappointed not by American intransigence but by one of the outstanding diplomatic blunders made by a Foreign Secretary. It was Canning who, in his most irresponsible manner and apparently out of sheer dislike of everything American, recalled the ambassador Erskine and wrecked the negotiations, a piece of the most gratuitous folly. As a result the possibility of a new embarrassment for Napoleon turned into the certainty of a much more serious one for his enemy. Though the British cabinet eventually made the necessary concessions on the score of the Orders-in-Council, in response to the pressures of industrial lobbying at home, its action came too late. Long before this the Americans had tired of attempting to organise their own economic sanctions against both France and Britain, and Napoleon had seen the chance to win them over by withdrawing his own measures against them. In these circumstances the war which broke out in June 1812 was inevitable. Had Napoleon acted sooner he could in fact have added a crippling burden to the British economy, which in 1810-11 was in desperate straits. The loss of the North American markets could have been the decisive blow. As it was by the time the United States declared war the Continental System was beginning to crack, and the danger correspondingly diminishing. Even so, the war, inconclusive though it proved in a military sense, was an irksome and expensive embarrassment which British statesmen could have done much more to avert.

By the beginning of 1813, fortunately for Britain the European situation was changing dramatically. Alexander I had finally defied the Continental System and broken with his ally of Tilsit. Napoleon had invaded Russia, had failed to bring the Tsar to terms, had carried out his long and wearing retreat, and was preparing to regroup his forces in Germany. The Prussian government was being nudged closer to alliance with St Petersburg, not least by the activities of its own army officers. The Austrians, newly allied to the Emperor of France by marriage, were becoming dimly aware that they might after all have backed the wrong horse. In this situation it is easy to see the fall of Napoleon's empire as inevitable. Ahead lay the last and grand coalition, the great battle of Leipzig, which cost Bonaparte the control of central Europe, the steady advance on France itself terminating in the unseating of the emperor, the redrawing of Europe's territorial boundaries at the Congress of Vienna, the Hundred Days, and Waterloo. Yet these developments did not follow inevitably or even logically from the failure of Napoleon's efforts to discipline Russia. At best the clock had been turned back to the days before Tilsit; Napoleon still had enormous resources at his command and still represented the greatest threat to Europe's liberty in centuries. His defeat was anything but a foregone conclusion.

Luckily by 1812 Britain had at last found a Foreign Secretary worthy of the Younger Pitt's mantle. Wellesley had gone after a futile attempt to bring in his friends the Grenvilles and the Whigs, and the Perceval ministry had been disrupted by the assassination of its leader. When a new and initially rather fragile government was formed under Liverpool, Castlereagh, who was Wellesley's replacement, remained at the Foreign Office after Canning declined to serve in that post. Castlereagh's term was one of the most important in the history of the office, and his capacities amply fitted him for the awesome responsibilities of these years. He was admittedly not without faults. As a parliamentary performer he was abysmal, a substantial disadvantage at a time when so much depended on the ability of individual ministers to carry the House of Commons. Moreover his judgement of men was in some respects extraordinarily aberrant. The choice of his own brother Sir Charles Stewart and Lord Cathcart, two unsophisticated soldiers, for the conduct of negotiations with the other powers in 1813, not to say the mission of the young and inexperienced Aberdeen to woo the artful and cynical Metternich, were of a piece with the disastrous choice of Lord Chatham to lead the Walcheren expedition back in 1809.

However in other respects Castlereagh showed himself to be infinitely superior to the Wellesleys, Harrowbys and even Cannings

of his day. More than anyone else he grasped the essential nature of
the priorities imposed by the circumstances of 1813. The failure of
the Fourth Coalition could well lead to the final extinction of European liberties for a generation. Many shared Lord Grey's view that
'the present Confederacy' would be 'the last certainly, if unsuccessful,
that Europe will see'.[1] The need for absolute unity and a clear concept of the arrangements which must be made to prevent future
mischief on the part of France was overwhelming. In this respect,
however, there was nothing strikingly new about Castlereagh's
ideas which drew heavily on the earlier schemes of Grenville and
Pitt. The achievement of Castlereagh was successfully to steer the
great powers towards the actual attainment of the goals which
previous coalitions had barely espied, let alone accomplished. This
meant a continual battle against adverse tendencies on the Continent.
Though Prussia and Russia both confirmed their determination to
bring down Napoleon in the Treaty of Kalisch in February 1813,
the different notions of their respective rulers as to the terms of a
postwar settlement, not to say their temperamental idiosyncrasies,
made reliance on their firm and consistent support dangerous. Still
more doubtful was the attitude of the Habsburg monarchy, which
now found itself in the same position of critical importance as
Prussia at the inception of the previous two coalitions. As Liverpool
remarked, 'If Austria would now declare, We might really hope to
put an End to the Tyranny which has been so long oppressing the
World'.[2] Unfortunately the Austrians were by no means certain on
which side to throw their weight. Having recently allied with
Napoleon, and remaining exceedingly sceptical as to the latest
coalition's prospects of success, they and especially Metternich were
more intent on mediation than participation. The results could have
been fatal, and indeed Britain was only narrowly saved from
isolation in the face of mediated peace between France and its
enemies.

The point of greatest danger undoubtedly occurred in the spring
and summer of 1813. At that stage Napoleon had recovered his

[1] Historical Manuscripts Commission, *Fortescue MSS*, x, pp. 351–52.
[2] *Metternich and the British Government from 1809 to 1813* by C. S. B. Buckland
(London 1932), p. 526.

confidence by winning two small but significant victories at Lutzen and Bautzen, and extracting an armistice of six weeks from his adversaries. With Britain's representatives left in the dark, Metternich convinced the Prussians and Russians at Reichenbach of the need to negotiate a generous peace with Napoleon. The future of Europe hung on a fateful meeting at Dresden between Metternich and Napoleon. Fortunately the latter, whose incapacity to make timely concessions was the despair of those who surrounded him, took a truculent attitude. Almost simultaneously there arrived news of Wellington's brilliant and conclusive victory at Vittoria. The relative importance of Napoleon's folly and Wellington's victory in heartening the allies and impelling the Austrians in the direction of the other powers is not easily determined. Wellington himself had no doubt that 'Vittoria freed the Peninsula altogether, broke off the armistice at Dresden, and thus led to Leipsic, and the deliverance of Europe'.[1] Others felt that it was Metternich's final realisation that Napoleon would not budge an inch until forced to do so that proved decisive. In any event the result was the effective formation of a coalition which for the first time included all the great powers, and the liberation of Germany at Leipzig. Not that this was the end of the danger. Metternich had no desire radically to recast the shape of Europe and his Frankfurt proposals, in November 1813, would have left Napoleon with the Rhine as a frontier and the future menace of France intact. Only when Castlereagh himself took a hand on the Continent, and joined the monarchs of eastern Europe as they approached the French frontier, was the loose alliance pulled into a coalition such as Pitt and Grenville had once dreamed of. 'We have now the bull close pinioned between us,' he declared, 'and if either of us lets go our hold till we render him harmless, we shall deserve to suffer for it'.[2] The great alliance of Chaumont, which was nothing if not a monument to Castlereagh's personal diplomacy, was signed on 1 March 1814. By it the four great powers, a term used officially for the first time, undertook to

[1] *Metternich and the British Government from 1809 to 1813* by C. S. B. Buckland (London 1932), p. 525.

[2] *The Foreign Policy of Castlereagh, 1812–1815* by C. K. Webster (London 1931), p. 152.

combine for the complete destruction of Napoleon and the elimination of any future threat to the security of Europe. All were subsidised with British funds, and all accepted Britain's basic war aims. 'What Castlereagh has achieved', one of the diplomats involved wrote, 'is really wonderful. But for him I do believe we should have been off, the Devil take the hindmost'.[1]

Achieving the demolition of Napoleon's empire, which was brought about within weeks of the signing of the grand alliance at Chaumont, represented only the beginning of Castlereagh's problems. The stabilisation of Europe, after some twenty years of almost continuous warfare was a complex and perilous business, and was not assisted by the fact that Napoleon had to be defeated once again at Waterloo after his return from Elba. Nor was the actual settlement concluded in one process. Quite apart from the Treaty of Ghent, which terminated the Anglo–American war in January 1815, largely on the basis of a return to the *status quo ante bellum*, there were two Treaties of Paris of 30 May 1814 and 20 November 1815, respectively representing the terms obtained from the allies by France before and after the Hundred Days, the Congress of Vienna which produced the definitive settlement of Europe outside France, and the Quadruple Alliance, signed in November 1815 and settling the basis on which the affairs of the Continent were to be conducted in the future. It is a tribute to Castlereagh's extraordinary primacy that it was his view on the substantive points at issue which was adopted. Hampered not a little by factors at home ranging from the unpredictability of public opinion, and according to Stratford Canning especially 'the Methodists and the women',[2] to the anxiety of his cabinet and parliamentary colleagues as to his activities far from their direct supervision, Castlereagh was able to achieve the most complete control ever exercised by any British diplomat over continental deliberations.

On the central question of France and its future this was particularly important. Especially after the Hundred Days there was a strong feeling in some quarters, notably Prussia, that France must

[1] *The Foreign Policy of Castlereagh, 1812–1815* by C. K. Webster (London 1931), p. 219.
[2] ibid., p. 239.

be squeezed until the pips squeaked. Though ultimately forced to retire to her frontiers as defined in 1789, that is with none of the Revolution's territorial gains, and compelled to yield up their ill-gotten art treasures, as well as paying indemnities, the French did not suffer the indignities which they were to submit to after the war of 1870. Internally affairs were confused. Some among the allies, like Alexander, had extreme doubts as to the wisdom of restoring the Bourbons at all, while others, like Louis XVIII himself, expected to have France returned to the days of absolute monarchy. In this situation the ultimate restoration of a relatively moderate and constitutional monarchy, owed not a little to Castlereagh, admittedly aided by Talleyrand. Externally it was Britain's old desire to encircle France with adequately strong buffer states, in place of the feeble neighbours who had collapsed so completely at the onset of the Revolutionary wars, which triumphed. The House of Orange was restored to a kingdom consisting of the Belgian as well as Dutch Netherlands, while Prussia was strengthened on the Rhine and Savoy in the Alps. In retrospect, given the eventual secession of Belgium, the growth of Prussian power, and the Italian distractions of the Savoyards, these measures are not without their objections. Yet at the time they were a logical response to the problem of future French aggression. Basically Britain's own gains were limited to some West Indian acquisitions (Trinidad, Tobago and St Lucia) and the colonial conquests which were of overriding importance for worldwide communications within the empire—Malta, the Cape and Mauritius. In addition she obtained some measure, though a limited one, of international agreement on the eventful abolition of the slave trade, an abiding cause for concern at home.

The greatest difficulty was experienced in the settling of central Europe. In this area Castlereagh was moved by a desire to see Prussia and Russia strengthened without becoming over-mighty members of the continental community; he was also under pressure from home where there was growing opposition to the aggrandisement of the eastern powers at the expense of lesser states and indeed nations. Already Britain had been forced to sacrifice Norway to Sweden, by way of honouring the promise with which Bernadotte had been brought into the last coalition, and the danger of similarly

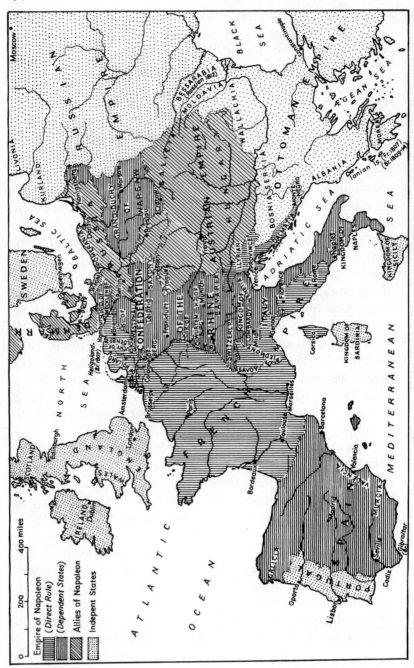

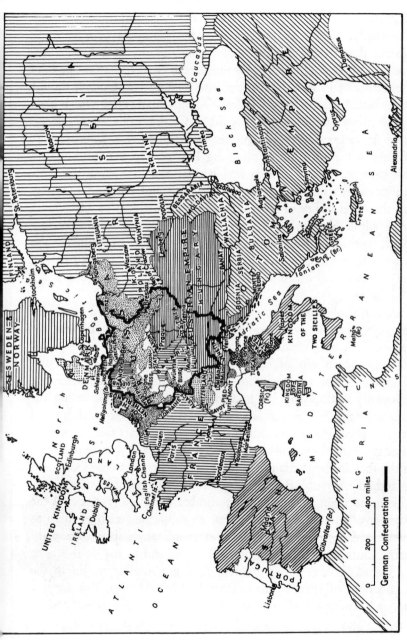

Maps 7a & b. Europe under and after Napoleon

sacrificing the Poles to Russia and Saxons to Prussia was considerable. Eventually, after a major storm at the Congress of Vienna, so violent that a new alignment of Britain, France and Austria was brought into play to exert pressure on the two recalcitrant powers, the extent of Prussia's expansion into Saxony was limited, though little could be done for the Poles. The diplomatic crisis which blew up on these questions was arguably Castlereagh's most difficult one. At home Liverpool and his colleagues were feverish with anxiety at the prospect of plunging Europe into yet another war, this time to restrain Prussia and Russia, and in Vienna the tense emotional reactions of Frederick William and Alexander, not to say the unreliability of Metternich and the intrigues of Talleyrand, were admirably dealt with by a cool and eventually victorious Castlereagh. Not every item in Britain's war aims, as defined at this stage, was secured, but no one could have obtained more, or more deeply imprinted his conception on Europe than the British Foreign Secretary.

Britain's role was in some respects one which mystified observers. In the Napoleonic wars, and above all in the last years of war, she had made a commitment to the Continent in men, money and material which out of sight exceeded anything ever previously exhibited. Even in the 1790s the strain had been considerable, repeatedly multiplying the budget and enormously increasing the national debt. But in the last coalition a level of expenditure had been reached which was extraordinary. Quite apart from the strain of maintaining the world's largest and dominant navy, and employing in the Iberian Peninsula the biggest force ever sent to the Continent or indeed overseas, Britain had committed herself in the Grand Alliance to maintaining the same number of troops (150,000) as the other powers, and at the same time to subsidising each of them to the tune of £5 million. 'What an extraordinary display of power,' wrote Castlereagh. 'This I trust will put an end to any doubts as to the claim we have to an opinion on continental matters'.[1] In the negotiations of 1814–15 his opinion had indeed been the decisive one in continental affairs. And yet it had scarcely been used to

[1] *The Foreign Policy of Castlereagh, 1812–1815* by C. K. Webster (London 1931), p. 228.

Britain's obvious advantage. Napoleon's thoughts on these years, at any rate those transmitted to the public, have to be treated with caution, but there was much that was typical of the continental viewpoint in his mockery of Castlereagh. 'What great advantage, what just compensations, has he acquired for his country? The peace he has made is the sort of peace he would have made if he had been beaten. I could scarcely have treated him worse, the poor wretch, if it had been I who had proved victorious! . . . Thousands of years will pass before England is given a second opportunity equal to this opportunity to establish her prosperity and greatness'.[1] Even at home Castlereagh was to some extent misunderstood. Compared with Canning he was to seem a hopeless reactionary, intent on restoring the *ancien régime* where possible, and involving little England in international affairs in order to buttress the international class structure.

Neither criticism is a relevant one. What many found difficult to understand was that in 1815 Britain's real interests were naturally negative and defensive. At least since the War of American Independence there had been little desire in London for territorial aggrandisement, and colonies were regarded, in Perceval's words, as a 'source of expense and weakness'.[2] Such conquests as were desired were purely those designed to protect trade and communications. In Europe the sole aim of British policy was to maintain a balance which would prevent continental conflicts of a kind likely to endanger Britain's international trade or involve her in recurrent warfare. Though this involved certain territorial requirements, they were all negative; the independence of the Low Countries, the defensive ring around France, the permanent equality of the eastern powers, all these were aims which involved no direct accession to the military or economic power of Britain. They also included a new and important element which was Castlereagh's most distinctive legacy.

Above all it was Castlereagh's concern not merely to complete the destruction of Napoleon's empire but to find means by which Europe could save herself from the erection of new empires. At the time and since, his part in the creation of the Congress System, the

[1] *The Congress of Vienna* by H. Nicolson (London 1946), p. 237.
[2] *Spencer Perceval: The Evangelical Prime Minister, 1762–1812* by D. Gray (Manchester 1963), p. 48.

means by which the great powers were to police Europe for the future, has been seen as that of a mindless reactionary intent on quashing liberalism in all its forms. Nothing could have been further from the truth. In fact Castlereagh's was not an unreasoning conservatism. 'It is impossible', he told Lord William Bentinck, 'not to perceive a great moral change coming on in Europe, and that the principles of freedom are in full operation. The danger is, that the transition may be too sudden to ripen into anything likely to make the world better or happier'.[1] In any event, he had nothing to do with Alexander I's mystical Holy Alliance, and was not one of those who saw the Congress System as a machine of reaction. The items in the settlement of 1814-15 which related to the establishment of a permanent concert of Europe were seen by Castlereagh as a purely peace-keeping device. His crucial state paper of 1820 is decisive on this point. 'When the Territorial Balance of Europe is disturbed, she [Great Britain] can interfere with effect, but She is the last Government in Europe, which can be expected, or can venture to commit Herself on any question of an abstract Character. . . . We shall be found in our place when actual danger menaces the System of Europe, but this Country cannot, and will not, act upon abstract and speculative Principles of Precaution'.[2] In short the concert of Europe was intended to defend peace not privilege. Admittedly the trends in European politics after 1815 were evidence that Britain's ultimate capacity to restrain the ambitions of powers as determined and as self-interested as Prussia, Russia and Austria, was restricted. Yet Castlereagh's achievement was considerable. His boast to the House of Commons—'Never before was so much accomplished for Europe'[3]—was exaggerated and would not have earned the approbation of liberals in what was to become increasingly Metternich's Europe. But it amply revealed how much Britain had matured as a world power intent on something more than dynastic intrigue and territorial gain.

[1] *British Diplomacy, 1813–1815* ed. C. K. Webster (London 1921), p. 181.
[2] *Foundations of British Foreign Policy from Pitt (1792) to Salisbury (1902) or Documents, Old and New* ed. H. W. V. Temperley and L. M. Penson (Cambridge 1938), pp. 62–3.
[3] *British Diplomacy, 1813–1815* ed. C. K. Webster (London 1921), p. 403.

16 Conclusion

One central problem remains. If anything is clear from a study of British foreign policy in the period 1688 to 1815, it is the extraordinary level of overall success attained, at any rate compared with the record of the seventeenth century. In the nineteenth century of course, the British were to achieve a degree of world hegemony which exceeded the wildest dreams of Englishmen in earlier ages, largely on the basis of the enormous economic advantage created by being the first industrial nation. In the eighteenth century the British did not obviously outdistance their European rivals in economic or demographic terms, yet they achieved a power status far beyond their apparent strength. Apart from the isolation and defeat of the 1760s and 1770s, itself a temporary setback, and perhaps the still more temporary impotence of the 1730s, the record was one of great growth as a world power; and at times, in the War of the Spanish Succession, in the Seven Years' War, in the Napoleonic Wars, the spectacle was one which astonished continental contemporaries.

The growth of British power in world affairs is not accounted for by any single or even any very obvious factor. The one which statesmen themselves would like to have selected is certainly ruled out. There was nothing fundamental to distinguish British diplomacy or strategy, though both had their high points certainly in Marlborough and in the Elder Pitt, perhaps in William III, Stanhope, the Younger Pitt and Castlereagh. But these were exceptions. The eighteenth century was a period of often glittering continental talent—witness Louis XIV, Fleury, Choiseul, Kaunitz, Frederick II, Catherine II and so on. In any rating of eighteenth-century statesmen, one or two British diplomats and strategists could expect to be

239

placed highly but there would be no obvious dominance in such a ranking. A consideration which in retrospect greatly strengthened Britain in the international contests of the period was one which to many seemed to weaken her. The National Debt, that remarkable creation of the reign of William III which on the one hand gave to Britain's finances a stability they had so evidently lacked under the Stuarts, and which on the other, climbed to such dizzy heights as a result of subsequent government borrowing, was alternately the pride and despair of British statesmen. Dubois was not alone in thinking that the French financial system was infinitely superior to the English, and as late as the 1780s there were those who were convinced that this was so. Jeremiahs who prophesied that the National Debt would mount without control until it finally burst, like a greater and much more devastating South Sea Bubble, had a great deal of support. Indeed it was widely considered that the massive burden of debt involved in Britain's unique fiscal system positively hindered the makers of foreign policy. 'So long as the Nation labours under so great a load of Debt,' one pamphleteer observed in 1737, 'it is impossible it should maintain its Honour and Rights', with the same vigour as formerly'.[1] None the less the machinery of taxation and borrowing in Britain, which, with periodic modifications, went back to the 1690s and the strain of the Nine Years' War, proved adequate to every task imposed on it. Contemporaries were appalled by the expense, for example, of the Seven Years' War and the War of American Independence, and the interest charges thus permanently laid to the nation's account. Yet in the Revolutionary and Napoleonic Wars there seemed to be almost no limit to the extent to which British ministers could borrow to support their arms and their allies. There were admittedly crises, notably in the shock of 1797 when the Bank of England was compelled to suspend cash payments, and during the bullion crisis of 1810; but eventually the system won through, a remarkable tribute to its financial flexibility. No other state in Europe had a machine capable of raising money in such quantities, at such short notice, with such little political difficulty, and with such obvious security. So attractive was the National Debt that even foreigners, notably the

[1] *The Financial Revolution in England* by P. G. M. Dickson (London 1967), p. 21.

Dutch, found themselves investing in it in peacetime, a phenomenon which itself created considerable anxiety in London.[1] These fears were grossly exaggerated, but they represented, at least by implication, a compliment to the superiority of the British financial system.

Financial strength was important because the British as a nation were profoundly reluctant to invest manpower in high strategy in the manner of other nations. This refusal to squander human flesh and blood significantly reduced the strain of war upon the economy and was one of those factors which permitted Britain actually to increase her share of world trade during a period of continual warfare, and at a time when most of her rivals were extensively damaged by the economic effects of war. Hence the readiness of eighteenth-century governments to subsidise the employment of German, Russian, Austrian, Sardinian, indeed almost any troops not their own, and hence the vast subsidies which made Britain 'a pretty good milch cow' as Grenville termed it in the 1790s. Yet it was Grenville who insisted, in response to criticism of the great quantities of treasures poured into the Continent that 'it was certainly cheaper and more politic to pay foreign troops, than to take our own youth from the plough, and the loom, and thereby not merely put a stop to all domestic industry, but also drain the island of its population, and diminish our natural strength'.[2] This is not to argue that the Royal Navy and the army did not absorb a significant proportion of national resources; on the contrary, particularly at the time of the Peninsular War, Britain was making a large and onerous contribution even in men to the European war effort against Napoleon. But at no time in the period did government resort to the mass conscription and massive deployment of manpower which all the continental states regarded as a normal state of affairs. In such circumstances a sound financial and economic base was crucial.

Economic strength was not merely a matter of money. British industrial and commercial growth even before the celebrated period

[1] See A. C. Carter, 'Dutch Foreign Investment, 1783–1800' in *Economica*, xx (1953).

[2] *Guineas and Gunpowder: British Foreign Aid in the Wars with France, 1793–1815* by J. M. Sherwig (Cambridge, Mass., 1969), pp. 37, 44.

of take-off in the 1780s, was rapid and impressive. The revolution which has been discerned in the pattern of British commerce, growing by leaps and bounds as the emphasis switched from textiles to manufactured goods and from the traditional markets of Europe to the ever increasing demands of the Americas and the Indies, helped both to mould and sustain the conduct of British foreign and strategic policy. It has been seen that the statesmen saw commerce as a crucial consideration in their calculations, and the conviction of eighteenth-century Englishmen that the wealth derived from trade and industry was the key element in British power, was by no means without justification. Under the strain of blockade and war the economy creaked alarmingly in 1810 and 1811; yet in the event it survived, and in doing so made a vital contribution to the maintenance of European liberties. Historians are clear that the wars of this period held back the growth of industrialisation, but also that they did so far less in Britain than in France and the rest of Western Europe. By 1815 Britain was beginning to vie with France and Russia even in terms of population, and in terms of economic strength had completely overhauled all rivals. The way was open to the establishment of that total industrial supremacy which characterised the following decades.

The rise of Britain in world affairs did not, however, derive merely from her financial and economic strength. It was also related to a significant extent to her political system. As has been seen, it was generally considered that Britain's limited monarchy and mixed constitution, whatever their benefits to the subject, were a hindrance to the successful conduct of relations with foreign states. In fact the element of consent which they provided for all major diplomatic strategies throughout the period was an admirable corrective to the ingenious schemes of over-subtle statesmen and the ill-considered commitments of imprudent ones. Popular fury sometimes hurried ministers into error and parliamentary curiosity sometimes weakened their credit with their continental colleagues. But in the last analysis the fact that foreign policy could only be conducted with the full and voluntary consent of the propertied, the political, the ruling classes, whatever they are described as, instilled a welcome touch of realism. Admittedly mindless prejudices had sometimes to be pandered to. On the other hand, if the national purse had to pay for policy, it was not a bad idea to consult the views of those who held the purse strings. Consensus politics are not always the best but they did little harm and a great deal of good in the eighteenth century. The realism which entered British foreign policy, for example, in 1710, in the 1740s, in 1763 and in 1782, was largely the result of the force of opinion at large. The unlimited aggressiveness of the Whigs in the War of the Spanish Succession, the devious and intricate intrigues of Carteret in the War of the Austrian Succession, the excessively bellicose spirit of Pitt in 1761–62, the desire of George III to fight the American colonists to the death, all involved risks of the kind which continental statesmen often took and to which statesmen with strong views were often tempted, and all were circumvented in Britain by the taxpayers' power to influence events. And when a determined and continuous sacrifice was truly needed, as it was to combat the totalitarianism of the French after the Revolution, the support of the community was not wanting. That dependence on the nation at large which statesmen such as Frederick II so despised helped not a little to preserve British security and British interests, while even states as strong as Prussia collapsed in the face of a novel menace.

One final consideration is worth mentioning, one which in a sense is ever present in any discussion of British foreign policy, and one which at the same time was not the particular objective of governments in the ways that commercial gain or strategic advantage were. The balance of power was a term frequently on the lips of politicians and no doubt much misused. But British concern with the balance of power did reflect an important, indeed central strength of British foreign policy; namely that as a nation the British were concerned with Europe only to a limited degree. Every continental state, without exception, had natural and fundamental interests in continental questions for obvious geographical reasons. For an equally obvious geographical reason Englishmen, once they had been weaned from the deluded fantasies of absolute monarchs intent on rivalling the feats of their continental rivals, had few such interests. If Holland or Hanover were invaded, if the trade of the Mediterranean was restricted, then intervention might be required. And equally if one power, notably France under Louis XIV and again under Napoleon, attempted completely to overturn the European state system, similarly intervention was inevitable. Hence so many of the wars of the period. As Sir James Harris commented, 'The history of the present century afforded repeated proofs, that the English fought and conquered less for themselves than for the sake of their allies, and to preserve that equilibrium of power, on which the fate of all Europe depends'.[1] But to intervention of this kind there were crucial qualifications. Britain's role was basically defensive. As Auckland put it, 'the English nation is unwilling to enter into any war for an indirect object of Continental politics'.[2] She could and sometimes would be dragged reluctantly into European affairs, but she was rarely tempted to remain in them longer than was absolutely necessary. The temptations which lured other European statesmen were to a great extent foreign to those in London. Moreover Britain's lack of vested territorial interests on the Continent put her in a strong position to influence others, as the peace settlement of 1815 demonstrated. It also enabled her to exploit that concern with overseas objectives which her subjects, if not always her statesmen, had long seen as their priority. The eighteenth century finally witnessed that realisation of Britain's natural capacity for aggressive commercial and industrial expansion overseas, which Tudor and Stuart monarchs had only intermittently favoured and frequently obstructed, and which was to provide the basis for Victorian hegemony. Eighteenth-century ministers often blundered, and in the War of American Independence almost catastrophically so, in their misunderstanding of commercial and colonial strategy. But the one thing that cannot be said of the British in the eighteenth century is that they undervalued maritime and overseas objectives, or overrated the lure of the Continent. And Victorians were to owe much to their predecessors' understanding at least of this fundamental fact of political and economic life.

[1] *Britain, Russia and the Armed Neutrality of 1780* by I. de Madariaga (London 1962), p. 204.
[2] Historical Manuscripts Commission, *Fortescue MSS*, ii, p. 57.

Bibliography

The following is intended as a brief guide to the principal literature with the emphasis on books rather than learned articles, and with monographs in foreign languages largely excluded. It is divided into sections which correspond with the major divisions of the text.

Part 1

There are few general works on British foreign policy in the eighteenth century. Easily the best is D. B. Horn's *Great Britain and Europe in the Eighteenth Century* (Oxford 1967). By the same author *The British Diplomatic Service 1689–1789* (Oxford 1961) which may be supplemented with M. A. Thomson *The Secretaries of State, 1681–1782* (Oxford 1932), is an admirable account of the machinery available to British diplomats. *British Diplomatic Representatives*, ed. D. B. Horn, S. T. Bindoff, etc. (Camden Series 1932, 1934) provides a comprehensive guide to the biographical details of the men involved. The seventeenth-century background is helpfully described in G. M. D. Howat, *Stuart and Cromwellian Foreign Policy* (London 1974), and in J. R. Jones, *Britain and Europe in the Seventeenth Century* (London 1966), while the nineteenth-century sequel is dealt with in P. M. Hayes, *The Nineteenth Century 1814–80* (London 1975) and K. Bourne, *The Foreign Policy of Victorian England 1830–1902* (Oxford 1970). Among the general accounts of eighteenth-century Britain which contain useful summaries of foreign policy are B. Williams, *The Whig Supremacy, 1714–1760* (Oxford 1962, 2nd edn.), J. Steven Watson, *The Reign of George III, 1760–1815* (Oxford 1960), J. B. Owen, *The Eighteenth Century, 1714–1815* (London, 1974), and D. Marshall, *Eighteenth Century England* (London 1962). For the pattern of European diplomacy generally in this period the best short account is *Histoires des Relations Internationales, Les Temps Modernes, ii. De Louis XIV a 1789* by G. Zeller, and *iii. La Revolution Francaise et l'Empire Napoleonien*, by A. Fugier. In English the original

Cambridge Modern History is more detailed on political history than the New Cambridge Modern History. Among the many short histories of eighteenth-century Europe generally, easily the best is M. S. Anderson, *Europe in the Eighteenth Century, 1713–1783* (London 1961).

There are a number of accounts of relations with particular courts which extend over more than one of the periods covered below, viz. M. S. Anderson, *Britain's Discovery of Russia, 1553–1815* (London 1958), Sir R. Lodge, *Great Britain and Prussia in the Eighteenth Century* (Oxford 1923), J. O. McLachlan, *Trade and Peace with Old Spain, 1667–1750* (Cambridge 1940). Among other general studies are S. Conn, *Gibraltar in British Diplomacy in the Eighteenth Century* (New Haven 1942), and A. C. Wood, *History of the Levant Company* (London 1935). On themes particularly important, though not directly connected with foreign policy, are P. G. M. Dickson, *The Financial Revolution in England* (London 1967) and R. Davis, 'English Foreign Trade 1700–1774' in *Ec. Hist. Rev.*, xv (1961–62). A valuable set of essays on various themes is to be found in studies in *Diplomatic History: Essays in Memory of David Bayne Horn*, ed. R. Hatton and M. S. Anderson (London 1970). Useful as readily accessible selections of key documents are the series published by the Camden Society as *British Diplomatic Instructions, 1689–1789*, and *Recueil des Instructions données aux Ambassadeurs et Ministres de France* (Paris, 1884–   ).

Part 2

Two collections of essays contain many of the best contributions to an understanding of post-Revolution foreign policy. In *Britain after the Glorious Revolution, 1689–1714*, ed. G. Holmes (London 1970), G. C. Gibbs deals with the impact of the Revolution, A. D. McLachlan with the Peace of Utrecht. In *William III and Louis XIV. Essays 1680–1720 by and for Mark A. Thomson*, ed. R. Hatton and J. S. Bromley (Liverpool 1968), there are some excellent examples of Thomson's own work on the 1690s and 1700s as well as a variety of other contributions to diplomatic history. Straightforward accounts of William III's policy are to be found in D. Ogg, *England in the Reigns of James II and William III* (Oxford 1955), and S. B. Baxter, *William III* (London 1966). For the following reign G. M. Trevelyan,

England under Queen Anne (London 1930) remains useful. St John's role is displayed in H. T. Dickinson, *Bolingbroke* (London 1970), and among the many works on Marlborough, W. S. Churchill, *Marlborough: His Life and Times* (London 1933–38) is, despite flaws, valuable. On the early years of George I, W. Michael in *England under George I: The Beginning of the Hanoverian Dynasty* and *The Quadruple Alliance* (London 1936 and 1939) presents an admirably comprehensive account. Also useful are J. J. Murray, *George I, the Baltic and the Whig Split of 1717* (London 1969) and B. Williams, *Stanhope* (Oxford 1932). There are a number of works on special aspects. G. N. Clark deals with the economic implications in 'War Trade and Trade War, 1701–1713', *Ec. Hist. Rev.* i (1927–28), 'The Character of the Nine Years' War 1688–97', *Cambridge Hist. Jnl.*, xi (1953–55), and *The Dutch Alliance and the War Against French Trade, 1688–1697* (Manchester 1923). For relations with the Dutch later, R. Hatton, *Diplomatic Relations between Great Britain and the Dutch Republic 1714–1721* (London 1950) is essential. Privateering is admirably discussed in essays by J. S. Bromley in *Statesmen, Scholars and Merchants: Essays in Eighteenth Century History presented to Dame Lucy Sutherland*, ed. A. Whiteman, J. S. Bromley, P. G. M. Dickson (Oxford 1973) and in *Historical Essays, 1600–1750, presented to David Ogg*, ed. H. E. Bell and R. C. Ollard (London 1963). The celebrated Methuen treaties are the subject of a book by A. D. Francis, *The Methuens and Portugal, 1691–1701* (Cambridge 1966). Two good selections of documents are *An Honest Diplomat at the Hague: The Private Letters of Horatio Walpole, 1715–1716*, ed. J. J. Murray (Bloomington 1955) and *The Correspondence of John Churchill, First Duke of Marlborough and Anthonie Heinsius, Grand Pensionary of Holland*, ed. Van'T. Hoff (Hague 1951).

Part 3

For the foreign policy of the Townshend–Walpole era, J. H. Plumb, *Sir Robert Walpole: The King's Minister* (London 1960), is invaluable and may be supplemented by B. Williams' pieces on Walpole in *Eng. Hist. Rev.* xv, xvi (1900–02). P. Vancher, *Robert Walpole et la Politique de Fleury (1731–1742)* (Paris 1924) and A. M. Wilson, *French Foreign Policy during the Administration of Cardinal*

Fleury, 1726–1743 (London 1936), cast much light on the 1730s. There are excellent essays by G. C. Gibbs, 'Parliament and the Treaty of Quadruple Alliance' in *William III and Louis XIV*, etc., 'Parliament and Foreign Policy in the Age of Stanhope and Walpole', *Eng. Hist. Rev.*, lxxvii (1962), 'Great Britain and the Alliance of Hanover', *Eng. Hist. Rev.*, lxxiii (1958), and useful ones by Sir R. Lodge, 'English Neutrality in the War of the Polish Succession', *Trans. Roy. Hist. Soc.*, 4th Ser., xiv (1931), 'Sir Benjamin Keene: A Study in Anglo-Spanish Relations', *Trans. Roy. Hist. Soc.*, 4th Ser., xv (1932), and 'The Treaty of Seville', *Trans. Roy. Hist. Soc.*, 4th Ser., xvi (1932). For the 1740s there is a poor biography of *Carteret* by W. B. Pemberton (London 1936), and a thorough set of essays on the diplomacy of the War of the Austrian Succession in Sir R. Lodge, *Studies in Eighteenth-Century Diplomacy, 1740–1748* (London 1930). On the diplomacy of the post-war years see D. B. Horn, *Sir Charles Hanbury Williams and European Diplomacy (1747–58)* (London 1930), 'The Origins of the Proposed Election of a King of the Romans, 1748–50', *Eng. Hist. Rev.*, xlii (1927), 'The Cabinet Controversy on Subsidy Treaties in Time of Peace, 1749–50', *Eng. Hist. Rev.*, xlv (1930), and R. Browning, 'The Duke of Newcastle and the Imperial Election Plan, 1749–1754', *Jnl. British Studies*, vii (1967–68). R. Browning's *The Duke of Newcastle* (London 1975) is also useful. On commercial diplomacy D. K. Reading, *The Anglo-Russian Commercial Treaty of 1734* (New Haven 1938), N. C. Hunt, 'The Russia Company and the Government 1730–42', *Oxford Slavonic Papers*, vii (1957), P. G. M. Dickson, 'English Commercial Negotiations with Austria, 1737–1752' in *Statesmen, Scholars and Merchants*, etc., and E. G. Holdner, 'The Role of the South Sea Company in the Diplomacy leading to the War of Jenkins' Ear, 1729–1739', *Hisp. Am. Rev.*, xviii (1938), are all helpful. There are some useful documents in Sir R. Lodge, ed., *Private Correspondence of Chesterfield and Newcastle 1744–46* (London 1930), and *Private Correspondence of Benjamin Keene* (Cambridge 1933).

Part 4

For the mid-century warfare R. Pares, *War and Trade in the West Indies* (Oxford 1936) and 'American versus Continental Warfare,

1739–63', *Eng. Hist. Rev.*, li (1936) are outstanding; his *Colonial Blockade and Neutral Rights, 1739–1763* (Oxford 1938) is more technical. The most useful of a poor group of biographies of Pitt is B. Williams, *The Life of William Pitt, Earl of Chatham* (London 1913). D. B. Horn deals with the diplomatic revolution in 'The Duke of Newcastle and the Origins of the Diplomatic Revolution' in *The Diversity of History. Essays in Honour of Sir Herbert Butterfield*, ed. J. H. Elliot and H. G. Koenigsberger (London 1970). Relations with Spain in the 1750s are covered in J. O. McLachlan, 'The Seven Years Peace, and the West Indian policy of Carvajal and Wall', *Eng. Hist. Rev.*, liii (1938). For the problems of peacemaking after the Seven Years' War, see Z. E. Rashed, *The Peace of Paris, 1763* (Liverpool 1951) and W. L. Grant, 'Canada Versus Guadeloupe, an Episode in the Seven Years' War', *Am. Hist. Rev.*, xvii (1911–12), and for the vexed question of the desertion of Prussia, W. L. Dorn, 'Frederick the Great and Lord Bute', *Jnl. Mod. Hist.*, i, (1929), and F. Spencer, 'The Anglo-Prussian Breach of 1762; An Historical Revision', *Hist.*, xli (1956). On the 1760s there are a number of short but extremely penetrating studies. Notable are the introduction to F. Spencer, ed., *The Fourth Earl of Sandwich, Diplomatic Correspondence, 1763–1765* (Manchester 1961) and M. Roberts, *Splendid Isolation, 1763–1780* (Reading 1970). Similarly helpful is an essay by H. Butterfield, 'British Foreign Policy, 1762–5', *Hist. Jnl.*, vi (1963). Anglo-French relations are treated, primarily from the French angle, by J. F. Ramsay, *Anglo-French Relations, 1763–70* (Univ. California 1939). On limited aspects D. B. Horn's, *British Public Opinion and the First Partition of Poland* (London 1945) is excellent; J. Goebel, *The Struggle for the Falkland Islands: A Study in Legal and Diplomatic History* (London 1927), less so. The diplomacy of the American War is treated fully in S. F. Bemis, *The Diplomacy of the American Revolution* (Bloomington 1967) and incidentally in P. Mackesy, *The War for America, 1775–1783* (London 1964). Less central but also useful are further monographs by Bemis, *The Hussey–Cumberland Mission and American Independence* (Princeton 1931), and 'British Secret Service and the French–American Alliance', *Am. Hist. Rev.*, xxix (1923–24). The peace negotiations of 1782–83 are unravelled in detail in R. B. Morris, *The Peacemakers* (New York 1965) and V. T. Harlow, *The

Founding of the Second British Empire, 1763–1793 (London 1952, 1964). Relations with Russia are covered in M. Anderson, 'Great Britain and the Russo-Turkish War of 1768–1774', *Eng. Hist. Rev.*, lix (1954), W. H. Reddaway, 'Macartney in Russia, 1765–67', *Cambridge Hist. Jnl.*, iii (1931), and I. de Madariaga, *Britain, Russia and the Armed Neutrality of 1780* (London 1962). M. Roberts deals with Sweden in 'Great Britain and the Swedish Revolution, 1772–73', *Hist. Jnl.*, vii (1964). Among collections of documents, that illustrating the armed neutrality, *Documentary History of the Armed Neutrality 1780 and 1800*, ed. Sir F. Pigott and G. W. T. Omond (London 1919), is useful. Letters bearing on Anglo-Russian relations are to be found in *Despatches and Correspondence of John, second Earl of Buckinghamshire*, ed. A. d'A. Collyer (Camden Soc., 1900–02), and in Historical Manuscripts Commission, *Lothian MSS*.

Part 5

The foreign policy of the Younger Pitt is admirably treated in J. H. Ehrman, *The Younger Pitt: The Years of Acclaim* (London 1969) and *The British Government and Commercial Negotiations with Europe 1783–93* (Cambridge 1962), though the 1790s have to be sought elsewhere, for example, in J. H. Rose, *William Pitt and the Great War* (London 1911). The period generally is covered in A. W. Ward and G. P. Gooch, ed., *The Cambridge History of British Foreign Policy, 1783–1919* (Cambridge 1922) and in R. W. Seton-Watson, *Britain in Europe, 1789–1914* (London 1955). An excellent study of the 1780s is A. Cobban's investigation of the Dutch crisis, *Ambassadors and Secret Agents* (London 1954). On a related theme by the same author see 'British Secret Service in France, 1784–1792', *Eng. Hist. Rev.*, lxix (1954), and 'The Beginning of the Channel Isles Correspondence, 1789–1794', *Eng. Hist. Rev.*, lxxvii (1962). The Nootka Sound episode is analysed in J. M. Norris, 'The Policy of the British Cabinet in the Nootka Sound Crisis', *Eng. Hist. Rev.*, lxx (1955), and W. L. Cook, *Flood Tide of Empire: Spain and the Pacific Northwest, 1543–1819* (New Haven and London 1973). A variety of useful works on the Revolutionary and Napoleonic wars are J. M. Sherwig, *Guineas and Gunpowder: British Foreign Aid in the Wars with France, 1793–1815* (Cambridge, Mass., 1969), A. B. Rodger, *The War of the Second Coalition, 1798–1801* (Oxford 1964), P. Mackesy, *The War in the Mediterranean, 1803–1810* (London 1957) and *The Strategy of Overthrow 1798–1799* (London 1974), R. Glover, *Britain at Bay: Defence against Bonaparte, 1803–14* (London 1973). Among the many articles on particular aspects are R. Glover, 'Arms and the British Diplomat in the French Revolutionary Era', *Jnl. Mod. Hist.*, xxix (1957) and J. Sherwig, 'Lord Grenville's Plan for a Concert of Europe, 1797–99', *Jnl. Mod. Hist.*, xxxiv (1962). Espionage activities are described in H. Mitchell, *The Undergound War against Revolutionary France* (Oxford 1965). Relations with America are treated in H. C. Allen, *Great Britain and the United States* (London 1954), in C. R. Ritcheson, *Aftermath of Revolution, British Policy towards the United States, 1783–1795* (Dallas 1969), in B. Perkins, *The First Rapprochement: England and the United States, 1795–1805* (Philadelphia 1955) and *Prologue to War: England and the United States, 1805–1812* (Berkeley 1961), and with Russia in M. S. Anderson, *The Eastern Question* (London 1966). A number of political biographies covering the period cast considerable light on foreign policy. Particularly valuable are J. W. Derry, *Charles James Fox* (London 1972), C. J. Bartlett, *Castlereagh* (London 1966), P. V. J. Rolo, *George Canning* (London 1965), P. Ziegler, *Addington* (London 1965) and D. Gray, *Spencer Perceval: The Evangelical Prime Minister, 1762–1812* (Manchester 1963). The best accounts of Castlereagh's activities are to be found in C. K. Webster, *The Foreign Policy of Castlereagh, 1812–1815* (London 1931) and C. S. B. Buckland, *Metternich and the British Government from 1809–1813* (London 1932). For collections of relevant documents, see *Journal and Correspondence of William Eden, Baron Auckland, from 1771 to 1814* (London 1861–62), *Despatches from Paris 1784–89*, ed. O. Browning (Camden Series, 1909–10), *Diaries and Correspondence of the First Earl of Malmesbury*, ed. 3rd Earl (London 1844), C. K. Webster, ed., *British Diplomacy, 1813–1815* (London 1921), Historical Manuscripts Commission, *Fortesque MSS*, and H. W. V. Temperley and L. M. Penson, eds. *Foundations of British Foreign Policy from Pitt (1792) to Salisbury (1902) or Documents, Old and New* (Cambridge 1938).

Index